UNDAUNTED

MY STRUGGLE FOR FREEDOM
AND SURVIVAL IN BURMA

ZOYA PHAN
WITH DAMIEN LEWIS

Free Press

New York   London   Toronto   Sydney

FREE PRESS
A Division of Simon & Schuster, Inc.
1230 Avenue of the Americas
New York, NY 10020

First Free Press hardcover edition May 2010

FREE PRESS and colophon are trademarks of Simon & Schuster, Inc.

For information about special discounts for bulk purchases,
please contact Simon & Schuster Special Sales at 1-866-506-1949
or business@simonandschuster.com.

The Simon & Schuster Speakers Bureau can bring authors to your live event.
For more information or to book an event contact the Simon & Schuster Speakers Bureau
at 1-866-248-3049 or visit our website at www.simonspeakers.com.

Designed by Carla Jones

Manufactured in the United States of America

10 9 8 7 6 5 4 3 2 1

Library of Congress Cataloging-in-Publication Data
    Phan, Zoya.
        Undaunted: my struggle for freedom and survival in Burma / Zoya Phan with Damien
Lewis.
        p. cm.
        Previously published: London; New York: Simon & Schuster, 2009, with title Little
daughter: a memoir of survival in Burma and the West.
        Includes index.
        1. Phan, Zoya. 2. Phan, Zoya—Childhood and youth. 3. Burma—History—1948—
Biography. 4. Women political activists—Burma—Biography. 5. Women refugees—Burma—
Biography. 6. Women refugees—Great Britain—Biography. 7. Karen (Southeast Asian
people)—Biography. 8. Karen (Southeast Asian people)—Burma—Government relations.
9. Karen (Southeast Asian people)—Burma—Social conditions. 10. Democracy—Burma—
History. I. Lewis, Damien. II. Phan, Zoya. Little daughter. III. Title.
    DS530.68.P48A3 2010
    959.105'3092—dc22
    [B]   2009038546

ISBN 978-1-4391-0286-2
ISBN 978-1-4391-3473-3 (ebook)

This book is dedicated to my late mother, Nant Kyin Shwe, and father, Padoh Mahn Sha Lah Phan.

—Z. P.

For Eva

—D. L.

CONTENTS

Contents

ABOUT BURMA

B urma is in Southeast Asia, with Thailand and Laos to the east and Bangladesh, India, and China to the north. The population is estimated at around 50 million. There are eight main ethnic groups and more than one hundred subgroups, making it one of the most ethnically diverse countries in the world.

It is a country rich in natural resources but also one of the poorest in the world, as the dictatorship spends up to half its annual budget on the military.

Burma gained independence from Great Britain after World War II, but even under democratic rule the central government oppressed and discriminated against ethnic groups.

In 1962 General Ne Win took power in a military coup, and the country has been ruled by dictatorships ever since. A student-led prodemocracy uprising in 1988 was brutally suppressed by the regime, and a new dictatorship—the State Law and Order Restoration Council (SLORC)—took over. A combination of internal and international pressure led the regime to hold elections in 1990, which it expected to win. But instead the National League for Democracy (NLD), led by Aung San Suu Kyi, won 82 percent of the seats in Parliament. The regime refused to accept the results and instead arrested and tortured members of Parliament and democracy activists. As of October 2009 there were more than 2,100 political prisoners in Burma, many of whom had been tortured, kept in solitary confinement, and denied medical treatment.

Aung San Suu Kyi is now in her third period of detention and is the world's only Nobel peace laureate in detention. She is denied visitors, her phone line has been cut, and she is not allowed to send or receive mail. She has grandchildren she has never been allowed to see.

Burma is a record breaker for all the wrong reasons. It has the highest number of child soldiers, one of the highest levels of infant mortality in the region, and the lowest levels of spending on health and education. The regime has been accused by the United Nations of a crime against humanity for its use of slave labor, the highest in the world. It is engaged in ethnic cleansing in eastern Burma, it is one of the few governments in the world that still uses land mines, and it denies international aid to its own population. Burma also regularly comes first in tables on corruption and media censorship.

BURMA TIMELINE

1947: Karen National Union (KNU) is formed and lobbies unsuccessfully for an independent Karen State.

1948: Burma gains its independence from Great Britain.

1949: The KNU begins armed struggle after attacks by Burmese Army and communal violence against Karen civilians.

1962: General Ne Win seizes power in a military coup.

1976: The National Democratic Front (NDF) is formed by ethnic groups opposed to the dictatorship.

1976: The KNU drops its demands for an independent state and joins other ethnic organizations in calling for federalism in Burma.

1988: There is a democracy uprising across Burma. The Ne Win regime is toppled, but thousands are massacred in the student-led uprising. A new and even more brutal regime takes power, calling itself the State Law and Order Restoration Council (SLORC).

1989: SLORC renames Burma Myanmar. The democracy movement and many governments refuse to accept the name change, saying it has no right to decide what the country is called.

1990: Elections are held. The National League for Democracy (NLD), led by Aung San Suu Kyi, wins 82 percent of the seats in Parliament, but the regime refuses to hand over power.

1995: The Burmese Army overruns the KNU headquarters at Manerplaw.

1997: SLORC renames itself the State Peace and Development Council (SPDC).

2004: The SPDC and KNU make a "gentleman's agreement" to end hostilities. The KNU sticks to it, but the SPDC does not.

2005: The SPDC gives just a few hours' notice that it is moving from Rangoon (Yangon) to a new capital, Nay Pyi Taw.

2007: January: China and Russia veto a resolution on Burma at the UN Security Council.

2007: August–September: A democracy uprising led by Buddhist monks is brutally suppressed by the SPDC.

2008: February: Padoh Mahn Sha Lah Phan, general secretary of the KNU, is assassinated by agents of the SPDC.

2008: May: Cyclone Nargis strikes Burma. The SPDC fails to warn the population that the cyclone is coming and then blocks international aid.

2008: May: A rigged referendum is held on a new constitution for Burma that will enshrine military rule. The SPDC claims 92 percent support.

2009: May: Aung San Suu Kyi is put on trial after an American man swims to her home and refuses to leave. She is charged with breaking the terms of her house arrest. In August she was sentenced to a further eighteen months under house arrest.

2010: The regime plans rigged elections that will bring in a rubber-stamp Parliament and a new constitution that legalizes the dictatorship, keeping it in power.

INTRODUCTION

There are two Burmas. One you may have heard of, where a recipient of the Nobel Peace Prize, Daw Aung San Suu Kyi, leads our struggle for democracy against one of the most brutal dictatorships in the world, where monks marched for freedom but were met with bullets, and where victims of the 2008 cyclone were denied international aid by the military dictatorship. But the other Burma, the Burma I am from, is less well known. I hope that through my story you will learn about this other Burma.

I am Karen, one of the ethnic groups in Burma. Out of sight in the mountains and jungles of eastern Burma, the Burmese dictatorship has been trying to wipe out my people. Millions have been forced to flee their homes. More villages have been destroyed in Burma than in Darfur in Sudan, but the world has seemed content to ignore our suffering. It's been going on for more than sixty years.

Before the Burmese Army came to our land, I had a happy childhood. Karen land in eastern Burma seemed like paradise to me, a green mansion in which I played with my sister and brothers. Both my parents were activists in the struggle for democracy, and their work kept them very busy, but they loved us dearly.

But when I was fourteen years old my village was attacked by the Burmese Army. I had to run for my life, knowing that capture would mean being raped, used as slave labor, and then killed. After weeks of hiding in the jungle my family ended up in refugee camps in Thailand, which seemed more like prison camps, surrounded by barbed wire.

I am luckier than many of my fellow Karen. I managed to escape Burma twice after my home was attacked and to escape the refugee camps on the Burma-Thailand border, winning a scholarship to study in the United Kingdom.

Though I am safer now, living in London, I still don't feel completely safe. I am on a hit list because of my political activities, and three attempts have been made on my life. The regime has not been successful in killing me, but they assassinated my father. He had been elected leader of the Karen resistance movement and was living in a small town on the Burma-Thailand border. On February 14, 2008, Valentine's Day, he was shot dead in his home by gunmen sent by the dictatorship.

My father named me Zoya after a female Russian resistance fighter, Zoya Kosmodemyanskaya, who had fought the Nazis during World War II. When I was born he prayed that I would grow up to help my people in their struggle for freedom and democracy. I have done my best to fulfill his wishes. I now work with Burma Campaign UK, an organization campaigning for human rights, democracy, and development in Burma.

Burma is a beautiful country, full of people from diverse cultures and religions who want to live side by side in peace, different but equal. Like the Tibetans, whose indigenous culture is being systematically eradicated, the Karen lived for centuries in a peaceable isolation. Now we have been forced into a diaspora, our villages destroyed, our lives and traditions uprooted from the land in which they are anchored and to which our spirits are still tied. I am in constant communication with friends who still hope to return to Burma from the refugee camps on the Burma-Thailand border, with concerned humanitarians working to get aid into the interior where impoverished Karen and other minorities are still preyed on by Burmese soldiers. I return to Burma often in my dreams and thoughts, remembering my dear parents and their determination to help our people and our fight for democracy. I want to take you there, too, so you can feel the preciousness of our beautiful culture, so that you recognize in our struggle the struggle of all people for dignity, self-determination, and freedom.

The generals ruling Burma don't want you to know what they are doing. They have tried to kill me to stop me speaking out. Please don't let them have their way. Read on . . .

Chapter One

Grandfather Bent Back

The problems in Burma are widely misperceived by people outside the country to have started in 1962, when the first dictator came to power. Others remember only as far back as 1988, when students protesting in Rangoon were massacred on the streets and an even more brutal dictatorship took over. But for the Karen people, my tribe, persecution has been going on for centuries and escalated from the moment Burma gained independence.

Our legends tell that in ancient times Pu Tau Meh Pa, the first leader of the Karen, led his people south from Mongolia searching for a new homeland. On the way, the Karen divided into two. One group, known as the Pwo Karen, or "Mother Side," traveled through central Burma and settled in what is now the Irrawaddy Delta. My family is descended from the Pwo Karen. The Sgaw Karen, or "Father Side," followed the Salween River and settled in an area of mountainous jungle in what is now the border region of Burma and Thailand. We called our new home Kaw Lah, "Green Land."

A Karen elder led our ancestors to the area of present-day Rangoon, with its beautiful, lush plain. Pu Ta Ku, "Grandfather Bent Back," hoisted a makeshift flag, a fishing rod with a traditional Karen tunic on it. Back then the settlement was called Way Ta Ku, "Bent Back City," after Pu Ta Ku. Centuries later, the British came along and renamed it Rangoon. They created an official border along the Salween River and split our tribe in two.

Our own name for ourselves is Pwa K'Nyaw, which means, quite simply, "The People." When the Burmans, now the predominant ethnic group in Burma, arrived, they gave us the name "Kayin." "Karen" is most likely a name that the British adapted from Kayin.

Over the centuries, the different ethnic groups in Burma expanded. More people settled in the country. As they did, they came into conflict with one another. The Karen people were subjugated and persecuted by the ethnic Burman and Mon groups.

Burmese kings were from the Burman ethnic group, and were all-powerful and ambitious, wanting to expand their empire. They looked on Karen people as animals and treated us as slaves. Poor and uneducated, constantly living in fear, Karen people were not permitted to learn to read. If a Karen person could read, he was executed.

When the British colonized Burma, the Karen were treated more equally, and many Karen considered that life was better under British rule. For the first time Karen people could get an education and be more open about their culture. Justice under British administrators was fairer as well. Karens were promoted in the army, which made many Burmans resentful. The perceived closeness of the Karen to the colonizing British exacerbated existing prejudice that many Burmans had against the Karen.

These differences became more extreme when the Karen sided with the British in fighting the invading Japanese during World War II. During World War II, the British promised the Karen they would be given an independent country once Burma gained independence; it was a promise that we would be free from oppression. But the British broke their promise and left the Karen in Burma when the country gained independence in 1948. So began decades of oppression and discrimination against the Karen people.

Aung San, the leader of Burma's independence movement and the father of Aung San Suu Kyi, had joined forces with the Japanese to drive the British out of the country. He later switched sides and fought against the Japanese, but some Burmese considered the Karen to have collaborated with their oppressor. Karen people were not given equal rights, and the government incited communal clashes, accusing the Karen of being lackeys of British colonialism.

In 1947 Karen community and religious organizations from across the country united to form the Karen National Union (KNU). They wanted a united voice to demand equality and an independent state. On February 11, 1948, hundreds of thousands of Karen marched in cities across Burma. Their slogan was "Give the Karen State at once; For the Burman one kyat [dollar], for Karen one kyat; We do not want communal strife, we do not want civil war." But the protests were ignored. Later that year the Burmese prime minister, U Nu, told Karen leaders that the only way they would win rights and independence was to fight for it. Community violence escalated, with Karen villages being burned, villagers shot and women raped, and reciprocal attacks taking place. Karen organizations were outlawed and Karen leaders arrested. In January 1949 Karen leaders called on their people to take up arms to defend themselves.

The struggle for freedom was led by the Karen resistance movement, the Karen National Union. The Karen resistance named their traditional lands, parts of east, south, and central Burma, where most Karen lived, Kaw Thoo Lei, or "Land of No Evil." This is from where so many resistance fighters were drawn, my parents among them. I was born in Manerplaw, headquarters of the Karen resistance. In our language Manerplaw means "Victory Field." There was a wild romance about my parents' journeys to Kaw Thoo Lei and their finding love there. My parents loved telling us stories of their differing journeys to join the resistance.

My parents came from the same village, one situated deep inside Burma on the Irrawaddy Delta. The Burmese Army attacked when my father was a young boy, and he and his family fled into the forest, where they hid for many days. There he lost his younger sister to dysentery, and soon afterward his mother succumbed to smallpox. The disease made her skin fall off in great lumps, and because it was so contagious, she could not hug her children good-bye before she died.

After these deaths, my father and his brother were brought up by his father, who owned a plantation of betel nut palms on the outskirts of the village. All across Burma people chew the nut of the betel palm, mixed with lime leaves and betel pepper, as a mild stimulant a little like coffee. The Burmese Army had burned down the village when it attacked, but the plantation had survived. My father's father used the money he earned from selling betel to give my father a proper education.

After high school my father went to the university in Rangoon. He was very bright and quickly fell in with a socially conscious group of students who were interested in democracy and equality for all the people of Burma, not just the Karen. He was nineteen years old and studying hard for his history degree when Army general Ne Win seized control of the country. All student unions were banned, as were trade unions, and my father led angry students demonstrating on the streets. The military cracked down hard, and there were hundreds of arrests.

Luckily, my father escaped the soldiers, and he went on to join the Karen National Union (KNU). Of course, that organization—like all resistance movements—was banned, and so it had to operate in secret. As soon as my father graduated, he decided to join the resistance in Manerplaw.

As a child my mother was so poor that she only ever owned two dresses. The eldest daughter of impoverished parents with seven children, she was twenty years old by the time she finished year seven of her studies because she had to spend so much time caring for her other siblings and keeping the family together. My grandparents didn't have the money to keep her at school, so she decided to do something to help her family. She had heard that the KNU ran courses training young women to be nurses that lasted for two years and were free.

The Burmese government did not provide training, but the KNU did, and she enrolled to learn how to help the sick. As a trainee nurse she was drawn into the struggle, helping those who had been injured in attacks by the Burmese Army as well as injured soldiers and people who were sick. The more she saw her people's suffering firsthand, the more committed she became to stopping the violence. She had planned to return to her village after the course to nurse people and earn money to help put her siblings through school, but because she was in the KNU, it was not safe for her to return. She was only in her early twenties and would never see her home village again.

My mother joined the Karen National Union and became a member of an army company operating in the southwest delta region. Her talent and commitment were appreciated by her commanders, and she was promoted to command a company of female soldiers.

As the Burmese Army sent more soldiers into the region, it became more and more difficult for my mother's company to operate, and the order came from KNU headquarters that they should join the main Karen Army in the east of the country to avoid their all being killed. My mother was heartbroken to be leaving the delta, for she feared she would never see her mother or father again. In Karen culture parents depend on their children when they are old and infirm, and she felt terribly guilty for leaving them, but she had a responsibility to the struggle and the soldiers in her charge.

There was no direct route by which my mother's unit, Delta Battalion, could join the main Karen Army in the east, so they embarked upon a perilous journey into lands most had never seen before. My mother never for one moment imagined that the journey ahead would take five years and be one of the most challenging undertakings of her entire life.

Several hundred fighters traveled north into the rugged Arakan

Mountains. My mother didn't speak much about this journey, except for a few stories that she would tell. As the months passed and they left Karen lands far behind them, the soldiers started to run short of food. One day they came to a place where there were herds of wild elephant. Elephants have a special place in Karen culture, and no one would normally think of killing and eating one. But the soldiers were desperate. It was either that or starve to death.

The soldiers shot and killed two elephants. Whenever she told me this part of the story, my mother used to stress how odd the elephant meat tasted. It smelled pungent and musty, like the jungle, and was tough as old leather. The trunk was the oddest thing to eat, for it was all cartilage and bony bits. Yet because there were around two hundred soldiers in Delta Battalion, the two elephants were barely enough to keep them going.

My mother had some thirty female soldiers under her command and was determined that not one of them would die of starvation or be killed by the enemy. One morning she went out from the camp searching for vegetables and fruit. All of a sudden she spotted an enormous python in the undergrowth—it was asleep, and it hadn't seen her.

As quickly as she could she returned to the camp and explained to her soldiers her plan to kill the snake for food. Four of them would go; any more, and they might waken it. She would creep up and jump on the beast's neck in an effort to hold it down and keep it from swallowing anyone. The others would rush in and beat it with bamboo sticks. By the time my mother was back at the python's nest, she had realized what a truly scary prospect it was. She didn't like the idea of wrestling with such a beast, but she steeled herself, and on the count of three, she jumped. As soon as she landed on its thick and powerful neck, the python awoke. Surprised and angry, it thrashed about, trying to get its jaws around my mother. She held on with all her strength while the others beat it with bamboo sticks. On and on the battle went, the python thrashing and the women screaming and beating it, until eventually they overcame the giant snake.

6

The story of her battle with the python was one of my mother's favorites. She used to tell it to us in the evenings when my father was away and my brother, sister, and I were sitting with her near the cooking fire. She used to act out the battle, with the python thrashing and thrashing and squirming beneath her. We would listen in rapt attention, marveling at how she could ever have been so brave. It wasn't that unusual to find snake curry on the menu in our home, although it was never giant python. Most of the snakes we ate were about the length of a man's arm, and they were captured in the bush that surrounded the village. My mother would smoke the snake meat over the cooking fire before frying it in oil, with onions, garlic, salt, and chili. The curried flesh tasted like fish crossed with chicken and was quite delicious.

Because she was such a soft and loving mother, I used to wonder how she could have been so fierce. And I wondered why she hadn't just shot that python and killed it. Surely, it would have been far easier—and safer—than beating it to death? One day I asked her, and she explained to me that ammunition had been in short supply. Karen soldiers had been rationed only a few bullets each and were allowed to use a bullet only in an effort to kill the enemy. Shooting the python would have been considered a dereliction of duty.

Before my mother's battle with the python, the Delta Battalion's commanding officer had fallen sick, so he remained in the camp along with the main body of soldiers. While she and her troops went for food, the Burmese Army attacked the camp and quickly overran it. When my mother and her soldiers returned, they found the commander dead. He had been killed with a knife thrust to the stomach.

My mother and her troops knew they had no reason to stay and in fact needed to try to escape from the Burmese troops, who were still surely nearby. They set off into the jungle with the aim of scaling a high peak that lay to the north of their position. Many exhausting days later they discovered a beautiful cave, which seemed totally deserted. There was no sign that any humans—the enemy included—had ever been there. They decided to rest up in that cave and try to recover their strength. They made a fire at the entrance, and as darkness descended they told each other what had happened to them when the Burmese Army had attacked.

All of a sudden there was a deafening roar, and a huge tiger came bounding out of the darkness. Before anyone could react, it snapped its jaws shut around the head of one of the soldiers sitting by the fire. As it tried to drag him away, the man thrashed and fought through the flames, and the fire flared up fiercely. The tiger kept shaking the man's body, making the flames grow higher and higher. The cave was filled with smoke and sparks, the tiger's roaring and the man's screaming echoing horribly all around. Eventually, the tiger succeeded in dragging his victim away. My mother and the rest of the Karen soldiers realized then why the Burmese Army had never used that cave as a camp.

Once more they set off into the forest, and finally they came out of the Arakan and Pegu Mountains into the central plains of Burma. All they had to do was cross the Sit Taung River, and they would be into the eastern highlands, which were controlled by the Karen forces.

It was the rainy season, and the Sit Taung River was high and strong. It was impossible to wade across, so the soldiers set about building rafts to ford the river. The forests of Burma are full of bamboo, and in the intense, steamy heat each can grow to the thickness of a man's thigh. For its weight bamboo is incredibly strong, and the Karen are renowned for building just about anything with it, including rafts. My mother ordered her troops to work quickly, as she feared the Burmese Army was still on their tail.

It started raining hard, a torrential downpour drumming on the leaves. The harder it rained, the more difficult it became to cut the bamboo and lash the rafts together. They had to weave rope from bamboo fibers and craft paddles from split bamboo stems. My mother sent the first raft into the strong current, soldiers climbing aboard and striking out for the far side. But just as it neared the center of the river, shots rang out from the jungle behind. The Burmese soldiers had found them.

My mother asked for volunteers, and soldiers stepped forward to face the enemy. They headed off to set up a defensive cordon that would buy those escaping some time. My mother mustered her remaining troops for the crossing.

As they pulled away from the riverbank, she shouted orders that the volunteers holding off the enemy should try to swim for it. Most had never seen a river as wide or as powerful as this. When my mother's raft reached the safety of the far side, she counted how many she had lost. Fifteen had drowned in the river, many of them from her own unit.

My mother had vowed not to lose a single one. She was heartbroken, feeling as if she had failed them all. There was a mother-and-daughter team in her unit, and she discovered to her horror that both had drowned. My mother would often tell me that she would never forget that loss no matter how long she lived.

But those who had died hadn't given their lives for nothing, she explained. A few months after that fateful river crossing she and her soldiers reached the safety of Karen territory— the heartland of the resistance.

My mother was thirty-two years old when she and my father met again in Manerplaw. They had known each other as childhood playmates, and the discovery of a person from so close to home was a great comfort to them both. They began spending time together to reminisce about home, but their feelings quickly became more than neighborly. My father started to court her but did so in a way that no other Karen man would have tried. Traditionally, a man would write a letter to the woman he liked. It would be worded very simply: "I feel love for you; do you feel the same for me?" The man would get a go-between to deliver the note, and the courtship would be pursued through the exchange of such letters. Eventually, if they really liked each other, they might meet.

But my father did things very differently. He gave her flowers, wrote romantic poetry, and offered her a pillowcase with a message of love embroidered on it. While it is a Karen tradition for lovers to give pillowcases, because the pillow is the place where they might both eventually lay their heads, it is the woman who is supposed to give it to the man, not vice versa! My father was proud of the way he had won my mother's love. He often told me the story of how he had done so, and all throughout their married life he always brought her fragrant bunches of flowers.

My mother and father were married in 1976. The Karen Revolution had begun in the delta of central Burma and in and around the capital, Rangoon. The bigger and better-armed Burmese Army had driven most Karen resistance fighters into the mountains of eastern Burma, as it had my mother and her troops. There new headquarters were being established and new administrative systems set up. The KNU was not just a resistance movement; it also provided local administrations, schools and health clinics, a justice system, a newspaper, a postal system, and trade and taxation.

But the onslaught of the Burmese Army was relentless. It was constantly attacking and was particularly targeting civilians, even though civilians had nothing to do with the resistance. Just being Karen was enough to make you a target.

CHAPTER TWO

THE ALMOST-DYING

When I was two years old, I died and came back to life again. It was my first brush with death, although it wouldn't be the last. One morning my mother discovered me lying in our bamboo hut unconscious from a high fever. She had hoped that overnight I would have slept it off, but as I had always been a sickly child, she now feared that she had lost me.

She covered me with a damp cloth, scooped me into her arms, and ran as fast as she could to the Per Hee Lu village clinic, a small bamboo hut three minutes from our house. One nurse ran the clinic, which served the three hundred people in the village, and my mother prayed that the nurse would be there and not out treating someone.

Panicked, she rushed inside. Luckily, the nurse was in, but she took one look at the little unconscious bundle that was me and declared that it was hopeless to treat me.

"I'm afraid your daughter is dead," she said. "I'm sorry, I can't help her."

My mother was beside herself. She refused to believe that I was gone. Having served five years as a soldier in the Karen National Liberation Army, she was tough, and she refused to give me up without a fight.

"No way!" she cried. "No way has my Little Daughter died, just like that. No way!"

She scooped me up again and started running to the neighboring village, Pway Baw Lu, which was forty minutes away, to see if the nurse there might help. There was only a faint path through the jungle, but she was sure she could make it. Never mind that she was already nine months pregnant with my little brother; she knew that I needed help, and she would do everything possible to get it for me.

It was the dry season, and the Mu Yu Klo River, which ran past our village, was low. My mother was able to wade 160 feet through the thigh-high water. For forty minutes she fought her way through the jungle, until finally she burst into the clearing of Pway Baw Lu village. She rushed across to the clinic, tears streaming down her face as she ran.

The nurse there was far more sympathetic. She examined me closely and declared that I was in a deep, fever-induced coma. She put me on a drip and gave me the few drugs that she had in an effort to calm the fever. Then she told my mother to be patient. I was still breathing, and there was a chance that I might come out of this alive and well.

After I had been on the drip for three days my fever started to come down. My mother and I had the small clinic mostly to ourselves, and my mother soon knew her way around the medicines as she treated me herself. When I regained consciousness, none of the nurses was present, for it was Christmas Eve, and they had gone to a party at the village school. My mother was sitting beside me as I opened my eyes. She couldn't believe that I had come back to life.

As my mother gazed at me in wonder, she realized with a shock that my eyes weren't right. One was looking at the sky, the other down at the earth. She was convinced that I was brain-damaged. The shock sent her into labor, and the nurses had to rush back from the Christmas party to help her deliver the baby.

That's how my little brother came into the world. My mother decided to name him Slone Phan, "Shining Stone," because he brought light into the darkness of my almost-dying.

Slone and I stayed in the clinic for a few more days, while my older brother and sister stayed with neighbors back in our village. My mother was with us, trying to take care of us, and the nurses helped her, for which she was grateful. She was particularly grateful to the nurse who had saved me, of course, but she was angry with the nurse in our village who had said that I was dead. But that's what it was like to be a Karen woman in Karen State. That nurse was young and inexperienced, my mother said when she told the story, and didn't know how to do her job properly. My mother held her beliefs closely, and I know that it was her belief that I could pull through and her refusal to take no for an answer that kept me alive that day. My mother had to get by on her wits and use all the resources she could think of. Karen people are used to hardship. We don't complain, we just make the best of what we have, and we don't give up easily. It has made us tough and determined, and my mother was even tougher than most.

As children do, I recovered quickly from my almost-dying, but my eyes remained all askew. After a few days in the clinic, my mother was allowed to bring my brother and me home. My eyes healed slowly but did not quite go back to normal. My friends would laugh at me whenever my eyes went crooked, which they did especially when they got tired. I would get very annoyed. My vision would swim, things becoming all twisted and blurred. At its worst I would be seeing a cup or a bowl of food, but my eyes would appear as if they were looking in another direction completely.

Some weeks later, when my father came home, he took one look at me and exclaimed, "Oh, my Little Daughter, still so beautiful—even though you have *ta klay meh*!" In Karen culture calling someone *ta klay meh*, "wonky eyes," is very rude, although my father was only joking. It is considered really ugly to have crooked eyes. From then on my

13

sister and elder brother were always making jokes about my *ta klay meh* appearance.

Whenever I was teased like that, my mother would try to reassure me: "Little Daughter, you're still very beautiful, despite your funny eyes."

Over time I learned to get used to it. I learned how to bring my eyes back to normal by looking down at the ground and then slowly bringing them up again. Luckily, the older I got the less wonky they became, and by the time I was in my teens they were almost back to normal. That is how things were in my childhood; we worked hard to solve our problems any way we could, we made do with the hardships, and we prayed for the best.

My father was a loving, gentle man, and I was very close to him. Out of all us children, mine was the only birth at which he was present. He managed to stay with the family for six months after I was born, and I think that explains in part the special bond between us. He was of average height, slim but strong, with brown eyes framed by laugh lines and black hair. He would be clean-shaven whenever possible and used a cutthroat razor to shave. He always seemed to be dressed the same: a checked shirt, rolled up at the sleeves, with a Karen longyi—a *hteh ku*—wrapped around his waist. He was a leader in the Karen resistance against the Burmese military.

My father wasn't particularly handsome, but he was very intelligent, and he had a great sense of humor. He'd gone to university in Burma's capital city, Rangoon, and graduated in history. We had few university graduates in the Karen resistance, and in my mother's eyes this made him extra special.

My mother was considered a real beauty. She was tall for a Karen woman, almost as tall as my father. She'd wear a red Karen longyi—I think red was her favorite color, for she wore it every day. She had straight, jet-black hair, which she wore in a bun and would let down only when she washed it, when she'd leave it free to dry. I used to marvel at her hair. When she let it down, it fell in a glistening, glossy waterfall right to the small of her back.

My mother's complexion was a little darker than my father's; I had inherited his lighter coloring. Every day she would wear *tha na kah*—a traditional Karen face cream—on her cheeks. She used to make the *tha na kah* from the bark of the *tha maw glay,* the tamarind tree. She would take a smooth-worn stone and roll a length of bark backward and forward on it, adding a little water as she did so. Gradually, the bark would dissolve into a light yellow paste: the *tha na kah* cream. She would rub it onto her cheeks, using a circular motion, until it left a little yellow sun on each one. We Karen believe that *tha na kah* makes a woman look beautiful, and it also protects our skin from the sun. It was the only "makeup" I ever wore; the next closest thing was when my sister, Bwa Bwa, and I improvised lipstick by smearing some old vitamin tablets across our lips. My mother would rub *tha na kah* onto my cheeks, arms, and legs to keep me cool in the hot season. And when she grew old and less capable, we children did the same for her.

My mother did much more than the domestic tasks usually left to the women in Karen culture and was so much more than a housewife. From my earliest memories, Mum worked in the information department of the Karen resistance, in central Manerplaw, an area with several villages with the resistance movement offices in the center. Most villages were less than an hour's walk from the offices. My mother typed articles for the movement's newspaper, using an old manual typewriter, as there were no computers, and ran the office. With my father away so much, she had no one to help look after the children, so we children would often go with her to her bamboo-walled office and play quietly while she banged away on that ancient typewriter.

With my father away so much, my siblings and I had to help my mother keep the house running. My older brother, Say Say, helped her with the chores, and when both my parents were away on their resistance work, he took over as if he were a parent. He would wash, cook, and clean for the three of us. When I was very small, he would carry me everywhere he went strapped in a longyi on his back.

Say Say was adopted. He had a pointed face, whereas my mother and father had rounded features, more like my own. He came to our family when he was about ten and I was just four months old. One day when I was little, my father told me the story of how Say Say had come to be with us: The Burmese regime had a notorious policy called the "Four Cuts," which was designed to crush the Karen. The Four Cuts policy was brutally simple: it aimed to cut off all supplies, information, recruits, and food to the Karen resistance.

Burma's central government discriminated against Karen people and provoked communal violence, forcing Karen people to take up arms to defend themselves. Once the country was taken over by a dictator in 1962, the attacks on Karen escalated and the Burmese Army increased its attacks on civilians, raping, killing, and torturing, burning villages, looting, and using villagers as slaves and human minesweepers. By now the resistance movement had retreated into the mountains of Karen State and the Tenasserim region in the south. Thousands of soldiers from the Burmese Army rampaged through the jungle, shooting people on sight, even children.

Whole villages in the Kler Lwee Htu district were on the brink of famine because Burmese troops had destroyed their crops and burned their stored food. Starving families were reduced to eating the flesh of banana trees.

One day a man who worked for the resistance approached my father. He told my father that he had seven children and that he wanted at least one to get a proper education. But the Four Cuts policy had destroyed all the schools in the area. He asked my father to take one of his oldest sons, Say Say, and give him an education in our home village. My mother and father had only one child at this time—my eldest sister, Bwa Bwa—and my father felt a deep sympathy for his friend. He agreed to take Say Say as one of his own children, and thus Say Say became my parents' adopted son.

When Say Say came to live with us, he started attending the village junior school. He was a ten-year-old boy in year one, and most of the other children were half his age. But Say Say didn't mind. He was happy just to get an education, and he studied hard and tried to make up for lost time. Say Say's parents tried to visit once a year, if they could afford the time to make the long journey. Whenever they did, they were so happy and proud to see how well their son was doing in his studies at school.

When I was four years old, Say Say started taking me to school with him so I could be looked after. The schoolroom was little more than a bamboo-walled hut with open windows and rows of rough wooden desks. There were no child care facilities in the village, so while Say Say studied hard I would play quietly at his feet. By the time Say Say was in his fourth year, people used to joke that I was the only four-year-old already in year four!

Say Say came from an isolated jungle village, and he understood the nature of the forest -its moods, its promise, and its dangers. Whenever my siblings and I went to the jungle without Say Say, we'd invariably get lost. We'd leave from one side of the village and return from another, never knowing where we'd been. But Say Say had a sixth sense; he always knew the way home.

My sister, Bwa Bwa, took after my mother in looks and was taller than I, but emotionally, she was like my father. She cared about everyone, was touched by their suffering, and felt their pain in her own heart. She was very clever and was always at the top of her class. I looked up to my sister and wanted to equal her example at school.

My little brother, Slone Phan, was the spitting image of my father in looks, but he was very small for his age. Slone Phan was thin and small, but he was totally fearless. He seemed to compensate for his size with his temper, and growing up he was always angry. At times he would lie down and bash his forehead on the ground time after time after time, especially if he couldn't get our mother's attention. He'd keep smashing away, making a loud slamming noise. But as he got older, his quick temper took the form of leadership among his peers. His friends soon learned to respect his temper, and mostly they followed his lead. He was the boss of his gang because of his bravery. If they were to climb a tree, Slone would dictate which one they climbed. He'd be first up, directing the others to various branches and telling them which fruit to pick.

As I was growing up, it was my mother who was around to care for us and make sure that we were growing up well. My father loved us very much, but he was often away on his resistance work. The Karen National Union was like a local and national government rolled into one, and as a KNU official my father was responsible for running a local administration, including schools and health care, as well as providing political leadership to the people. His area was several weeks' walk away, too far and too dangerous to take a young family, so often he was away for ten months of the year or more. Despite our bond, I didn't have the time to play with him or to get to know him properly, and I sometimes felt he was a stranger. When he returned when we were young, Say Say, Bwa Bwa, and I would have all but forgotten him. But I'd always be the first to go to him, and soon I'd be following him around everywhere. Often when my father returned home I'd notice that he looked exhausted and drawn. I'd watch as he devoured the leftovers from the previous meal. My mother would tell him that she was making a fresh curry for him, but my father insisted on eating every last scrap of the leftovers. There was no food where he had just come from, he said, and people there were being forced to eat putrid, rotten rice. I tried hard to listen when he and my mother spoke about the world outside our village, but as a small child I couldn't understand everything he told us. I knew people were starving to death; I also knew there was an enemy doing this to us and that it was human, just like us. But I was scared and I didn't want to think about it. In an effort to reassure myself I'd whisper, "Well, we've got food, and it's a long way away . . ."

My memories of my family together from my childhood are few but precious. One day when I was little my father tried to teach me to swim in the mighty Moei River. Few Karen can swim; it's not something that comes naturally to us. My older brother and sister were screaming and laughing with joy, but I was crying because of my fear of the water.

Zoya's father and mother, with (from left to right) Say Say, Slone, Zoya, and Bwa Bwa

My father tried to soothe me: "Little Daughter, don't worry, you are with me right here in my arms. Don't worry, Little Daughter, you're safe."

I was still afraid, but having my father so close filled me with courage, I allowed my father to pull me along, with my legs kicking through the clear, fast-flowing water.

Once I had learned to swim properly, I loved playing in the river and resting on the riverside beach. Say Say would climb on top of one of the giant water buffalos that wallowed in the shallows and start dancing on their horns. The gentle creatures never seemed to mind, but to me it always seemed like such a bold act.

Most days at dusk Say Say would grab some nets and take me fishing. He'd cast the nets into the river and leave them out overnight. Very early in the morning he'd waken me, and we'd go together to see if we'd caught anything. Usually, the nets would be full of little tilapia fish. We would carry home our trophies and present them to our parents; even though we were young, we understood the importance of providing for our family whenever we could. My mother would curry the fish or mix them with water spinach to make a delicious stew.

Whenever it came time for my father to go away again, my mother would have to trick us into letting him leave. Often she would take us to play with the animals under the house so he could sneak away without our knowing. There was never a good-bye; he would just be gone. If she hadn't done that, we would never have let him leave.

"Don't go!" we'd have cried. "Don't go, Daddy! Please don't go!"

At times I wondered why my dad was absent so much. I resented it, and I used to ask myself—*why?* Why was he so rarely with us?

My little brother, Slone Phan, didn't take very kindly to my father's absence. One day when Slone was around three years old, my father returned from a long period away. Slone didn't know who the strange man was and started to beat my father with a bamboo rope, to make him leave the house.

My mother tried to stop him. "That's your father! Your father! Stop it! Stop it!"

Eventually, she had to take the rope away to make Slone stop. My father laughed about it, but inside I think he was crushed. He was dedicating his life to improving our country for us and to making the world a better place for us, yet we didn't even know him. It must have been so hurtful for him to realize that his children didn't recognize him as their father.

In spite of his absences, my father tried to show his care for us in many ways. Whenever he came home, he would bring us something that he'd crafted with his own hands: a woven bamboo hat; spoons, forks, and bowls made out of wood; sometimes even a carved toy. We would cherish these as our most precious possessions.

Every day he was home my dad would show his love for us by grabbing us and kissing us on the cheek. He might reach out and catch us for a hug and a kiss at any time, sometimes five times a day. I used to complain about his stubbly face, but in reality I adored his kisses.

My mother and father were born to families who were animists. Animism is a traditional belief system that assigns things in nature—trees, rivers, mountains, the sky, and stars—souls and a consciousness. My parents rarely explained to us the nature of animist beliefs: instead, they preferred to show by example. We had no set scriptures or prayers and no holy book, but individual, personal relationships with the spirits of the universe. If a boy drowns in the river, we believe that the river spirit must be angry and we have to make an offering to the river spirit and ask for forgiveness.

In the culture of the Karen people, families don't usually have surnames. Children have only the one name that they were given by their parents, and there is no name passed down through the generations. But when my father left his home village and came to join the Karen resistance, he abandoned the name that his parents had given him in favor of a resistance name. Resistance fighters did this largely to protect their families back home from reprisals by the Burmese military regime, and he became known as Mahn Sha Lah Phan, "Mr. Star Moon Bright." He chose "star" and "moon" because he believed the heavens were the light of the future, and "Phan" because he believed that the future would be bright.

When my father was young, there was a Karen leader named Mahn Phan Shaung, "Mr. Bright Unity." He was a great military commander and resistance fighter, and he was my father's role model. Mahn Phan

Shaung believed in freedom for the Karen people and human rights and democracy for all. My father took "Phan" as his own "surname" to keep this man's spirit alive. When we were born, he passed that name on to us to sustain his memory through future generations, and also to remind us of the bright future he believed was in store for us all.

As I mentioned above, my name, Zoya, is not a Karen name. My father named me after Zoya Kosmodemyanskaya, a Russian partisan who had fought the Nazis in World War II, and who had been captured and executed.

When I was little, none of this meant much to me. I wasn't really interested in that Zoya: I was interested in me. And I had no idea where Russia was, who the Nazis were, and what the war had been about. It was only years later that I would understand just how prophetic it was for my father to have named me Zoya.

For he had named me after who and what I would become.

CHAPTER THREE

TOUCHING THE PIG

D espite what was happening in the rest of Burma, our village, Per Hee Lu, was a tranquil paradise. It nestled on the banks of the Mu Yu Klo, a tributary of the mighty Moei River. The Moei was fringed with towering mountains, and it was deep, with dark, emerald green waters. Our area was not so mountainous, and the Mu Yu Klo was shallower, with a lighter, jade green hue. Most years during the rainy season the Mu Yu Klo would flood its banks, thick brown water gurgling into the village. But we would sleep safe and sound above the flood, in our bamboo house on stilts. At such times we would roll up our Karen skirts, or longyis, making a pair of "shorts" so we could wade through the waters.

The village consisted of bamboo huts strung out along the riverbank, each set on stilts some six feet above the ground, with a bamboo ladder leading into it. The space underneath was both a wood store and a place for animals.

When we were growing up, no one had locks on his doors. We had a culture of honesty; no one would have dreamed of stealing. We did have latches on the doors, but only to prevent the chickens from going into the house when everyone was out and eating leftover food.

We didn't have any clocks in the village, either, because the rooster was everyone's timekeeper. He would crow at specific times of the day. The first crow was around two in the morning, and we called it *hsaw oh oh ter tablaw*, "the first crowing of the cock." That was the signal for the farmers to get up and start pounding their rice for breakfast.

At three o'clock he would crow again: *hsaw oh oh kee blaw tar blaw*, "the second crowing of the cock." This was the time to start cooking breakfast. On the third crow, at four, people would eat and go to their farm. To us, the rooster was known as "the Karen clock."

My father and mother had built our house all by themselves. In fact, my father was a great craftsman, and he'd make tables, chairs, and beds for friends and neighbors. He'd make huge hats, woven from young, supple bamboo and interwoven with leaves that covered the whole body in order to keep off the sun in the hot season and provide shelter during the rains.

One day my father took me into the forest to show me how to cut bamboo, an important lesson, for bamboo is central to the lives of the Karen. We use it to make the floors, walls, roofs, and frames of our houses, to construct bridges over rivers, as fuel for cooking, to construct water pipes and water carriers, and to make furniture. We use bamboo staves as weapons, and bamboo leaves are the favorite food of the elephant.

Bamboo is the heart of the Karen people, and we have many names to describe the types of bamboo found in the forest. There is *wa glu*, the most giant bamboo you could ever find; *wa blaw*, a type that has a long separation between each of the internal walls; and *wa klay*, which is between the other two.

But bamboo is useful only to those who know how to use it. It grew in huge groves high in the forests that surrounded our village. My father showed me how to use a *gheh*—a machete—to clear the small branches and shoots away, so that we could get at the choicest stands of bamboo.

24

During the dry season I would help my parents collect firewood in the forest and store it under the house. Once we had filled up the space under the ground floor, my father would build an outer "wall" of firewood around each side of the house. This was to keep the rain out and the wood inside dry.

Our village also had its very own elephant. She was called Mo Ghay Bay, "the elephant with the beautiful skin." Mo Ghay Bay's main task was to pull heavy wood out of the jungle so it could be cut into firewood. Growing up with an elephant in the village was completely normal for us. As children we didn't even call her "the elephant"— everyone called her Mo Ghay Bay. We'd run and chase around her feet, and she'd be very gentle. She never harmed us, not even when we got in her way.

Mo Ghay Bay was older than most of the people in Per Hee Lu, so she was like a wise grandmother to the village. There were no vehicles and no roads, so everything had to be transported by elephant or on the river. Sometimes elephants would come from neighboring villages to help Mo Ghay Bay with her work. It was nice to see her having some elephant company.

Our house was right in the center of Per Hee Lu, next to the village square. The bamboo steps of our house led up into a living room to the left, and to the right was a bedroom. We used to sleep on rush matting laid out on the bamboo floor. To the right of our bedroom was a spare room with a couple of bamboo-framed beds in it, for guests. At the back of the house was the kitchen. It had an earthen floor for a hearth and three stones arranged in a triangle. Firewood would be pushed into the space between the stones and a cooking pot balanced on top. Above the hearth was a shelf for drying foods—chili peppers, vegetables, meat, and mushrooms—which we did to preserve them since we had no refrigeration.

My mother did most of the cooking, but my father was always interfering. When her back was turned, my father would taste the food and add some extra ingredients—salt and lemon, perhaps.

"You! Always interfering!" my mother would say. "Are you trying to teach me how to cook?"

My father would burst out laughing. "No, no, no—it's the other way around. I'm not your master—you're mine!"

One time my father added some seasoning from a bottle beside the cooking fire to the soup my mother was making for dinner. She returned to the pot to find it frothing over with bubbles. She couldn't understand what had happened until she checked the contents of the "salt" bottle—it actually contained the dregs of some washing powder. We were sitting there hungry, and now the food was ruined. But it was so funny that my mother couldn't help laughing. She had a laugh like mine: it sounded like the sharp cry of a bird. In spite of our hunger we started laughing along with her.

Manerplaw was just an hour's walk away from our village, on the far side of Teak Mountain. My mother would travel to Manerplaw during the week for her work, leaving us in the village with instructions on how to care for one another. If it was the wet season, she could get there easily by "long-tail" boat, which is like an enlarged canoe, with a car or truck engine mounted on the back and a long shaft with a propeller on the end dipping into the water. During the wet season, the river journey to Manerplaw would take thirty minutes or so, as the waters were deep and easily navigable. In the dry season it would take longer, as the boatman would have to find a way through. Sometimes the rivers would be impassable by long-tail boat, and my mother would have to take the path that led over Teak Mountain into the territory of wild elephants, which could be dangerous.

We children were often on our own during the week while our mother worked in Manerplaw and our father was off on his missions. When my parents weren't at home, the rest of us would have to wait to eat until Say Say came back from school. He was the only one old enough to deal with the cooking fire and big enough to prepare the food. But first we'd have to help Say Say feed the chickens and ducks and make food for the pigs, usually banana shoots pounded into a mash. Say Say didn't mind doing the cooking, and he tried to look after us well.

Most evenings, the only foods Say Say had on hand to prepare were rice, fish paste, and a water spinach salad—but it was good enough for us. On rare occasions, he would cook his specialty, a rich chicken curry, which was a rare treat. The staple foods for breakfast, lunch, and dinner were rice and fish paste. On a weekday, Say Say would get up very early in the morning—at the third crow of the cockerel—and start pounding the rice. Beneath the house was an ancient-looking rice pounder that my father had crafted of wood. Say Say would have to stand on the end of a wooden beam, using his weight to lift it and then letting it drop into the bucket filled with rice. A lump of hard wood set at right angles to the beam would smash down on the rice and break away the husks from the grains.

Say Say wasn't heavy enough to operate the pounder properly, so in the morning he'd wake me up, strap me onto his back, and start the rice pounding. As he worked, he would sing me back to sleep:

> *Sleep, sleep, my Little Sister . . .*
> *Sleep, sleep, my Little Sister . . .*
> *Sleep, sleep, my Little Sister . . .*
> *Sleep.*

By seven o'clock Say Say would have left for school. Bwa Bwa, Slone, and I would wake around then and eat the breakfast that he'd left us.

No one in our village was wealthy, but we did our best to ease one another's hardship. One of the big events of the year was the roof-building time, called *dut htaw hee koh,* "the time of covering the house with leaves." It took place before the start of the rainy season and always demonstrated how much easier our lives were when everyone pulled together. Word would go around the village that it was so-and-so's time to do their *dut htaw hee koh*. No one would pledge to come—it was all very informal—but on the allotted day there was always enough help.

The roofs needed replacing every year, and the aim was to get the whole job completed in one day. To prepare for the day, very early in the morning we would head off into the forest to collect the leaves of the tur lah trees, which are similar in size to teak and have similarly large leaves. We would pile the leaves into woven bamboo baskets with straps that stretched from the back around the forehead. My mother and father would each carry home a basket of leaves on their back.

Upon arrival, the basket would be emptied out and the leaves laid flat on the ground. We'd fetch bowls of water and weight the leaves down with a rock to soak. That made them last longer as a roofing material, but it quickly spoiled their beauty. My father and Say Say would be first up on the rafters, while we prepared the leaves down below. One by one the able-bodied boys and men of the village would come to join them. We passed up each row of leaves and hooked its leaf stem over a bamboo roof spar, to which they were lashed with bamboo rope, for extra strength. Row upon row of leaves was added to the roof, each overlapping the other.

My mother would prepare a special meal, *lu kay tha dot hsaw nyah*, "pumpkin and chicken curry." In Karen tradition this is the dish you feed to those who help with the roofing. She would keep everyone well fed as they worked. The more people came to help, the quicker the roof would go up—but the more pumpkin and chicken curry was required! People would be talking, cracking jokes, and laughing, and sometimes those above would be working at different speeds from those below and the roof would start to go all wonky, so the faster roofers would have to stop and move over to help others catch up. By nightfall, the roofing would be done. Such communal activities were the social glue that held the village together.

*   *   *

Each year in August, the whole village would come together for the most important event in the Karen calendar, Lah Ku Gee Su, "the Month of Wrist Tying." The wrist-tying ceremony takes place alongside Pwaw Htawt Ker Pa, "the Ceremony of Touching the Pig." This was a bittersweet time for our family. On the one hand, we enjoyed the way in which these ceremonies reaffirmed our Karen culture and identity. But on the other, they reminded my parents of how totally cut off we were from their home village and their extended family.

Both ceremonies are animist in origin and have been adopted as symbols of Karen identity. For the wrist-tying ceremony, the whole village would gather in the local monastery. The elders would sit in a row at the front, with the youngsters of the village facing them. Between the rows were baskets crammed full of mouthwatering food: coconut, sweet sticky rice, and delicious bamboo-cooked rice.

The elders would remain seated while the children came across to stand before them. The elders would tie a white cord around the youngsters' wrists, one woven in the traditional Karen way. After that they would offer a blessing, invoking the spirit of the young boy or girl to ensure he or she would have good fortune in the year ahead.

"Spirit, come back, come back to the body," the elder would say. "Spirit, come back to this boy, in peace and in hope, to give the body long life, health, and happiness. Don't stay under the bamboo or the tree, but come back to the body."

All the while the elder would be stroking the rope along the young person's wrist. Once the elder had completed the blessing, the youngster would do the same for his elder. Once everyone had been tied and blessed in this way, we would eat the feast, and the adults would drink rice whisky and rice wine. Rice whisky is fermented from boiled rice and rice wine from sticky rice. The eating and drinking would last long into the night.

After the village ceremony each family had a private gathering—

called Aw Gheh—which was terribly poignant. It was vital for all living family members to return to the family home for Aw Gheh. If family members were absent, the spirits could not be properly accommodated, a very bad thing in animist culture; little was worse than a family being separated at the time of Aw Gheh.

But of course, it was impossible for my mother and father to return to their family home. On becoming resistance fighters, they had been forced to sever all family ties. Any contact at all could be fatal, as the Burmese regime had spies everywhere and would not show mercy to a family that was found to have links with the resistance.

My mother and father had been absent from their families for more than twenty years, and for all that time they had been unable to hold a proper Aw Gheh ceremony. The only way around this impasse was to hold a ceremony to expel the missing family member, and then Aw Gheh could be held without them. It was difficult enough for my parents to be separated from their families physically, but the thought of being spiritually expelled was even more devastating.

One day a cousin of my mother came to visit. It had taken her months to find us, for she had had to go from village to village, asking after my mother's whereabouts. Though her family knew she had joined the resistance, they had no idea where she was living, or even if she were still alive. That cousin had come to ask if my mother was willing to come home, so that a proper Aw Gheh ceremony could be held.

I was very young at the time, but I still remember how inconsolable my mother was. At first she had been so happy to see her cousin, for it was the first family contact she'd had in many years. She wanted to see her parents and her siblings so very much, but she was torn.

"What will happen if I do try to go home?" she said. "I might never see my children again."

We were so upset at the thought of losing her, and we didn't want her to go.

"Don't go, Mummy," I begged her. "Don't go. Don't leave us."

I told my mother about a dream that I'd had. Maybe it was a premonition of the future, for I dreamed that my mother had disappeared. My father was away on work, and she had left the four of us—Say Say, Bwa Bwa, Slone, and me—all alone. It was evening and we were hungry and lonely, yet still our mother didn't come. I was so sad and worried, because I was used to being with her.

In my dream, the four of us sat by the door waiting as the evening sky grew dark and night arrived with all its loneliness and fears. We were wondering whether we should go to bed and see if she came home the following day, but I knew I wouldn't be able to sleep. I felt abandoned.

All of a sudden my mother appeared out of the gloom. She was carrying a bundle of the long grass that we use as an alternative kind of roof thatch. I ran up and hugged her, and told her how sad we were that she had left us. I was crying and crying.

"Po Mu Sit [Little Daughter], I didn't leave you," my mother replied. "I had things to do for the house; see, I came back with some new thatch."

My mother lit the fire and started to cook some rice. And it was then that I woke up from my dream. I looked wildly around for her, wondering if my dream had been real somehow. But all along she had been sleeping beside me, and she had woken with my cries. She gazed at me in sleepy concern.

"What's wrong?" she asked. "Po Mu Sit, have you had a bad dream?"

My mother had reassured me that she would never, ever leave us. And now, even though she faced being "expelled" by her family, the same was true—she could never leave. She had no choice but to agree to be "expelled" from her family. Of course, it was in name only: if ever she had gone back, they would have welcomed her in. But still she was very sad for a very long time afterward.

Because we were separated from our extended family, my father decided that we should have an Aw Gheh ceremony at home. Traditionally, a fat pig would be killed and roasted on a spit over a fire. Each family member would touch the roasting pig, starting with the eldest and finishing with the youngest. We couldn't afford a pig, so we performed our Aw Gheh ceremony with a turkey instead.

As the elder of the family, my father led the ceremony. He tied the traditional white chord around my wrist and started to pray.

Spirit, come back to my Little Daughter; come back and make her healthy, make her happy, and make the year before her a good one . . . Spirit, do not live under the tree; spirit, don't stay under the bamboo grove; spirit, don't hide on top of the mountain. Spirit, come back instead to my Little Daughter . . . Come back, come back to my Little Daughter . . .

After the tying and blessing, we ate roast turkey with sticky rice, and we drank the cool, sweet milk of coconuts with the tops lopped off. We couldn't "touch" the turkey, because that part of the ceremony *had* to be done with a pig. But it was the best we could do under the circumstances, and for us it was enough.

CHAPTER FOUR

THE BAMBOO PEOPLE

When my parents first moved into the village, they had nowhere to stay, so they lodged with the family of Ter Pay Pay, a Karen man in his thirties. Ter Pay Pay lived with his parents, and they were getting on in years. Over time he became a close friend of ours, and his parents became our honorary grandparents. Of course, they weren't related to us, but we loved them as if they were family, and they were the nearest we ever had to a real grandfather and grandmother.

Their house was on the opposite side of the school from us, just a short walk away. In Karen culture, adults are usually nicknamed after their oldest child. My father would be called Bwa Bwa Pah—"father of Bwa Bwa"—and my mother would be Bwa Bwa Moh—"mother of Bwa Bwa." Everyone called Grandma and Grandpa Ter Pay Pay Pah and Ter Pay Pay Moh, after their son, Ter Pay Pay. We never knew their real names.

Grandpa was a quiet man, but Grandma was the opposite. She seemed never to stop talking and was always telling us stories about her youth. She and Grandpa were in their eighties, and they had lived through the British colonial times. When she was in her twenties,

Grandma had worked as a teacher at a school founded by the British, called Per Ku School. Whenever we talked about the resistance, Grandma would share her own memories of how things had come to be. She recounted how the Karen and the British colonizers had gotten along well. The British did their best to respect Karen culture; while they were in Burma, the Karen were granted the right to have Karen New Year recognized across the whole of the country. It had been a long, long fight to reach this point, and it meant a lot to the Karen people.

Grandma told us vivid, terrible stories about the battles that she had lived through, the worst during the Second World War. She had terrifying memories of fleeing from the Japanese soldiers who had been joined by the Burma Independence Army (BIA) to drive the British colonizers out of Burma. The Japanese and BIA forces visited horrific cruelties on the Karen villages, their goal being to force the Karen to give up the leader of the British troops, Major Hugh Seagrim. From 1942 to 1944 Major Seagrim was leading a joint force of British and Karen soldiers, who were fighting a guerrilla war from the jungles. They would launch surprise attacks, then melt back into the hills, wreaking havoc on the Japanese and BIA forces.

Seagrim had stayed behind in the mountains of Karen State when the Japanese invaded Burma and drove out the British. He loved the Karen people, and the Karen people admired him and respected him as a deeply religious man.

The Karen steadfastly refused to betray Major Seagrim, but he gave himself up when he realized that the Japanese were taking revenge on innocent Karen villagers. We Karen had an affectionate name for General Seagrim: "Grandfather Longlegs." We didn't agree with Grandfather Longlegs giving himself up, but he was a brave and principled man. He wouldn't stand by and see innocents suffer. The Japanese executed Major Seagrim and several of his Karen brothers in arms, but this did not stop the terrible violence.

It seemed impossible that people could be so merciless. The Japanese and BIA continued to oppress the Karen people, burning villages and crops and shooting people on sight. Grandma told us how they would snatch Karen babies, throw them into the air, and impale them on their bayonets. Or they would get a pregnant Karen woman, force her to lie on her side, and pound her stomach with a rice pounder. It was so horrible. It seemed as if they were fighting a war on two fronts: one against the British and the Allied forces and the other specifically against the Karen people.

Yet still the armed resistance grew. The British air-dropped weapons and soldiers into the Karen jungles. Grandma remembered seeing many things fall from the sky: men and crates of weapons and ammunition. The fighting finally came to an end when the atom bomb dropped on Hiroshima and the Japanese troops were ordered to abandon the offensive and return to their barracks.

The British had promised the Karen some degree of autonomy in postwar Burma, as they had done with other ethnic groups that had fought on their side. It would be their reward for helping to drive the Japanese out of the country. But by the time the war was over those promises seemed to have been forgotten. In 1947, shortly after World War II, the Karen National Union had been founded, and it went on to become the heart of the resistance movement. After centuries of oppression as part of Burma, the KNU wanted an independent state for its people. It saw this as the only way to guarantee their rights and preserve their culture.

KNU leaders traveled to London to ask the British prime minister to keep his promise that the Karen would have their own state. But when Burma gained independence in 1948, no such guarantee was given. And so had begun decades of conflict and hardship for the people of Burma.

Grandma told us lots of tales like this. She did so because she never wanted it to be forgotten how the Karen had fought and suffered. I liked listening to the stories; somehow I felt it was important to hear such things, but I was very young and didn't understand what they really meant.

In my childish mind the war was all a long way away, and we lived in a beautiful, peaceful place. It was inconceivable to me that it would ever change. I had seen Grandpa die, but he was an old man—and I knew that all people had to die in the end. There was nothing dark or horrific about his death.

When I was nearing my fourth birthday, Grandpa died quite suddenly. He was the first person that I had ever known die. My mother explained to me that Grandpa was dead and that once he was buried I would never see him again. I was very sad. I loved Grandpa even more than Grandma. She was forever chatting away, but it was with Grandpa that I got the best snoozes and cuddles.

I had spent much time playing at Grandpa's feet when he was alive, and I wanted to touch them one last time. I went to their house and found Grandpa laid out in the living room, his body surrounded by candles. He was covered in a white cloth, with just his face showing. He looked so peaceful, and if I hadn't known better I would have thought him fast asleep. I went and tweaked the cloth, so it revealed just his toes. I played with each in turn, until I was sure they were all there.

After he was buried I asked my mother where Grandpa had gone. She didn't give me any easy answers—like he was in Heaven and we'd meet him again. Karen animists believe that once the body has died the spirit remains on Earth, so in that sense Grandpa was still with us. I liked the idea that Grandpa was still here, watching over me.

CHAPTER FIVE

THE FLOWER CHILDREN

When I was five years old, I started primary school. The school building was very basic: a large bamboo-framed hut, with open sides and rows of sawn-log benches facing the single blackboard. Still, it was all we knew, and from the very first I loved it. There was a set school uniform—a blue skirt and white blouse—but a number of families were so poor that they couldn't afford it. Their children were allowed to come to class in whatever clothes they had. I felt sorry for them in their make-do half-uniforms. Luckily, I had my sister's hand-me-downs.

Boys and girls had to sit in separate rows. We were told that the atmosphere was not to be one of competition between pupils and we should be pleased when others did well. In year one we had Karen language lessons, basic English, and handwriting. In those first few months I learned to write my name, "Zoya," in Karen. But I often got it wrong and spelled "Zo-gah" instead; I kept getting the Karen "y" letter upside down, which turns it into "g." Zo-gah means "broken," and my friends would laugh and tease me mercilessly. I was already unhappy, because my name wasn't a traditional Karen one. That just made it worse.

I loved school, though, and I wanted desperately to do well. During that first year the teacher asked us what we wanted to be when we grew up. I said, "a teacher," because that was about the most important profession that I could think of. Of course, my teacher was very pleased.

I came in first in my class in the year one exams. There was a big prize-giving ceremony on the school playing field. My mother was there, as were most of the other parents. When I was called to the front to receive my prize, I was thrilled. I was wearing one of my sister's hand-me-down skirts, and it was far too big for me. I went running up to the stage, all the while holding up my skirt with my hands. But when I went to reach for the prize I let go in my excitement, and down my skirt fell.

Everyone burst out laughing. I was shocked and confused, and I didn't know what to do. Should I first take my prize or pull up my skirt? Finally, it was the teacher who reached down and did it for me. She told me to grip my skirt with one hand and take my prize with the other. I did just that and turned around and went back to join my mother. She was glowing with a mixture of pride and embarrassment.

It was more than worth all the humiliation when I examined my prize, though—it was six exercise books and three pens. We had little or no money to buy such things, so they were precious to me. Ever since I can remember I was very independent, and when I won the school prize I kept my winnings to myself. I used to store my things in a backpack that I kept by my bed, and I didn't like other people touching it. In that bag were my few clothes, a wooden bowl my father had made me, a handful of precious photos that had been taken at village weddings, and my school prize materials. And those were all my worldly possessions.

We didn't appreciate it at the time, but we were incredibly lucky to be learning Karen in school. In areas controlled by the Burmese regime—which is dominated by the Burman ethnic group—no one was allowed to study Karen or any other ethnic language. In Burma there are eight main ethnic groups: the Shan, Arakan, Mon, Kachin, Chin, Karen, Karenni, and Burman. Then there are dozens of smaller ethnic groups, and each has its own language. But the only language other than English taught in schools controlled by the regime was Burmese. Rather than celebrating the nation's cultural riches, the regime tried to crush its diversity. Because our village was so close to the center of the Karen resistance, though, we got a better-rounded education.

Each week on a Friday we would have a lesson called "Citizenship Education." In it we were taught to respect older people, to respect our parents, and to help people who might be in need of assistance. If you were walking on a path and you saw an old woman carrying firewood, you should go and offer help. It was common sense, really, and a reminder to us of how we should behave toward others.

At school we studied the Karen flag and learned its meaning. It is made up of three stripes of red, white, and blue, with a rising sun with nine rays set over a Karen drum in one corner. During colonial times the Karen had to fight to get their flag recognized by the British, just as they had done with Karen New Year. We learned that the red stood for the courage of the Karen people. The white signified purity of purpose and honesty. And blue in our culture means loyalty. The rising sun signified that the Karen were a new nation, and its nine rays stood for the nine regions inhabited by the Karen people: Irrawaddy, Myawaddy, Tenasserim, and so on.

The school doubled as the village church and the village hall. There was a bell made of a triangular rod of iron that the headmaster would ring by bashing a metal pole backward and forward inside it. The harsh ringing would echo across the village, and that was the signal for morning assembly. It was also rung at the end of the school day and for Sunday school.

Our village was mixed Christian, animist, and Buddhist. No one ever tried to convert anyone directly, but Sunday school was an overtly

Christian affair. We were taught that if you weren't a Christian, you would go to Hell. That prospect frightened me, and I often came home looking for assurance from my parents that we were not all doomed.

My parents were very relaxed about religion. The Karen people describe animism as Pwa Aw Gheh, "the People Who Believe in the Spirit." But my parents never preached to us. They always said that I was free to choose my own faith. So I listened carefully to what the Sunday school teacher told us and tried to make up my own mind. They were not unique in being open-minded and flexible. Karen who were Buddhist or Christian still incorporated some animist traditions or beliefs into their religion, so even though Karen had different religions, we still shared certain beliefs and traditions, which helped unite us.

Our primary school teachers taught us the legends of the Karen people. One of the most important was a poem that narrated the story of the earliest times of our tribe. It tells that in the beginning there was an animist god, called Ywa. Ywa was neither man nor woman and was not in a human form. Ywa was the creator of the world and a force for good. There was also a force of evil, called Mu Kaw Lee. But Mu Kaw Lee was not a god and so was weaker.

Ywa created three sons in human form. The eldest was a Karen, the second a Burman, and the youngest a white man. To the Karen son Ywa gave a golden book, to the Burman a silver book, and to the white man Ywa gave a book bound in normal paper. When the rains began and the Karen son went to plant his rice field, he placed the golden book nearby, on a tree stump. But his younger brother, the white man, had grown jealous and coveted his beautiful golden book. When the Karen man wasn't looking, the white man came along and took it, replacing it with his own. Then the white man built a boat and escaped to a far-off country. He carried his prize with him—the golden book that contained the teachings Ywa had given to his eldest son.

After a long day working under the heavy rain, the Karen man went to fetch his golden book. The book that the white man had left in its place had fallen apart in the rain, and there was nothing left. A chicken had been scratching around the stump searching for food, and all the Karen man found was chicken scratch marks. He concluded that the golden book had been replaced by the scratch marks and that those must embody the message that Ywa had left him. So the Karen man taught himself to read and write in chicken scratch. Over time, he learned the truth about the golden book being stolen, but by then it was too late—chicken scratch had become the official language of the Karen.

Many Karen believe this story absolutely and believe that one day the younger brother—a white man—will come again to help save our people. In the nineteenth century, when the first white missionaries came to Burma, many Karen believed that this was the younger brother returning. They believed that the Bible must be the golden book that had been stolen so long ago, so they welcomed the missionaries. The traditional "chicken scratch" writing of the Karen had all but died out by the time the missionaries arrived, and they found it hard to convert people to Christianity without a recognized written language with which to read the Bible. So the missionaries invented a written language for the Karen, based upon the Burmese alphabet. That is what we use today.

I remember very clearly the first white people I ever met. I was around five or six years old when two French nurses came to our village. It was a man-and-woman team, and they were running a mobile backpack clinic. All the medicines they had with them had to be carried on their backs through the jungle. But to us it was just as though a real hospital had come to town, so impressive were their medical supplies.

It was also the first time that I'd seen white people. I was told they were "French," but that meant nothing to me. All I knew is that they were *gaw la wah*, "white people." Their hair was whiter than elephant ivory, and their eyes were bluer than the sky. As I gazed at them, with their pale faces and long noses, I couldn't believe how scary they looked.

They sat on pillows provided by the villagers and spread out their medical supplies. I had no idea why they were sitting on the pillows like that. In Karen culture a pillow is a highly respected place where you lay your head to rest. That's why we gave them as presents to lovers. No Karen person would ever place his or her bottom on one!

The French nurses called together the adults and announced that they'd come to vaccinate the children. We sat on the ground and waited, nervously, as the village nurse called us one by one. Eventually it was my turn. I went and sat on my teacher's lap and waited to see what would happen. A lot of the children before me had cried. The French lady turned to me and gave me an injection in the arm. It didn't really hurt, and I thought to myself, if that's it, it's not so bad.

I gazed up at her as she dabbed at my arm with a piece of cotton wool. It was her nose that I just couldn't get over. It was long and white and pointed, and burned red on top from exposure to the sun. I realized then that the other children hadn't been crying due to the pain of the injections; they'd been crying due to their fear of the nurse! I found her scary, too, but I didn't cry. I just wished my mother had been there to hold me.

Not all Karen people have converted to Christianity. Many are Buddhist, and it is the predominant religion in Burma. Even those of us who are not Buddhist still respect and appreciate the traditions. Once a year my parents would take me to the Water Festival, which happens every April. We'd take a long-tail boat to Ka Paw Lu—Spider Hill Village—on the bank of the Moei River. It was called Spider Hill Village because the villagers had found many huge spiders when they cleared the bush to build the first houses. The Water Festival was held in the Buddhist monastery that overlooks the village.

The Water Festival is like a captivating carnival. It takes place at the hottest time of year, and people are supposed to pour water over one another to cool down. But invariably, it turns into a big water fight! The monks dress in their saffron robes and ring their little hand bells as they start chanting, chanting, chanting. There are trays piled high with delicious food—rice, curry, cookies, and traditional snacks. And the smoke of burning incense hangs heavy in the air, with its spicy scent.

My favorite memories from these festivals were the hot-air balloons, each as big as an elephant. The monks made them out of brightly colored paper, with a small wood fire at the neck of the balloon. Hanging down was a long rope strung with gifts—children's clothes, soap, and sweets. The monks would release a balloon and it would soar skyward, everyone watching to see its direction of flight. As the fire died down, the balloon would start to descend. People tried to guess where it was going to land and set off at a run, chasing the balloon. The first to find it could take their pick of the presents.

Of course, we loved it; it was like a magical adventure. We went for the sheer fun of it, but my parents went to show their respect for Buddhism, a belief to which many Karen adhere. Throughout our childhood my parents would take us to hear the chanting of the Buddhist monks and the preaching of the Christian pastors, while at home they would follow their animist traditions. In this way they exposed us to the main faiths in Burma, leaving us free to choose our own ways.

The highlight of the Christian year was Christmas, and our village made it a very big deal. As with the Water Festival, it was a magical time of year. With the help of Mo Ghay Bay, we'd drag a big tree out of the forest. Mo Ghay Bay was so strong she could pick up a tree using only her trunk. With her help we'd erect the tree in the school playground and decorate it with balloons and presents. On Christmas Eve we had a Nativity play, with one student acting as Joseph and one as Mary, and a model stable with a baby in a cradle. Others acted as the Three Wise Men, following the star to the stable, and as angels, shepherds, and sheep. When I was young I wanted to be a sheep, covered in a white cloth and crawling on all fours. But eventually I got bored with that, and then I wanted to be an angel, singing with an angelic voice in the choir.

Christmas morning was for opening presents. Parents didn't generally give their children many presents, as no one could afford it. Instead, our parents would buy us gifts of biscuits, sweets, or soap, which we were supposed to give to our friends. The teachers would write the names of all the children on scraps of paper and put them into a hat. Each of us had to pick a name, and that was the child to whom you gave your present.

By lunchtime the entire village would have congregated at the school. Each family would have brought their own Christmas lunch—usually bamboo-cooked rice, sticky rice, and chicken. Bamboo-cooked rice was my favorite food at Christmas. To make it one had to cut a bamboo the diameter of a man's arm and about three or four feet long. The inside would be packed half full of rice and topped up with water. Then you'd lay the bamboo in the glowing embers, so that 75 percent of it was in the fire and you could keep turning the free end. As the bamboo blackened in the fire, the rice inside would be cooked. Finally, you'd remove it and split it open. The rice would come out in a pillar contained in the inner membrane of the bamboo. It would be steaming hot and delicately flavored.

But the best thing about Christmas was Santa Claus. Santa would be dressed in a red suit made of light cotton and wearing a pointed hat with a white ball on the end. As he ho! ho! ho!'d, he'd throw handfuls of sweets and cookies. We'd go mad fighting to get them, running and falling and laughing fit to burst.

Sometimes Santa would start doing a silly dance, which would make us laugh all the more. He wore an enormous white beard, and at first I believed absolutely that he was for real. In my mind he was a kindly human from a far distant land who came to make Karen children happy on Christmas Day.

It seemed to me that in my village we lived in a kind of paradise. Animists, Buddhists, and Christians lived together peacefully; it never even occurred to me that things might be different in other parts of the world. But, sadly, not even paradise lasts forever.

CHAPTER SIX

RIVER OF DARKNESS

When we weren't at school we had to invent our own entertainment, as there were no televisions, computers, or movie theaters in our village. Because our school was a village school, most of my classmates were also my neighbors and my playmates. My closest friends were Day Nyah Paw, "Lily Flower"; Tee Ser Paw, "Sweet Water Flower"; and Nightingale. Nightingale was called Nightingale in English, and she didn't have a Karen name. It wasn't that unusual for Karen children to be given English names, especially among the families of the resistance. Nightingale lived next door, and she was the same age as me. Her house was between the river and ours. Her mother was a housewife, and her father worked in the resistance. We were very close, and we'd always be playing at each other's houses.

I was the gang leader of my group of friends most of the time. In part this was because I was always thinking up new games to play. But I also had an advantage in that the floor of our house was unusually high, leaving plenty of room beneath it for us to play. Often, our gang would go climbing the guava trees. Bwa Bwa might be with us, and Slone might come with Nightingale's brother, his best friend. If Naw

Paw was there, we would be seven—all of us swinging in the branches, grabbing the fruit, and playing.

I was good friends with the leader of the boys' gang, Lah Ka Paw, "Moonlight." Moonlight was a bit of an angry child, like my little brother, Slone. He channeled that anger into being in firm control of his friends. If Moonlight made a decision, the others had to follow. Like Slone, he wasn't a particularly big child. But he was very smart, and that's how he kept control of his gang.

One sunny day we broke lessons for lunch. On the way home Moonlight and I started playing in the sun, wheeling around with our arms outstretched as if we were birds. I soon forgot completely about lunch. Once afternoon school was over, Moonlight and I finished off our flying game. By the time I got home my mother was worried sick. She'd even sent Say Say to search for me.

"Little Daughter, where have you been?" she exclaimed. "You didn't come for lunch, and you're home so late!

"I wasn't anywhere, Moe," I said. "I was just playing with Moonlight in the sunshine."

After that everyone was convinced that Moonlight and I had a little romance going and that we were destined to become sweethearts. His family and my family teased Moonlight and me remorselessly. My sister was the ringleader, amply assisted by Say Say and Slone. I was shy, and I didn't like being teased like this. As for Moonlight, when his brothers and sisters teased that I was his girlfriend, he used to get so annoyed.

The craziest adventure I ever went on was led by my older sister. Bwa Bwa announced that she was going to collect mangoes, and I said that Nightingale and I were going too. Bwa Bwa argued that it was a long, long way and we were too young. But we refused to be left behind. When Bwa Bwa and her friends set off, we followed after. Soon we were deep in the forest. The path petered out, and no one was sure in which direction the mango trees lay.

We'd been walking for hours, and we reached a small rice farm. One of my sister's friends said she thought the mango trees were just downhill from there. My sister tried to send us back, but I kept insisting that we were fine. We went down the steep hill, clinging to bushes and branches as we descended a slippery slope. All we had with us was a basket and a knife for cutting the mangoes. We had no water, and we were so thirsty.

We paused while my sister cut into the side of a banana tree. We cupped our hands and drank the banana water as it came pouring out. It tasted like diluted ripe banana and was wonderfully cool and refreshing. We pushed on, and eventually we reached the mango trees. Fruit were lying everywhere. These were a small variety of mango, each about the size of a plum, and they were delicious. We gathered the mangoes and ate our fill. By the time we were done, there weren't enough left to fill the basket.

Someone suggested that we should whistle up the wind, so that it would blow down more of the ripe fruit. Many Karen believe that by making a whistling noise like the wind in the trees, you can cause the wind to blow. We all tried to whistle, but no matter how hard I tried I couldn't manage it.

"It's probably because your lips are too big," Bwa Bwa announced. "Look at the size of them! No wonder you can't whistle."

The others followed Bwa Bwa's lead and started to tease me about my lips.

"They may be big, but they're beautiful," I retorted. "In fact, they're the perfect size for calling up the wind!"

Just then, and as if by magic, the wind started to blow. It blew and blew, and down fell the mangoes. We collected as many as we could, and then we turned for home. We tried to retrace the route we had taken on the way out. But we'd lost track of the time, and dusk settles quickly in the forest. At night the jungle is a completely different beast from the day, and we didn't want to be out in the dark. We hurried ahead, fearful of losing our way. It was a huge relief when we reached the village in the gathering darkness. My parents had warned us about going into the forest without Say Say. We decided it was best to keep that mango-hunting expedition very quiet.

Although we children were often left to our own devices, we all knew how much our parents worried about us. There were so many dangers living in the jungle: dangerous animals and diseases, poisonous plants, even the river that we relied on so much, which could sweep us away. Those of us who were truly adventurous would play in the forest and rivers that surrounded the village. There was one area where the trees were draped in vines of all shapes and sizes, and it was like a natural playground. There were thin vines and ones as thick as your wrist, and smooth ones and knobbly ones, and even vines that were covered in spines. That last was best avoided, for our favorite game was to climb a tree and go whooshing down one of the vines.

If we were feeling really brave, we could jump on a vine and swing out over the river, hanging on for dear life as the water flashed past below. Of course, this game was very dangerous, as the vine could break and we'd end up in the middle of the river. But we didn't consider such things as children. We had little sense of fear.

My father, however, was quite aware of how dangerous it could be, so he built us a wonderful tree house in the garden. He constructed it in the heart of a beautiful, spreading tamarind tree, using remnants from the sawmill plus bamboo. I think he figured that if we fell out of his tree house at least we'd end up on the ground and not be swept down the river. We loved that tree house so much. We felt so special because we had the only one in the whole village. Slone and I spent hours playing in it, and Bwa Bwa too. We pretended it was our home. We designated some of the branches as bedrooms and others as the kitchen or living room. We'd climb all around the tree to collect the tamarind fruit and bring it back to the house and have a meal. We'd dip the fruit in salt and chili and have a tamarind feast. We'd eat and dip, and eat and dip, until we couldn't eat any more.

Beneath the floor of our house my father built us another plaything, a kind of giant wooden cradle. It was suspended from the rafters above with bamboo rope, and it was big enough for five or six of us to cram into. With one person chosen to push, we'd swing backward and forward, backward and forward, laughing as we did so. Eventually we'd always swing too high or fool around too much, and someone would go tumbling out. One time I fell and ended up under the cradle as it came swinging down again. It crushed my left arm, and I suffered for months in real pain. I couldn't lift my arm above shoulder level or move it backward or forward very much. But I didn't want my parents to know, for then they might ban me from playing with my friends. So I did everything I could to disguise the fact of the injury.

We used to eat with our right hand and take spoonfuls of curry or other food with the left. As I couldn't use my left arm very much, I had to use my right for both. But in our culture that's considered very rude, because your right hand is invariably covered in food from whatever you've been eating. When my mum noticed me doing so, she demanded to know where all my manners had gone. I was afraid to tell her the truth, so I forced myself to use my left arm more and more. Eventually, it seemed to repair itself of its own accord.

But when I was about six years old our happy games suddenly turned very dark. I was playing with my brother and sister down by the river. It was the hot season, and we were splashing about in the cool shallows. The roots of a big tree formed an underwater loop, and you could dive down and swim through the loop and up again. It was a tight squeeze, even for someone as small as me, and you had to wiggle a lot. Neither of our parents knew we were playing this game, or I don't think they'd have been very happy.

It was nearing evening, and the sun was dipping below the mountains. As we played in the darkening water, we suddenly caught a whiff of something very bad. None of us had ever smelled anything like it before. Instinctively I was scared, but at the same time I was curious, and I wanted to know what it was. I let my big sister and brother go first as we edged our way forward, closer to the furthest tree roots. All of a sudden we were screaming in horror. In front of us was a man facedown in the river, his body all swollen and bloated. He was lodged under a tree root, which was what was stopping him from floating away downstream. The smell was sickening, incomparable to anything I had smelled before, so bad, and we turned as one and fled back to the house.

"Daddy! Daddy! Come! Come!"

"There's a dead person in the river!"

"It smells so horrible!"

He led us back toward the river. I was scared and didn't want to go too close this time. Slone and Bwa Bwa were braver, and they went close enough to show my father exactly where the body was. My father told us all to keep back as he went to deal with it. I watched in horrified fascination as he grabbed a stick and leaned out and pushed the body until it went under. A moment later it bobbed up again, a little further out, and slowly it was dragged into the current.

As it floated away I could see that the man's back was torn to shreds and crisscrossed with angry red slash marks. It was so horrible I had to look away. What on earth had happened to him? I wondered. Had he been attacked by a wild animal? Even though I had turned away and hidden my eyes, the horrible image stayed in my mind. I knew for sure then that I was going to have nightmares.

Dad told us it was time to come in now, and he led us back to the house.

"How did that man fall in the river and die?" I asked him quietly.

My father glanced at me. I could tell that he was trying to decide what answer to give me. Finally, he must have decided to tell me the truth.

"Far away up river there are other Karen villages," he explained. "Sometimes the Burmese Army go into those villages and kidnap people. They use them as forced labor—as porters to carry their heavy loads. Those poor people get no proper food to eat or any rest. When they are exhausted and cannot continue carrying the loads of weapons or food, the Burmese soldiers throw them in the river. That's how that man ended up here."

"But why was his back so horribly hurt?" I asked. "How did that happen?"

"The Burmese soldiers beat the porters, to make them keep going," my father replied. "When they cannot go on anymore, sometimes they do very bad things to them. They do it to show the other porters what will happen to them if they stop carrying their loads. Once they're done, they throw them into the river to die."

That kind of cruelty was so unimaginable. My father knew that the dead man had to be a Karen, as the villages upstream were all populated by our people. This was my most direct experience of the war to date, and it was so up close and personal. We had found that dead body, and we'd found it in one of our sunniest, most favored play spots. It was not something that a child should see, and for many weeks it cast a dark shadow over us. One night I overheard my mother and father talking about it in hushed tones. They sounded worried, and this in turn worried me. They were discussing the fighting and how it was coming closer than ever to our own lands.

My mother seemed to be the most disturbed; whenever the war lurched a little nearer she felt its threat and its darkness impinging upon our happy lives. As a soldier herself, she knew from bitter experience the trauma of war and did not want us to know it.

I used to think that I could never be a warrior like her, a true Karen hero. Seeing that dead body in the river had made me even more fearful. It became harder to watch my parents leave us time after time now that I understood what was at stake and what the risks were. The image of that dead body stayed in my head for a long time. It haunted my dreams.

After that we stopped playing in the river for a long, long time.

Chapter Seven

Victory Field

Not long after we had found the dead man floating in the river, my father decided that we needed a house in central Manerplaw. My mother worked there so much, he said, it only made sense for us to be able to be closer to her. So we built a bamboo one, similar to the one in the village. Next to it was a small rice paddy, which my father converted into a flower garden. In the past, Karen resistance workers had been given food rations by the Karen National Union (KNU) instead of wages. But it was always rough, unhusked rice, so my mother and father had to grow extra food. But in recent years things had improved. The KNU had had time to improve administration and the local economy and was also making money taxing cross-border trade to and from Thailand in areas it controlled. Now the KNU ration included proper husked rice, salt, tea, and fish paste.

My father loved flowers, and he was thrilled to be able to cultivate a garden of his own. He loved their beauty and their spirit, and he loved them because the very sight of them and their scent made people happy.

While my father nurtured his flower garden, my mother used the land around the house to grow vegetables. She planted coriander, water spinach, onions, garlic, and green beans. She teased my father that when it came to mealtimes he should have to eat his flowers instead of making her share all the fruits of her labor. In response, he planted pineapple, mango, lemon, plum, and banana trees, so he had an excuse that he was really making an orchard. His real passion remained his flowers, but we children were thrilled to have such a bounty of food.

My father's flower garden ran right down to the banks of the Moei River. People traveling on the busy river used to comment on how lovely it looked and wonder who might live there. One dry season my father built a bamboo summerhouse in the midst of the garden, with a view of the river. When it was hot we'd go there to read, and it was somewhere to take visitors. That was my father's idea of how to make people feel truly welcome.

For my father, no flower garden was complete without an ornamental pond. It took him two days to build one at our Manerplaw home. When he finished, he filled it with tiny gray-and-silver fish that sparkled when the sunlight fell on the pond. The pond was beautiful, and we spent the whole first day sitting by the water just watching the fish dart through the clear water.

Unfortunately, the ducks my mother kept loved the pond almost as much as my father did. When my parents were at work, there was no one to protect the pond, and the ducks quickly caught and ate all the fish. When my father came back from work, all he saw was the ducks waggling their backsides contentedly and an empty pond.

He turned on my mother in exasperation. "Look! Look what your ducks have done! I gave up all that time to dig that pond and put those fish in there, and—"

"Why didn't you put a fence around it?" my mother countered. "Anyway, you're happy to eat duck whenever I cook it, aren't you?"

"Well, don't you like sitting around the pond and watching the fish? How're we going to do that now?"

My mother snorted. "As if I ever get the time! I'm always working in the garden, growing the vegetables to cook with the duck curry!"

It was a rare occasion when my parents argued like that, and when they did we just kept quiet. The arguments never became that heated, and the most that would happen was that one of them would storm out. After the ducks ate all his fish my father's ornamental pond became a duck pond, and the water got very dirty . But it was lovely while it lasted.

My sister and I spent hours in my father's flower garden catching butterflies. We'd pop the prettiest ones into a clear plastic bag until we had a rainbow of fluttering colors in there. Once we had enough, we'd set up a "market stall" selling butterflies to our friends and passersby. People would come and try to barter flower petals for our butterflies. Everything had its worth according to color: The yellow one was "the golden butterfly," so it was the most expensive. Blue was the "sky butterfly" and less expensive. Green was the "leaf butterfly" and so the least costly of all. Of the currencies we accepted, the purple flowers were worth the most, followed by red and then yellow. From the flowers we bartered for our butterflies we'd make a petal-and-lily-leaf salad and pretend to eat it. The butterfly and flower market was one of the best games of all.

My mother reared pigs, ducks, turkeys, and chickens. The duck and chicken eggs were to supplement our diet, but she sold some of the produce to earn extra income. If she killed a piglet, she'd earn around 300 Thai baht, the equivalent of six dollars, from selling the meat. A fully grown pig might go for 2,000 baht. She used the money to pay our school fees and to buy school uniforms, or to buy things to sell at her stall, such as cheroots.

The only way to earn any money was to have a little business on the side, so my mother ran a small shop in Manerplaw. It was a little stall under the house, which she opened in the evening and on weekends. She sold fruit, homemade snacks of rice flour and raw, juicy sugarcane, and chunks of crunchy brown sugar, called *ghan da gah*. And she stocked *tha blu yah,* betel nut mixed with lime paste and a red spicy powder. This was a mild stimulant that people chewed. Doing so produced mouthfuls of saliva and stained the teeth a dark red.

With what little money she earned my mother would buy some cut-price *moh htoo,* Burmese cheroots, which she would sell for a small profit. *Moh htoo* are like a very rough cigar, with dry, flaky tobacco rolled up in a long leaf. Often when people smoked them a glowing ember would fall out and land on their clothes or legs and burn them.

There was always a lull in the fighting during the rainy season, as the jungle would become impassable. Then there would be military training on the sandy beach below our house. One soldier would swim across the river, hoist a rope out of the water, and tie it around a tree so it was stretched taught. One by one the soldiers had to link their arms and feet around the rope and climb across. Once they'd done so, they had to swim back again. From our garden we had a ringside seat, and we'd watch in fascination, hoping that no one would fall. The Karen soldiers used to dock their long-tail boats in the lagoon below our house. It was like a little harbor, and often they would pause for a rest in my father's flower garden before continuing up the hill to their base. Since my mum had been a soldier and often told me her soldier's stories, I knew what they were fighting for. They were the army of the people, and they were very brave.

We had two lives now: our village one and the weekend one, which we often spent in Manerplaw. I was seven years old when our Manerplaw life started to attain more importance for us. One evening in 1988 my father came home with four Burmese students. He announced that they would be staying with us until they managed to build a home of their own.

I had never met a Burman before. It was very strange having them in the house, especially as my siblings and I couldn't talk to them or they with us; they spoke Burmese, and we spoke Karen. My parents could speak Burmese, though, and they spent many hours talking with the students. One evening one of the students explained to my parents exactly why they had come to join the resistance. My parents listened to him and then explained to us what he was saying in Karen. I didn't understand everything, but this was the gist of it.

Until August 1988 General Ne Win was the head of the military dictatorship in Burma. It was widely suspected that he was somewhat unbalanced. As if to prove this was so, he had suddenly announced that all banknotes except for the 45- and 90-kyat notes were no longer valid. (The kyat is the Burmese currency.) From now on, only denominations divisible by nine would be legal tender, because nine was a lucky number, General Ne Win declared.

Overnight, most people's savings were wiped out. It was the last straw for a population that had been suffering under his dictatorship for years. People began protesting on the streets, and the driving force behind the protests was the students. The marches grew bigger and bigger, quickly spreading across the country, until hundreds of thousands of protesters were marching in all the major cities and towns. The protestors came from all religions, cultures, and backgrounds, but they were united in their calls for an end to the military dictatorship and for the country to be returned to democratic rule. The students who came to stay with us were among those protestors. They had hoped to see an end to military rule, for there to be democracy, but it was not to happen.

On August 8, 1988, the military launched a bloody and horrific crackdown. Thousands of unarmed demonstrators were gunned down in cold blood and countless more arrested. Saffron-robed Buddhist monks—who until now had always been universally respected in Burma—were among those beaten, arrested, and killed. This became known as the 8/8/88 uprisings.

After the uprisings, a new and even more brutal dictatorship had taken power. It called itself the State Law and Order Restoration Council (SLORC). (In 1997 it changed its name to the State Peace and Development Council, after being advised by an American public relations firm.) Democracy activists had formed the National League for Democracy, led by Aung San Suu Kyi, the daughter of General Aung San, who had led Burma's independence movement. They continued the campaigns for democracy, and this, combined with international pressure, led to the regime's being forced to agree to elections, which were held in 1990.

Despite the government's trying to rig the elections by setting up lots of political parties as fronts, using state media for propaganda, and detaining opposition leaders, including putting Aung San Suu Kyi under house arrest, the NLD won 82 percent of the seats in Parliament. Instead of handing over power, the government launched a new wave of repression, arresting and torturing newly elected MPs.

I was proud that the Karen had given sanctuary to the democracy activists, but I was also worried about the escalation of the attacks on us. I heard people talking about Aung San Suu Kyi, but I was just a child and no one explained to me who she was.

Aung San Suu Kyi had been living in the United Kingdom but returned to Burma in 1988 to look after her sick mother. Student leaders went to her to ask her to lead their struggle. She agreed and was so popular among the people that the generals, terrified of her, placed her under house arrest. She has now spent most of the past twenty years in detention but is still loved by the people and has become a symbol of Burma's struggle for freedom.

My father was given the special duty by the KNU to work with other pro-democracy organizations and individuals who came to Manerplaw. That's how the four students living in our house had ended up with us.

Upon hearing the students' story, I realized that the Karen were not alone. Other ethnic groups—including the Burmans themselves—were suffering under the harsh rule of General Ne Win and his junta.

It was a surprise to learn that the Burmese junta was oppressing its own people as much as it was ethnic groups like the Karen. I couldn't understand how people could treat one another so viciously.

My father counseled the Karen National Union leadership to welcome the 8/8/88 refugees. One by one, offices of the democratic resistance groups sprang up around Manerplaw. Their young men started to train to join the armed resistance, fighting alongside our own Karen soldiers. My father was the perfect candidate to help coordinate all these activities: he spoke fluent Burmese; he was an animist and so religiously "neutral"; and he had been educated in Rangoon, so he was familiar with the ways in which the urban resistance functioned.

Manerplaw was transforming itself into the heartland of the democratic resistance movement in Burma, and my father was appointed a special adviser to General Saw Bo Mya, the president of the Karen National Union, to help advise on the transformation.

None of this meant much to me at the time, and it really affected my life in only one glorious way: with my father's new appointment, he was pulled out of the frontline areas. Now he would spend the week working in Manerplaw, and most weekends he would be back in the village with us. In short, my father was coming home.

It was from this time that I really started to get to know my father and to understand his belief that one day Burma would be free. He wanted peace and democracy for all the people in Burma and to live in a Burma where ethnic people could be free from oppression and celebrate their culture openly and without fear. The influx of the 8/8/88 refugees had instilled a new spirit of hope and resistance in Manerplaw. That spirit was all around us.

But it also had a darker side, for it would draw the attention of the junta ever closer to us.

Chapter Eight

The River Spirits

My parents didn't try to hide the truth of the war from us, but they didn't force us to confront it either. Life went on largely as it had before, with laughter and with light.

However, around this time I did notice other changes in Manerplaw. Our village wasn't as silent as before. Many new houses and offices were being built, more people were around, and more foreigners were around, as publicity about the uprising had finally gotten journalists interested in what was happening in Burma. There were also many more ethnic representatives than before, as Manerplaw became the effective headquarters of the whole country's resistance to the dictatorship. I hadn't really understood about other ethnic groups before. Different ethnic people had tended to stick to their own areas. Most were poor farmers, but even if they had wanted to travel around the country, it wasn't possible as the dictatorship didn't allow it.

My parents seemed even busier than before. Even though my father now lived with us, he was always at meetings or in his office. My mother was also very busy with her work. Villagers commented on how even though we were left alone so much, we didn't run wild. We were usually well-behaved children. I didn't really think much about why they were always working; I was having too much fun playing in the jungle, and I loved school.

In my family my father was the one who showed his emotions more. Often he saw terrible things during his work, and it would really upset him. My mother was the opposite. Whatever she saw or whatever might happen, she generally kept it all bottled up inside.

Although they must have been under a lot of pressure, it was rare for them to let us see it. Occasionally my father could be grumpy, but if they argued, it was unusual for us to see it. I can see that they must have made a big effort to try to protect us from what was happening to our people, the dangers we were in. They wanted us to have as good a childhood as possible in the circumstances, and they succeeded. Almost all my childhood memories are happy, and in my dreams I still go back there often.

If we played in the river, my father would worry that we'd get washed away and drown. He'd tell us we weren't allowed down there without him. But we didn't pay much attention to his warnings when he was away. One time he came home unexpectedly and caught all three of us diving in the river. He was really, really angry, but his anger masked his fear that one of us would get hurt or even drown.

My father's fears were well founded, but we quickly forgot his warnings until one terrible day. There was a new game that someone had invented—jumping out of a tree that overhung the river and landing in a huge splash. It was fantastic fun, and we'd been playing this game for most of the day. Eventually we left our friends playing by the riverside and went home. But a few hours later we noticed that a crowd had gathered at the water's edge. We hurried down there and heard that one of the children was missing.

As it was the dry season the water was low, so it could be waded in all places. We watched aghast as the line of adults moved slowly up the river, feeling with their bare feet as they went. When they were almost at the overhanging tree, one of them cried out that he'd found something. He reached under the water and emerged with the body of the missing boy cradled in his arms.

The boy must have been under the water for thirty minutes or so, but still they tried to save him. They carried him up the riverbank, held him upside down, and tried to shake out the water. People gave mouth-to-mouth resuscitation, his father included. But finally it was clear that the boy was dead, and the village headman told everyone that it was time to give up. The father gave him one last desperate breath and then laid his son's head back on the wet earth. He let out a cry of loss, and his wife burst into tears. It was a dark day for the village. After that we took our father's warnings very seriously. We were so scared we stopped playing in the river for months on end.

Gradually, our childhood innocence was being tempered with a knowledge of the dangers of the world. First, I had seen Grandpa die, and that had acquainted me with death through old age. Then I had witnessed the horror of the dead body in the river, which had alerted me to the dangers we faced from a faceless, and still distant, enemy. And now I had witnessed the death of my childhood playmate, which had shown me that none of us was ever too young to die.

It was in 1989 that I first noticed people with missing limbs in and around the village. The first time I saw a man with his leg ending in a stump at the knee I was so shocked. I asked my mother what had happened. Her answer led to the first thing I did, aged eight years old, linked with our struggle for freedom Once again, it was one of those moments where my mother had to wrestle with a difficult decision— just how much should she tell a child about the horrors that were ravaging our people and our land?

My mother went on to explain that the Burmese regime planted land mines in Karen villages. These were like small bombs hidden in the earth. When people trod on them they exploded, injuring whoever might be near. Sometimes the Burmese soldiers forced Karen villagers to walk ahead of them, acting as "human minesweepers," my mother said. They might have forgotten where they had planted their mines, so they would force people to clear the way. Others just trod on the mines by accident, when they were going to and from their farms. This was all part of the Four Cuts policy, and the Burmese soldiers even planted mines in the doorways of people's homes and in the churches. Why would people hide things so as to blow other people's legs off, I wondered, especially when they didn't know who was going to get hurt? It was so cruel and senseless.

The Burmese Army didn't care who trod on its land mines. The victims were mostly villagers, but also some Karen soldiers. There were no children, perhaps because they are smaller and would be killed by a powerful mine rather than losing a limb. Families would come with the victims, as they would be there for months recovering.

The land mine victims were sad but also seemed resigned. Life has always been hard for the Karen. When bad things happen, we put it down to fate and carry on as best as possible. Perhaps it is the way we have learned to cope with so much hardship.

My mother's explanation led to the first thing I did, at eight years of age, linked with our struggle for freedom. Bwa Bwa and I talked about it a lot. We felt so sorry for the victims of the land mines and wanted to know how we could help. The KNU had set up a workshop for the handicapped in Manerplaw, and people came from all over Karen State to have artificial limbs fitted. The prosthetics were made of plastic and wood, with a hinged steel cage providing leverage and support. The artificial legs had a fake foot, upon which people could wear a shoe to match that worn on their good leg.

Most of the amputees remained in Manerplaw until they had learned to use their artificial limb, and then they were able to return to their home village. But for those who suffered from the worst injuries, who had lost both legs or arms, the workshop and surrounding area became their permanent home. They and their families were given a place to live close to the workshop, where they could plant vegetables and rear some animals. These families were the poorest of the poor. Their children started turning up at school, and they were often so sad. They knew their fathers weren't like other fathers anymore—they had parts of their bodies missing. We all did our best to help out when we could, sharing our food or even just welcoming the children into our circle of friends. It made us feel that we, too, were doing our part for the resistance.

In the village we mostly had to make our own entertainment. There was only one television set, which was owned by Aung Ba, the village headman. No TV broadcasts could be picked up where we lived, so all one could watch was videos. Aung Ba was our neighbor, and if he was feeling in a generous mood he would invite us in to watch. But as soon as he let *us* in, all the children in the village would try to cram into his living room, followed by the adults.

One evening we watched a Burmese government movie supposedly about the war between the Karen and the Burmese Army. Aung Ba hadn't realized what it would be like. In that movie the Karen soldiers burned villages, beat and killed civilians, and raped women. By contrast, the Burmese soldiers were the nice guys, helping the villagers escape from the marauding Karen troops. It even showed Karen soldiers planting mines to blow off the limbs of innocent villagers.

We were all shocked and surprised. That film was a travesty. It was a total reversal of reality. We were the ones being attacked. It was propaganda produced by the regime. We were very angry after watching it, for we knew the reality of what was happening out there in the remote Karen villages.

My parents were not around and had not seen the film, and without them there to talk to about it we quickly forgot our outrage. We were back at school and playing games. But all too soon, that terrible reality became part of our own lives.

CHAPTER NINE

THE NAMING

One day my mother was taking us back to the village, after a weekend spent in Manerplaw. The river was low and difficult to navigate, so we decided to walk. It was a Sunday afternoon, and we began our lazy ascent of Teak Mountain. There was no hurry as long as we reached home before nightfall. It was thirty minutes or so before we reached the mountaintop. We paused to catch our breath, looking forward to an easy descent to the village. We were chatting and fooling around, when suddenly there was a massive spout of water just ahead of us. We knew instantly what it was: the deafening eruption could only come from an elephant, and we must have stumbled upon it in the midst of having its bath. The tame elephant we had grown up with in our village was one thing, but wild elephants were quite another. They were unpredictable, did not like humans, and could be extremely dangerous if caught off guard.

I could see fear and shock written across my mother's features, as she yelled at us to run. For an instant I turned to see what the elephant was doing, and there right next to us a whole herd was crashing through the water. The last thing I saw was one turning its mighty head in our direction and flaring its ears in anger. Then I ran, pounding along the slippery path with my heart pumping so fast I was afraid it would burst.

All of a sudden I saw my mother fall to the ground. She let out a muffled scream before dragging herself to her feet and trying to stumble onward. I cried out to her, but she told me to run and not to stop until I reached home. I did as she'd said, and ten minutes later I burst out of the forest into the village clearing. Bwa Bwa and Slone were there panting just ahead of me, but my mother was nowhere in sight. We were terrified, knowing how many things could go wrong if she hadn't been able to get away. I tried to remind myself how strong and fearless she was, how she had survived so much in her life. It seemed like an age before finally a figure appeared, hobbling out of the forest shadows. It was my mother, and she was clearly having trouble walking.

As she emerged into the sunlight, I could tell she was in great pain. We rushed up to her. She had blood pouring from a gash in her foot where she had fallen. We had no medicines as such, but we knew where to find the plant that my mother had used to heal our wounds. Say Say went to fetch some, and we bound up my mother's damaged foot with the leaves. Then we helped her home.

It took a month for my mother's wound to heal, and even then it left a painful and angry scar. Every day she had to re-dress the wound with fresh leaves. We worried that the sharp boulder that had cut her had infected the wound. Our worries proved well founded, for this injury would come back to haunt my mother, and at the worst of all possible times.

Manerplaw was now the heartland of the entire Burmese resistance movement, and the military regime redoubled its efforts against us. I started to notice lots of long-tail boats arriving below our house. Long green bundles were unloaded on the beach where we played and carried up past our house. We made a game of guessing at what could be in the bundles but soon got bored and asked my mother.

It turned out that each bundle contained a wounded or dead Karen soldier. Most were slung in a hammock from a single bamboo pole, making a makeshift stretcher. I tried to hide whenever I saw the boats coming, but sometimes it was impossible to miss them. There would be two or three "bundles" in each. I looked into one of those hammocks only once and have never forgotten what was inside: a face bloodied, swollen, and pockmarked with shrapnel, the gentle brown eyes all but gummed shut with congealed blood. But worst of all was the young man's hands, which ended in stumps wrapped in bloody rags. It was horrible.

None of us children had seen anything like this before. I had never seen so many of our soldiers so badly hurt or killed. I went to ask my mum about it and found her working in her vegetable garden.

"Mummy, where are all those soldiers coming from? And how have they gotten so horribly hurt?"

My mother paused and straightened her back. She seemed tired. She looked me directly in the face and tried to give me a reassuring smile.

"There's been a lot of fighting, Little Daughter. But it's far, far away from us. Those soldiers have been hurt or killed in the war. Their friends bring them back here to be treated in the hospital, and they bring back the dead to bury them."

"But why is there so much fighting?" I asked. "And where is it happening? It is far away, isn't it?"

Of course, I wanted the war to be far, far away. I imagined it to be so in my mind. The very idea that it might come to us, here, had never occurred to me. But now that the soldiers were close enough to be brought to us with their terrible wounds, I began to wonder if the danger wasn't closer than my parents wanted us to believe.

My mother put her arm around me. "Little Daughter, it *is* far away, so don't you worry. It's at a place called Mae Ther Waw, and it's been going on for a long time. Mae Ther Waw is a long way away from us."

But the following week there was some terrible news. My friend

Moonlight's father was a Karen resistance fighter, and he'd been killed in the battle for Mae Ther Waw. My parents took us to pay our last respects at the funeral in Manerplaw. We were taken inside the soldiers' barracks to see the body. I stuck close to Bwa Bwa as we crept toward the coffin.

Moonlight's father's face stared up at us, ghostly white and gaunt. He looked pale and pinched, as if all his blood had drained away. Moonlight was standing near the coffin, his face streaked with tears, his distraught brothers and sisters standing on either side of him. I couldn't imagine how they felt with their father lying there dead. I was devastated for them, yet a small part of me was grateful that it wasn't my father who'd been killed. As soon as that thought entered my head, I felt so guilty.

Moonlight was crying; his brothers and sisters were crying; and their mother was crying. I wanted to cry with them, but somehow I couldn't. I didn't want to be consumed by emotion or to break down. I was trying to protect myself from the horror. The coffin was draped in a Karen flag, lifted up, and carried to the graveside. A guard fired off a volley of shots and bugled the coffin into the ground. Of all the dead bodies I had seen by the time I was nine, this was the one that haunted me the most.

We began a relay with our neighbors in the village as each took turns to keep Moonlight's family company. Each night for a week there were ten or more people staying in Moonlight's house, providing solace to his mother, comforting the children, and helping with the cooking and other chores. We did this to give the family the proper time to grieve. In our culture we always do this. I spent time with Moonlight and his sisters, but I tried to avoid talking about their father. Instead, I talked about school, the games we played, or anything else that came into my mind.

Moonlight was one of eight children, and now his mother would have to bring them up as a widow. It was a terrible thing. At school we tried to continue as before, but there was an unspoken, underlying sadness now, for everyone knew about Moonlight's loss. We were just children; we wanted to play and do well at school, to forget all about the war and put sadness behind us. In our minds it was still a distant, invisible threat, and we wanted it to stay that way.

We didn't understand it at the time, but Mae Ther Waw was a major defeat for the Karen resistance. It was a major trading corridor and so provided important revenue for our struggle. Our soldiers had been trying to keep Mae Ther Waw as a stronghold and beat back attacks by the Burmese Army.

We had lost hundreds of soldiers in the battle for Mae Ther Waw after months of bitter fighting. Our soldiers were finally forced to give up Mae Ther Waw and retreat to new positions. The Burmese Army had seized hundreds of Karen villagers as porters. As with the dead man in the river, those porters were being abused in terrible ways before being left for dead. The fighters who came back from the front line looked exhausted. Many seemed relieved just to have survived a battle in which so many of their friends had died.

A few weeks after the defeat, an early-morning parade was held for the returning troops. The Karen flag was hoisted and buglers played a fanfare as the soldiers lined up in their best uniforms. Young women and schoolgirls lined up to offer the soldiers garlands of bright yellow and orange flowers. Each soldier had to step forward and bow his head so that the girl could place the flowers around his neck. As those young men turned away to march back into line, many had tears in their eyes.

I had been chosen as one of the flower girls, as had Bwa Bwa. It was a real honor, and I was very nervous; I understood that the ceremony was meant to honor the sacrifices that the soldiers had made for our cause, and I wanted to make sure to do it justice. You were more or less free to choose whom you gave your garland to, although the Karen Women's Organization was there in the background, making sure that no soldier was left out.

There was a soldier who looked to be in his early twenties, and he was really quite handsome. I smiled at him, and he smiled at me. The drumming of the military band was so loud that we couldn't speak. Instead, I moved forward and offered him my garland. He removed his bush hat so that I could place the garland over his head. He had to bend low to receive it, and for one nerve-wracking moment it got stuck on his forehead. I wondered what on earth to do, and then he reached up and pulled it down himself. He smiled at me again as I stepped back, and my heart filled with warmth and appreciation for what that young man had experienced while fighting for our freedom.

In that parade we celebrated that these soldiers had returned alive. That afternoon there was a memorial service to pay tribute to those who had fallen in the battle and to honor their sacrifice. It wasn't something for children, and I didn't attend. Even so, the deaths of so many brought home the reality of the war to us as never before.

While trying not to scare us, my mother warned us, in her own quiet way, to be prepared in case there was an attack on the village. Several crude air-raid shelters were constructed, each consisting of a hole in the ground covered with stout tree trunks and earth. My father set about constructing our own shelter in the garden. The inside was about three feet high and three feet wide, and it was just long enough for my mother to lie down in. It was only just big enough for us all to squeeze into. It was a big contrast to what my father usually liked to build, ornamental fishponds and beautiful flower gardens.

I had always known that my name had a special place in my father's heart. He used that name—Nant (Miss) Zoya Phan, *my name*—as his pen name when writing articles on the struggle for freedom in Burma. He was prolific in his writing, and he often used to show me what he'd published. I had never thought to ask him why he published under my name. I just felt so happy and proud that he and I shared the same name. Not long after the battle for Mae Ther Waw, my father sat me down to explain exactly how significant my name was to him. When my father was at university in Rangoon, he had read a book about a young Russian woman whose story had struck a chord with him, a seventeen-year-old Russian girl named Zoya Kosmodemyan-skaya who had joined the World War II Soviet resistance. She had led sabotage and reconnaissance missions behind German lines, and her life story had become one of the most enduring tales of heroism from that war.

In 1941, midway through a night mission in German-occupied territory, Zoya Kosmodemyanskaya was captured. She was tortured as her captors tried to extract information from her on the activities and membership of the resistance. But she refused to talk. When they saw that they could never break her, the Nazis sent her to the gallows. As she stood with the noose around her neck, she turned to her captors and leveled a warning at them:

"There are two hundred million of us. You cannot hang us all!"

After the execution her body was left hanging from the gallows, as a warning to others.

When the war was over, Zoya Kosmodemyanskaya was declared a "Hero of the Soviet Union." She was the first woman ever to receive that distinction. My father was moved by the similarities he saw between Zoya's struggle and that of the resistance in Burma. Just like the Burmese junta, the Nazi regime had been a brutal, totalitarian one. Its efforts to exterminate the Jews and other minorities mirrored the junta's efforts to exterminate the Karen and other ethnic groups. And the struggle to resist the Nazis had been a long and costly one in terms of lives, just as it had proved to be in Burma.

Of course, I'd heard snippets of this story before, especially when visitors asked my father why I had such a strange name. But my father had never given me such a direct and personal explanation as to why he had chosen to name me Zoya. He went on to explain that the name originates from the Greek *zoy*, which means "life," and that was another reason he had chosen it. But mainly, he hoped that I, like the original Zoya, might fight for the survival of my people.

Once my father had explained to me the full significance of his naming me Zoya, my childhood aspirations to become a teacher seemed somehow inappropriate. I felt that in my father's hopes for my future—that I might struggle for the survival of my people—lay my true calling. I began to listen more closely when he and my mother spoke about their work and to pay more attention to the many ways the battles were affecting our lives.

Bwa Bwa was twelve years old, and she had just taken the exams that all Karen students had to take in order to get a place at secondary school. The results were compared across the whole of the Karen State, and Bwa Bwa was declared the top pupil overall. She was given a scholarship and publicly congratulated by the Karen education minister, Padoh Shwe Ya Heh, who was the equivalent of the U.S. secretary of education.

It was such an honor, and I felt so proud of my sister, as did my parents. Both she and I were showing great academic promise, and we had dreams of getting a further education.

By my last year of primary school I was studying science, mathematics, geography, Burmese, English, Karen, and basic politics. That last subject included lessons on democracy—what it was, why it was worth fighting for, and what it would mean for us if Burma became a free and democratic country.

The Karen have no single word for democracy, so we call it *ka mler a tar bah tha*, "the will of the people." We were taught that in a democratic country the government is elected by the majority of the people; and we were taught about self-determination, which we called *naw ka sar ta per law tha*.

Though I was taught about such things, I didn't always understand them. The Karen educational system was one in which you learned by rote. It wasn't designed to make you think, it was designed to make you learn. I just memorized our basic politics lessons, learning the words and definitions by heart in order to pass the exams. It was only by listening to my parents and observing what was happening around me that I was able to really comprehend how to apply all those lessons to real life.

I had a dream of going to university after completing my Karen education, which could go no further than secondary school. That dream was inspired in part by my father, who had been so transformed by his time studying for a degree in Rangoon. I wanted to follow in his footsteps, although I had no idea how I was going to do so. But I lived in the hope that I would manage somehow.

CHAPTER TEN

PARADISE LOST

I t was around my fourth year of schooling when my father brought my mother a special gift—a tiny longwave radio. It was only a cheap thing, but to us it was precious. One day we were listening to the Karen-language radio, a Karen-run service that broadcasts out of the Karen free state. A famous Karen singer named Julia Pan Bun, "Julia Flower Bud," was singing a song about students going to university and the joys of learning.

It was a catchy song, with guitar and drums, and Bwa Bwa and I sang along. Hearing it made us even more determined to get to university. As children of the resistance we couldn't study inside Burma, so our only option was to study overseas.

Many of my school friends shared this dream of education and a bright future, even though the gulf between our situation and where we hoped to end up was enormous. We had practically nothing in our village: no way to earn an income, a very basic educational system, and all but nonexistent health care. We had no practical plans to overcome the many obstacles—financial, educational, geographic, and political—that lay in the way of our dreams, but that did not stop us from dreaming.

73

The sheer business of daily survival was more than enough of a challenge. One day, Naw Paw, "Miss Flower," fell ill with fever and was sent home from school. It wasn't uncommon for children to fall sick with terrible fever, and more often than not it was malaria. Most of us recovered over time, even though there were few or no medicines available.

Naw Paw's father was a famous resistance fighter, but he had been captured by the Burmese Army and was jailed. Her mother was also in the resistance, and she was away at the time that her daughter fell ill. Other members of the village would check in from time to time, but Naw Paw stayed at home to recuperate, while her brothers and sisters continued their school studies.

About three days into her illness, her siblings returned home to discover that poor Naw Paw had died. She must have had a horrible death, for we heard that her swollen tongue was clamped between her teeth, and her skin was lacerated and bruised from where she had thrashed around in her fever and cut herself on the sharp edges of the bamboo floor.

Naw Paw and I used to share our lunches at school, and we were very close, but I decided that I just couldn't go to her funeral. I was too scared of how my friend had died, the image of which seemed seared into my mind. But the night after her funeral, Naw Paw came to me anyway, in my dreams. She appeared as a ghostly white form standing over my bed.

She stared at me. "Zoya, I have come to live with you," she declared.

In my dream I was terrified. "No, Naw Paw, you can't live with me," I told her. "Don't you know you're dead?"

Naw Paw insisted that she had to come to live with me. I kept telling her she couldn't. "No, it's not possible—you're dead, Naw Paw, you're dead!"

I kept arguing with her like this for what felt like hours, until I suddenly woke up. I gazed all around me in the darkness. I couldn't see anything, but at least there was no sign of Naw Paw's ghost. My mother and father were away, and I couldn't get back to sleep again. I was too afraid of having that same dream.

I didn't sleep properly for months after that. My fear was that Naw Paw's restless spirit had decided to come to live with me in my world and that it would never leave. It was an irrational fear, a fear of the unknown and of death, but it haunted me all the same.

My father was away on a special mission at the time. He'd been sent to negotiate an alliance with the Wa, a tribe that, like us, had been fighting the Burmese junta for decades. The Wa inhabit an area far to the north of the Karen, on the border with China. As with us, their territory straddles the borderline: some of the Wa live in China proper, in Yunnan State, and others in Burma.

The Wa were once known as the "Wild Wa," because they were headhunters, and their United Wa State Army (UWSA) was a force to be reckoned with. My father's mission was to draw the Wa into an alliance with the wider democratic resistance. The Wa were considering signing a cease fire agreement with the dictatorship, and as part of a delegation from the National Democratic Front (NDF) of ethnic groups, he was trying to persuade them not to change sides. The negotiations were not successful. While he was visiting Wa State, my father was asked to adopt a young Wa boy, an orphan, and as with Say Say, the reason behind the request was to get the boy an education.

At first my father resisted. His return journey from Wa State would be as challenging as the journey there had been. He had trekked through the Karen jungle and hills, crossed large tracts of Thailand, and then traveled on foot and horseback into the remote Wa highlands. With a young Wa boy in tow, the journey back would be even more difficult. But because my father believed absolutely in the value of education, he eventually agreed to take the Wa boy—and that's how Ah Sai came to join our family. Ah Sai is a traditional name in the Wa language of the Wa tribe. Ah Sai was around twelve years old when he came to live with us and spoke not a word of Karen.

None of us could understand the Wa language, so at first Ah Sai could communicate with my parents only in basic Burmese. He called my father Poe-Poe, Burmese for "grandfather"; my mother was Pwa-Pwa, Burmese for "grandmother." And with us Ah Sai had to use sign language, plus the odd bit of Burmese that we had learned at school.

Ah Sai started his education in year one at junior school. He was a big, strong boy, and his complexion was much darker than that of us Karen students. He was like a giant in the class, towering over the other pupils, but he took it all in stride. He was getting an education, which was worth just about any sacrifice.

Ah Sai quickly learned to speak Karen. When he did his Karen homework every evening, he would read it out loud in a powerful, booming voice that would echo around the village. All the neighbors could hear, but we didn't mind. We were proud of his efforts, and by now Ah Sai had become like another brother to us.

Ah Sai came to join us just as the year was coming to an end. On January 31, 1993, we celebrated Karen Resistance Day, a yearly festival that marked the founding of the resistance. One of the biggest attractions of the day was *ta ker met su,* our martial art.

The famous Karen fighter Joe Ruby was going to fight. He was the overall champion at *ta ker met su.* Before the fight started, Joe Ruby and his opponent squared up to each other. They flexed their bulging muscles and performed their finest moves. Joe Ruby was famed for his skill in dodging and feinting to outfox his opponent. I was certain that he was going to win. The fight began in a flurry of punches to the head and stomach and kicks from the legs. It was fast and furious, and soon the fighters were lost in a cloud of dust as they fought. I was thrilled by the spectacle and could tell that my mother and sister and brothers were as gripped as I.

But after only a few minutes of the fight, I felt the earth shake and a frightening distant rumble cut the air. All around me people stiffened, as they strained their ears. And then it happened again; the faint *boom-crash,* muffled by distance and the thick jungle. And then the first cry went up from the crowd as someone spotted the black shapes of aircraft arrowing through the air. Instantly panic took hold of the crowd, with people running in all directions.

My mother grabbed me by the arm and called to my brothers and sister, "Quick! Run! Run! Back to the house as fast as you can!"

She had never forgotten the lessons she had learned as a soldier—the most important of which was to get into cover as quickly as possible. We ran as if our lives depended on it and hid in the underground shelter that my father had built for us. As we crouched there in terror, we could see the glint of the aircraft diving down onto the distant mountaintop and the tiny plumes of smoke below as their bombs hit.

The Burmese Army had launched an attack on Twee Pah Wee Kyoe, "Sleeping Dog Mountain," a high ridge to the west of our area. All along the ridge the Karen resistance had trenches and bunker systems, as Twee Pah Wee Kyoe was a key line of defense against the enemy. As the aircraft repeatedly dive-bombed the positions, the enemy on the ground started a booming mortar barrage that crashed into the jungle all around the ridgeline.

For the first time in my life I could actually see the enemy with my own eyes and hear them attacking us. I could see and hear their might—their sleek, shiny aircraft and big, booming guns. For the first time in my life, I felt terrifyingly small and insignificant, and vulnerable in the face of their power. I clutched my mother's hand and hoped and prayed that they would go away and leave us alone.

We crouched in the shelter for hours on end until the light was gone and the noise of the bombing faded away into the darkening silence. We didn't know then that this was just the start of the enemy assault on Twee Pah Wee Kyoe, an epic battle that would signal the end of happier times.

*   *   *

After that attack we tried as best we could to continue with our lives as before. I was doing better and better at school. I had to sit my final junior school exams. The result placed me second in the entire Karen area. A boy from another school had beaten me to first place, but I was really pleased with my rank, especially because I was awarded a scholarship to take with me to secondary school. I had won a Karen scholarship of 20 Thai baht a month—the equivalent of 40 cents—with which to buy notebooks, pens, and other school materials. In fact, I often found myself competing with Bwa Bwa to be the best student in the school.

One morning at school assembly, one of the teachers, Zipporah Sein, who would go on to become the leader of the Karen National Union, told us the story of a former pupil named Paw Paw, "Flower Flower." Paw Paw had traveled overseas to a country called Canada, where she had won a place at a university. Those of us who studied really hard might be able to do the same, she told us.

Bwa Bwa and I decided that we too were going to study overseas, but in England instead of Canada, because that was where Saw Ba U Gyi, the founder of the Karen resistance movement, had been to university, and we wanted to follow in his footsteps.

While Bwa Bwa and I studied across the river, Say Say's education was already over. He had grown into a kind, strong young man and one day announced that he planned to become a resistance fighter, inspired in part by my mother's war stories and in part by what he had witnessed growing up in his home village. Even though my mother kept telling him that she didn't want him to become a soldier, he had wanted to fight since his first years of high school. My mother and Say Say had cut a deal: if he would agree to complete high school, she would allow him to join the Karen resistance. Solemn promises had been made on both sides, so there was no way that she could go back on her word and stop him. I was proud of my elder brother when he joined the Karen Army. He qualified as a special forces soldier, join-ing an elite unit that carried out missions behind enemy lines. It was dangerous, and I knew there was a possibility that he might not come back alive from one of those missions. But there was no stopping him; the fight was strong in our family.

After that first attack on Karen Resistance Day, the rumbling of the battle had become a daily backdrop to our lives. I worried about Say Say all the time. I continued to do well at secondary school, but there was a real sense of imminent danger in our lives now. My parents were increasingly edgy and uneasy. The war was drawing closer, as the massive might of the Burmese Army tried to crush our resistance, de-stroying villages and forcing hundreds of thousands to flee. By now everyone knew someone whose father or brother had been lost to the fighting.

Every day more and more Karen soldiers were passing back and forth through our area. In spite of this, I never for one moment thought that we were in any real danger. Even though I knew that other villages had been attacked and taken over or destroyed, somehow my mind never connected this to thinking the same could happen to my own village. My parents had always kept us safe. I never expected that we would have to flee for our lives.

CHAPTER ELEVEN

SLEEPING DOG MOUNTAIN

The ongoing battle for Sleeping Dog Mountain was crucial for our safety. If the ridgeline was lost, little would stand between us and the might of the Burmese military machine. The mountain overlooked Manerplaw, with just a few miles of hills and jungle between them.

My father told me that the Burmese military had launched a major offensive, bombing from the air and shelling from the ground. Karen villagers were fleeing the area because the military were targeting civilians. Most hid in the jungle without food or shelter, but a good number were forced across the border into Thailand, as refugees. I often overheard my parents say that foreign oil companies were propping up the regime by investing in Burma. The military leaders purchased new weapons and funded their war against us using money provided by these investors. By contrast, our weapons were old and worn, some even dating back to World War II.

We villagers were being asked to help with the defense of Sleeping Dog Mountain in any way we could. The main tasks were to carry food and ammunition up to the mountaintop positions and make sure that the soldiers were well stocked. It was voluntary, but we all wanted to help. Much to Slone's annoyance, he wasn't allowed to participate because he was still in primary school. But Bwa Bwa was a strapping sixteen-year-old, and she volunteered right away. I wanted to go with her, but I doubted whether my mother would let me.

"Are you certain you want to?" my mother asked Bwa Bwa every night the week before Bwa Bwa's first trip.

"Yes, I am," Bwa Bwa replied.

"You really, really want to do this?" my mother insisted.

"Of course! My friends are going, and so should I."

Eventually, my mother gave in, but there was no convincing her when it came to me.

"You're too small, Little Daughter," she said. "If anything happens, you won't be able to run away."

"But Bwa Bwa can go, so why not me?"

"Bwa Bwa is older and bigger, and she can look after herself."

The students were divided into those who would carry the food to the ridgeline and those who would cook for the Karen soldiers lower down the mountain. Bwa Bwa took the more dangerous job, carrying food parcels wrapped in banana leaves to the frontline troops. Most of the men in the village volunteered to fight. On her first mission Bwa Bwa was away for several days. My mother was eaten up with worry and flinched every time we heard the faint boom of explosions from up on the ridge or saw the occasional enemy aircraft.

Bwa Bwa found her volunteer missions exhausting. It took a day to walk up to the ridgeline and almost as long to come back again. It was so high on that ridgeline that she had to gasp for air and was only ever able to carry a small load. She had been very thirsty during the climb but was determined to get the food to the soldiers, for she knew they were defending our very lives. She would return hot, dirty, and tired, with her head full of horrific images of the war.

Often she came back from her missions with very sad news. Saw Happy, "Mr. Happy," a young man from our village who had volunteered to fight, had been killed. It seemed impossible to us—he had been up there only a matter of weeks—but Saw Happy was gone.

Now the war had lurched closer, and it was a very real part of our lives. It was September 1994, and our tranquil little village became tense as the stress of the war increased. Unbeknownst to us, tensions between Buddhists and Christians within the Karen resistance were rising. A splinter group of KNU soldiers had started attacking our own boats at the confluence of the Salween and Moei Rivers, at Thu Mweh Hta village. The violence escalated; they arrested some KNU leaders and forced civilians at gunpoint to join them. The group declared themselves to be a new organization and gave themselves the name Democratic Karen Buddhist Army (DKBA). They allied themselves with the dictatorship. Their leaders seemed to have no agenda except attacking the KNU and obtaining power and money.

The first real sense we got of just how bad the tensions had gotten was when our church pastor, Pu Ghay Dweh, "Grandfather Handsome," gave an unusually impassioned sermon one Sunday. A very stern figure, he urged us all to pray as hard as we could, for the Karen were facing a severe challenge. The military junta was trying to use religion to divide us, he said, and we had to pray for unity. Religion might split the resistance asunder, and no one could afford that rift; if we could not put our differences aside to fight for a common goal, none of us could survive.

We children tried to comprehend the severity of what was going on within the resistance. Our father was one of a group sent to meet with the DKBA to try to defuse the problem. We were used to him going off to frontline areas on various missions, so we thought little of it when he disappeared this time. He was supposed to be gone only a couple of days, but after two weeks my mother began to sicken with worry. The injury caused to her foot when we had fled from the elephants had flared up again, looking angry and inflamed. She'd kept it from us, but the negotiating team—my father included—had been taken captive.

As the days passed, we learned fragments of the truth ourselves: our father and his fellow negotiators were being held in a prison beneath the monastery at Thu Mweh Hta; our own soldiers might have to go in to rescue them. My mother tried to convince us that he would be fine, even as she looked drawn and consumed by worry. A constant string of friends and villagers visited the house, and my mother kept asking if anyone had news of my father, but nobody had any information. Our neighbors started coming to spend the night with us, during which time they prayed with us for our father's well-being. In fact, they were acting exactly as they would have done if a family member had died and as we had done when Moonlight's father was killed.

Our mother had told us that Say Say's unit had been sent into the jungles around Thu Mweh Hta to launch a rescue, should one be necessary. They were in position to assault the monastery where my father was being held. But the DKBA had forced local people to move into the area surrounding the monastery, using them as a human shield against attack. The KNU had a strict policy of not harming civilians, and the KNU commander decided that the risk of killing so many innocent people in an assault on the monastery would be too great. It was such a difficult, dark time for us: my mother was ill and plagued by worry, my father was being held captive, and my brother was in a unit tasked with the rescue assault. Word had gone around the village that my father had been executed, though no one could find the courage to tell my mother, This seemed quite likely, as the DKBA often executed KNU leaders.

But after a few nerve-wracking days, one member of the negotiating team was released. They hadn't all been killed after all. My mother went to see him. My father was alive, he told her, and being held captive in an underground prison. There was still hope.

A few days later, a boat docked at the riverside below the village. All of a sudden I caught sight of my father walking up the path toward us. I screamed out to everyone that Daddy was home, and we all went rushing down to meet him.

"Daddy! Daddy! Daddy!" I yelled, as I threw myself into his arms. "You're home! You're home!"

My father smiled at me weakly and ruffled my hair. We were quickly surrounded by people talking all at once; half the village seemed to have gathered to greet him. During the weeks that he had been kept from us, it had been as if my heart were breaking. On the day my father returned to us, it was like sunshine flooding back into my life. It was a miracle that his life had been spared, and for the first time in months I saw my mother smile again.

Cuddling up to my father, I realized that I wasn't quite as small as I used to be. I could tell that I was tiring him, and eventually I got down and sat at his feet, gazing up at his tired features. How weak and exhausted he looked.

We barely had any time alone with him before people started flooding into our home to see him. He was hugged and patted on the back; people cried with happiness to see him returned and begged to know what had happened. People crammed into our living room as my father sat cross-legged on the bamboo floor. I realized then how much I loved him and how good it was to have him back with us alive and reasonably well. And for the first time I realized how special he was to others as well. For me he had always just been Dad, but now I could see how widely he was loved and respected. He was not just my dad, he was a leader to whom people looked for hope and inspiration. I was so proud of him.

"We went to listen to their demands and see how we could settle things amicably," my father began. "There was a monk who was the mastermind behind the DKBA, even though he is not a formal leader. We soon realized that he had been sent by the Burmese dictatorship to cause trouble, using religion to try to split our movement. He had been up to the frontline areas asking the Buddhist Karen soldiers why there was no pagoda there. Pagodas are where Buddhists pray. He said they needed to build a big, white pagoda to worship at, right where they were."

"Obviously they couldn't do that, as it would have given their army position away," my father continued. "But the monk told the soldiers that this was religious prejudice and proved that only Christians mattered to the Karen leaders. I'm certain that this was an operation engineered by the junta's military intelligence. Using a monk as an agent was a clever move; you know how people respect the monks, and this was the start of all the trouble. Underneath the monastery at Thu Mweh Hta the monk and his followers had built up a secret arms store. The monk called on the soldiers to revolt, and some of them joined him . . ."

My father paused for a second. "When we arrived, they arrested us and placed us in an underground dungeon, beneath the monastery. I tried to talk to the DKBA leaders, but they just told me they were going to do whatever the monk told them to. Most of those in the DKBA were just innocents—naive soldiers who believed every word the monk told them . . ."

My father described how he had been kept in the pitch black of the dungeon as his captors took away his fellow KNU leaders and executed them. At one point they had put a gun to his head and acted as if they were going to kill him.

"The regime has a big, active intelligence service, and they had set this up well," my father concluded. "But we hope that the innocents— the easily led soldiers and villagers—will see that they've been misled and come back to us. The resistance—Christian, Buddhist, and animist—has to be united, for only in unity can there be victory."

My father had tried to end his story with a touch of hope, to give the villagers something to feel happier about. In spite of what he had been through, he tried to give them something to believe in. I was so proud of him for surviving the ordeal and being able to put on such a brave face, and for trying to sound optimistic in order to keep up people's spirits. But he looked drained and fatigued as I had never seen him before. As I sat on his lap listening to him, I felt anger bubbling up inside me with a strength it had never had before. It was also only then that I truly understood how much danger he had been in, and I was so relieved he was alive and back with us.

A few days after my father's return the village headman rang the alarm on the village square. He announced that schools were to be closed immediately and until further notice, and those who hadn't already dug shelters were to start doing so. People were advised not to go out after dark, and if they spotted anyone moving around at night, they were to report it to him immediately.

Because we couldn't go to school anymore, it made sense to stay with our parents in the Manerplaw house. There we watched soldiers training. Sleeping Dog Mountain was clearly visible, as was, on some days, the eerie spectacle of the enemy aircraft launching their attacks. Fear gripped my heart.

Ever since the attack on Karen Resistance Day, our mother had made us stay in the shelter whenever we could hear or see the planes. Sometimes we were stuck in the shelter all day long, wishing we could be playing out in the sunshine. Sometimes we would play games, but most of the time we were very bored, remembering the days when we could climb trees and splash in the river.

The Burmese fighter planes would come several at a time, circling above the ridge like sleek black hawks. Then they would dive and release their bombs, and there would be the tiny puffs from the explosions below. I'd always ask my mother which area it was they were attacking. Often it was the positions right on the ridgeline itself, but sometimes it would be Karen villages.

The first time the aircraft came to drop their bombs on us I was in the toilet, which was a small bamboo hut outside the house. It was several weeks since school had been canceled, and by now we were used to hearing the drone of the enemy bombers circling in the sky. But all of a sudden a series of horrible, piercing screaming noises was right above us, and the aircraft dived to attack. The bombs we had only been watching on previous days were now falling on us. My heart leaped and my whole body shook with fear. I thought I was going to die. Each scream ended in the massive boom of an explosion—so close that the air shook and the bamboo walls of the toilet rattled with the shock waves.

As the terrible noise died away, it was replaced by my mother's screaming, "Into the shelter! Everyone into the shelter, now!"

I bolted from the bathroom and sprinted for the shelter, which was on the far side of the house. I was the last to reach it—Slone, Bwa Bwa, and my mother got there before me—and I could hear my mother desperately calling for me.

"Po Mu Sit! Po Mu Sit! Little Daughter!" she was crying. "Where are you?!"

We stayed in the shelter all that afternoon as the airplanes roared around in the skies above. I wasn't crying: I was more struck dumb with fear. I was so scared I wouldn't even venture out for a pee and had to hold it. As dusk descended over Manerplaw the sinister drone of the aircraft died away, and we decided it was safe to venture out. My mother left to prepare the evening meal.

Four bombs had landed nearby and some shrapnel had landed in our garden, but our mother would not let us look closely at the craters. We had seen war movies with bombing on the video at the village headman's house, but this was completely different. The scream of the diving aircraft had almost deafened me, piercing right to my heart. When my father came home that evening, he told us how he had been walking on one of the paths through Manerplaw when the planes had attacked. He had had no choice but to dive into a nearby patch of "water bush"—thick reeds that grow in the riverbeds—to take cover. When the bombing was over, he'd emerged covered in mud from head to toe. He tried to lighten the mood by mimicking emerging from the muck and walking the rest of the way, but we could tell that he was worried.

After eating a subdued meal my father told my mother how frightened he had been. Bombs had fallen all around Manerplaw, and no one doubted that the aircraft would return to attack us again. My father urged my mother to be careful and for us to always get straight into the shelter at the first hint of an attack.

"The situation just keeps getting worse and worse," my father told her quietly. "You must take good care of the children. Who knows where it will all end . . ." But just as we were beginning to despair, we got a wonderful, unexpected surprise: Say Say came home on leave for two days, bringing a friend with him. I had missed him so much and was so happy to see him. He had grown up a lot since I had last seen him. He was a man now, with a short military haircut.

But our joy at being reunited as a family did not last. We were sitting as a family having lunch just an hour or two after Say Say's return when suddenly the heart-stopping scream of a diving aircraft drowned out our chatting and laughter. Before we could even move, the first bomb exploded with a massive boom. In an instant Bwa Bwa and I were dashing through a door in the side of the house and had dived into the safety of the dark shelter. Say Say was the last to reach the shelter, and by then it was full. My mother kept trying to drag him in, but there was no way he could fit. The aircraft kept circling overhead and howling down upon us, each bomb shaking the ground terribly. I was so afraid for him. Only his head was in the shelter, and his eyes were wide with fear. Every time there was an explosion he cringed, expecting to be hit.

After half an hour, the noise of the aircraft died away to silence. We sat without speaking for a long time, staring at one other and trying to make sense of what had happened.

"What's Elder Brother thinking of?" Bwa Bwa finally demanded. "He thinks that even if a bomb falls on his backside he'll be okay, 'cause his head's inside!"

In spite of our fear, we all laughed. I poked my head outside, and the first thing I caught sight of was a smoking crater on the beach below the house. There was another just up the hill, right in the midst of my father's flower garden. No wonder the explosions had sounded so close—they had been!

As the rest of us set about finishing our chores, Say Say and his friend went out to inspect the craters. They returned with the tail fins of two bombs, each bright red and about the size of an adult's hand, with four fins splayed out from the center. They had a horrible, burning smell about them. As we inspected these carefully engineered steel bomb parts, I became more and more fearful.

When my father came home that evening, he was angered by the indiscriminate nature of the attack. The pilots weren't even trying to hit military targets anymore; they were trying to kill and maim civilians, deliberately trying to spread terror. I suddenly thought, this is real; it is really happening to us for real.

My parents spoke long into the evening in hushed tones. The following morning my mother sat us down for a talk. She told us that we had to pack a bag with some clothes and our important possessions in case we had to get away quickly. She tried to reassure us that it was only "in case." My brothers and sisters and I loved our home and tried to convince ourselves that we would never have to run away.

I decided to use my backpack as my emergency bag and packed my two good dresses, one blanket, a small mirror that I used for applying the *tha na kah* cream, and my school pens and notebooks. I grabbed my few family photos: one of me at four months old, another of me with Bwa Bwa standing in front of our house, and one or two group photos of the family. And that was it; my bag was packed. I hoped and prayed I would never need to use it.

My mother tried to reassure me. "Little Daughter, we'll be all right. I understand why you're scared, but we will get through this. Whatever happens, we'll be together and we'll get through it."

Her words were a comfort to me, but that night I had a horrible dream. I was coming home from school, and as I walked toward the village I saw a huge fire. As I got closer, I realized it was our house that was burning. I ran and ran to try to get to the house, but I could never reach it. The harder I tried, the more it seemed to keep moving away from me.

I woke up with a start, sitting bolt upright in fear. It was so vivid that I wondered for a second if our house was burning for real. First thing in the morning I told my mother about it. She told me not to worry, it was only a dream and nothing like that would ever happen to us.

But we Karen believe in foresight and the prescience of dreams. And despite my mother's comforting words, everyone was worried. Even the trees, the river, and the very earth seemed worried. The forest was quiet and brooding, as if the very trees were waiting for something bad to happen.

CHAPTER TWELVE

THE RIVER OF BURNING TEARS

Ever since the bombs had landed in my father's garden, I felt that war had become personal, and I was curious as to why the enemy was trying to get us. What had we done? Why us? Why our home?

My mother told me that the regime wanted to capture Manerplaw because it was the headquarters of the Karen resistance and the wider democratic resistance in Burma. After the elections in 1990 some of the members of Parliament had also fled to Manerplaw and established a government in exile. This had further infuriated the Burmese generals, and with their new planes and other weapons, paid for by increasing foreign trade and investment, they were determined to wipe us all out.

In January 1995 the word that I had been dreading for so long finally came. My father was home early, and he and my mother closeted themselves in the bedroom to talk. When they finally emerged, my mother announced that we had to leave. My father helped her pack some food, and we each took up our backpack and headed down to the river, where Karen soldiers were helping families escape. At the water's edge lots of people waited in turn for a boat.

My father seemed so worried about how we would be, but my mother was saying we would be okay, and we would be back. I was leaving everything I knew and loved and all my friends. We were leaving together, but I didn't know where we would end up. I still thought we would be leaving for only a short time.

As we were waiting in line to board a boat, suddenly my mother turned and rushed back to our house. After a few minutes we saw her emerge with some coriander seedlings, and she started planting them. Bwa Bwa, Slone, and I stared at one another in confusion: if we were leaving, why was our mother bothering to plant coriander? And what a time to choose! My father motioned for us to get into a waiting boat, and he hurried up the hill to our mother.

"Look, you have to leave," he urged her. "The boat's waiting for you."

"I'm just planting a little coriander . . ."

"We don't have much time, and you're wasting time planting coriander!"

"But when we come back it'll be ready for us . . ."

My mother stared at him desperately, then seemed to get hold of herself as suddenly as she had lost it. She shrugged, dropped what she was doing, and allowed my father to lead her down to the river. The other families in our boat were staring at my mother as if she were crazy, but my father bundled her into the boat and stood back to see us off.

"Hurry!" he urged us. "When you reach the other side, climb the mountain and head for Per Hee Lu. I'll catch up with you later. And remember to hurry."

His last words were lost in the snarl of the engine, as the boat driver gunned the throttle and backed us out into the current. As we pulled farther into midstream, I could see that the riverbank was lined with crowds of people, all of them laden with possessions and intent on leaving. Everything looked so sad: the people, the river, the beach, the trees, and the mountains beyond.

We had left everything apart from what we carried on our backs:

our chickens, ducks, and pigs; our house and our flower gardens. Who was going to feed the newly hatched chicks? I adored them, and I was more worried about them than I was for my father. He had promised to catch up to us, and I had no doubt that he would do so. But then the boat driver got to his feet, leaned his weight on the engine, and steered the boat into the current, and I saw my father hurry off, lacking even the time to wave good-bye. Suddenly, I felt as if I would never see him again, and my heart pounded in my chest. Over and over again in my head I said, "We will be back, we will be back," and it helped me calm down.

As we drifted away from the banks of the village, I tried to wrap my head around what was happening. In a way, my mother's gesture with the coriander was the only spark of hope I had left. Things were bad now, that couldn't be denied. But if she had been so intent on planting it, surely she, too, believed we would be back again?

When we disembarked, there was an explosion behind us, followed by the muffled chatter of gunfire from the forests to the north. Minute by minute, the noise of the fighting grew ever nearer. We had gotten out of Manerplaw just in time, but now we had to hope that we could get far enough upriver before we were spotted.

We were all scared now, even though my mother didn't show it. With her we always felt we would be safe, that she knew what to do. But never before had we heard the crackle of gunfire so clear or so close. Life itself was being torn apart. Slone set off on the path toward the village, which was forty minutes away, striding ahead as if he were an adult and urging my mother to hurry after. A little warrior, he marched ahead and ordered his elder sisters to follow.

"I'm scared," I breathed as I caught up with my mother. "And where's Daddy? Isn't he coming?"

The thought of him staying behind to face that gunfire was unbearable, but my mother's answer was drowned out by a mighty explosion as the first big mortar round slammed into the center of Manerplaw. We rushed on, too afraid of the bombs and bullets at our back to linger or to talk. As we climbed the mountain, the trees filtered out the noise, but the booming explosions still echoed around us, every one making me jump and hurry on, as if I were scrambling away from something horrid that was creeping up behind me.

We joined a stream of people heading toward the village, and everyone appeared worried and panicky. Parents kept urging their children to walk more quickly, to keep up. By the time we reached the village it was dark. Normally, people would light oil lanterns at dusk, but tonight a blackout had been imposed on the village, so that our position would be concealed from the enemy.

We made our way along darkened paths to our house. My mother set about boiling some rice, all the while calling out in a soft voice to our neighbors for any news they might have. We were all so exhausted from the shock of the evacuation that we went to sleep almost immediately after eating, with the fear that my father had been caught in the fighting in the back of my mind. My mother stayed awake and watched over us all night long.

It was not a good night. Every few minutes I'd waken with a start, as the boom of another explosion echoed through the forest. Then it would be quiet for a while, before the next crash. In the morning my mother fixed breakfast, and then she told us that we would have to move on. The village wasn't safe for us anymore. We would have to move farther, toward Thailand, to try to escape the Burmese soldiers.

I had no toys or any special mementos to take, no makeup or toiletries. My mother loaded each of us with as much rice, fish paste, and salt as we could carry, and then it was time to leave. We headed for the river, which we could follow southeast into Thailand. The route was very difficult on foot, for the water was channeled between several steep-sided gorges. But there were so many people waiting for the boats—thousands and thousands of them—and by the evening we knew that none was coming for us. We had to return to spend another fearful night in the house.

This time it was even worse. After dark, we could see the sky on the far side of Teak Mountain lit up an unearthly, fiery orange, and we knew that Manerplaw was burning. Victory Field, the heartland of the resistance, had been taken and laid waste by the forces of the military junta that ruled our land. Clouds of angry red smoke billowed skyward over the flames. It was heartbreaking, and we were terrified that the army would make their way to us next.

The village was gripped by an echoing silence even though nobody was asleep; we stayed up all night staring at the inferno. Our homeland was burning, and I was so angry. Bwa Bwa and Slone were deathly quiet as they watched that eerie glow spreading across the night sky. We were so traumatized that we couldn't even talk. I worried again about my father and wondered whether he had been caught in that fiery hell.

In the morning we were down at the river again, waiting. The noise of the fighting hadn't stopped completely, but it was more sporadic. The reek of burning had drifted down the river, too. It wasn't until late afternoon that a boat finally came for us, and even then people started panicking, worrying that there wasn't enough space for everyone. Luckily, the village headman intervened, establishing some order: women and small children went first; then women with teenage children; and finally the old and infirm.

Our turn came, and we got into the long-tail boat. It was already laden down with people, sacks of rice, and piles of possessions. The boat was dangerously full; it was only big enough for ten but fifteen were in it, so the able-bodied adults were told to walk. The way through the forest was difficult, there was no proper path, and the hillside was steep, but it was doable. Children had to be carried. Finally we set off up the river, the boat low in the water and the powerful engine straining to carry its heavy load.

As we drew away from my beloved village, I gazed back at it longingly. Long before I was ready to look away, it was lost from sight around a bend in the river. I couldn't believe that we were leaving. I told myself that we had to come back—the coconuts on our coconut trees were just about ripe now, and we would have to harvest them. My sister had become an expert at climbing them and plucking the coconuts so we could drink the delicious milk.

After a two-hour journey upstream the boat had to stop; the river was too dangerous to navigate any farther. We stopped in a high-walled, rocky gorge, through which the water was funneled in a series of angry rapids. In the forests to either side there were crowds of people, all of them, like us, fleeing from the attacks and carrying heavy loads in woven baskets strapped to their heads: pots, plates, and foodstuffs, all wrapped up in cloth bundles.

The gray-blue smoke of cooking fires drifted through the trees as people boiled a little rice to sustain them on their journey. My mother was unhappy with all the fires, as the smoke gave away our location, but those families had small children to feed. The boat pulled over, and we unloaded our possessions and joined the sixty people who had preceded us. Mostly, they were women and children scattered in family groups. Everyone had his or her own sad bundle of possessions and shared the same bewildered air, as if nobody could comprehend what our lives had suddenly become.

My mother, my siblings, and I threaded our way between the trees, searching for a spot where we could rest. As we did so, a voice cried out my name. It was Moonlight, and he was able to give me some hurried news of our friends. He had been there for a week, and Tee Ser Paw and Lily Flower had both passed through this place the day before, but they had moved on toward Thailand and the promise of possible safety. His family would be following them soon. There was no time for more questions, as he was helping some of the families, and he rushed off.

My mother told us that we would camp here for a little while, I presumed to wait for news of my father, and began work on a temporary shelter. An expert at building such things from her years living as a soldier in the jungle, she also had help from those who had already made their own shelters. Four bamboo posts were driven into the ground, to support a raised bamboo floor. A bamboo roof frame went above, sheeted over with a length of plastic that my mother had carried with her. Outside the front entrance she made a cooking hearth from three large stones. The shelter had no walls, but there was room enough inside for us all to sleep and stay dry.

It was the cold season, and the night air would carry a heavy fog up from the river. We could see our breath as we wrapped ourselves in blankets. That first night we had to share someone else's shelter, as ours was unfinished. It was crowded, but no one seemed to mind, and we huddled together to try to keep warm.

Apart from the roar of the river, the forest all around us was deathly quiet. Just a day's travel from the village we were in the midst of the dense jungle, and if the fighting was still going on we couldn't hear it. Even so, the atmosphere was subdued and fearful, and people communicated mostly in whispers.

For two weeks we stayed in this place with no name, living like ghosts in the forest. It was a tough and hostile environment in which to try to make even a temporary home. Each day we ate the rice, salt, and fish paste that we had carried with us. It was never enough, as my mother was rationing our food, and we were always hungry. But at least we were alive, and we had something in our bellies. We couldn't go far into the jungle looking for food, because of the danger from wild animals like poisonous snakes, so we had to make do with what we had packed.

At this time my mother never ceased to amaze me with her strength and resourcefulness. She was like a hero to us all. She knew how to survive; she could fell bamboo as well as any man, construct her own shelter, keep the fire going and the meals coming. She never wanted us to go far; she wanted us always to stay within her sight, worried that the Burmese Army would track and follow us and wanting our father to be able to find us.

She tried to create a sense of structure and security out of our fractured lives and even built a temporary toilet next to our shelter and advised other families to do the same; if we used the river as a toilet, it would be too dirty to drink from. We settled into a routine.

Although she was consumed with worry about us, my mother provided crucial guidance for many of the frightened people passing through the camp, quickly taking on an informal leadership role in this place with no name. People would come to her seeking advice. If they were tired, she would counsel them to rest for a few days, to rebuild their strength. Once they had slept and eaten, they could continue the journey with their heavy loads; even though they wanted to move quickly, they might be overcome with exhaustion in the deep jungle if they pressed on. She told the young mothers to try to stop their babies from crying by keeping them on the breast at all times—for a baby's cries might attract the enemy.

Everyone was asking the same thing: what are we going to do now? Some said there was a place of safety to which people were heading, a "refugee camp." We children didn't understand what that meant and talked among ourselves about what a refugee camp might be like: was it like the village, with a school and a church; did people there look after their neighbors?

Day by day our friends and neighbors from the village left this place with no name, until few remained. Bwa Bwa was tearful at seeing all her childhood friends leave, wondering if she would ever see them again. But I found myself unable to cry. I was crying inside, but I felt as if I should try to be strong. So I kept the trauma bottled up inside me.

I was now becoming a woman, and here in this place with no name was the worst place to be doing so. The total lack of any privacy was horribly embarrassing. I was shy about my body. When I went to bathe, I would wait until it was almost dark and ask my mother or sister to come with me. We would slip into the cold river wrapped in a longyi and try as best we could to wash the day's grime from our bodies.

It was a strange new life. I had always known everyone around me, but now we were surrounded by new people, who were from other villages in the area that had also been attacked. As those we knew from the village left, strangers kept arriving. Sometimes there would be a young mother with five or six children. The mother and the eldest children had to carry the infants and baby, so they had little strength or space for food. Some were starving. I had never seen children crying with hunger, but it became a regular, heartbreaking occurrence. Invariably, my mother would insist on their having some of our food, even though we didn't have enough ourselves. She would press on them a blanket or some other precious possession, and they would be so grateful for her generosity. My mother was so very kind, even in the midst of our own suffering. She would happily give away whatever she had if she felt it would help others.

We had been in this place with no name for two weeks and had just sat down to a lunch of boiled rice, when all of a sudden my father stepped out of the forest shadows. It was like a miracle. The last we had seen of him was a lone figure by the riverside at Manerplaw, before it had burned to the ground. It wasn't until I saw him walking toward us that I realized I had almost lost hope that he could have survived. Yet now we had been reunited. He was covered in dirt and grime from the forest and he looked totally exhausted, but he was alive!

That day, after we had begun to get over the shock and thrill of being reunited after so much, he told us his story. After we had left him he had prepared to evacuate with the Karen National Union leader, General Saw Bo Mya. Like most KNU leaders, the general had been based in Manerplaw. My father had worked for him for several years, and it was in part my father's responsibility to see that the general was safe and avoided capture or death at the hands of the enemy. My father had taken him on a long, difficult journey through the jungle, to a new location where the resistance could establish a new headquarters.

It must have been hard for my father to have to leave us during the evacuation, but he knew that his family, and all Karen families, would be safe only if there were freedom and democracy in our country. He also knew how strong our mother was and that she could take care of us.

My father couldn't tell us where the new headquarters was, because if we were captured and tortured by the enemy and revealed where it was, the consequences for the resistance would be catastrophic. Once my father was certain that the new location was safe and secure, he had set off again to find us. He had asked for news of us on the way, and one of the long-tail-boat drivers had been able to give him our exact whereabouts. I thought my father had come to stay with us, but about an hour after his arrival, he suddenly stood up and said he had to go. Shocked, I felt tears coming but held them back. I was so upset. I wanted him to stay with us so much.

Knowing that we would need help on the journey ahead of us, he had brought two young men with him who could act as escorts and protection. Both in their early twenties, Tu Chin and Eh Moo were Karen soldiers and friends of the family. Eh Moo had been injured and Tu Chin was very sick, so neither could be on the front line fighting right then, but because both were strong young men, it eased my father's mind knowing that they were with us.

From where we were, our only option was to follow the countless others who had headed into Thailand and the refugee camps. My father told us he would catch up with us there and see us again soon. Before leaving, my father told us how much he trusted our mother's ability to look after us. He told us to trust in her and support her on the journey that lay ahead.

As he readied himself to leave, it struck me how gaunt and troubled he seemed. He was weighed down by the responsibility he carried. He hugged and kissed each of us good-bye, and was gone.

The following morning, we set off at first light. I wasn't sad to be leaving the place with no name but was uncertain about what lay ahead. Having seen my father had lifted my spirits enormously, and having Eh Moo and Tu Chin with us was a real blessing. They hefted the heaviest loads as we set off into the deep jungle. We didn't have much left, though, just three sets of clothes each, some blankets, rice, salt, and fish paste, and a few personal possessions. I still carried my schoolbooks. Even then, I wanted to go back to school as soon as possible.

The path snaked through the dawn mists, sticking to the eastern riverbank and climbing steadily out of the gorge. A few minutes into the jungle, the terrain became rocky and slippery underfoot. To the left, a near-vertical slope fell to the crashing waters of the rapids below. One slip, and it would likely be our last. We were alone but followed the footsteps of those who had gone before, trusting that if they had made it then so could we.

By the end of the first day we had reached an area that was dominated by enormous trees. The forest canopy was high above, and little light filtered down to the forest floor, which was all but devoid of vegetation. There were plenty of places where we could rest for the night. From the banana leaves laid out under some trees, we could see where other families had slept here before us.

Beneath one of the largest forest giants we spotted a group of people in a makeshift camp. It turned out to be a friend from the village whose name was Winston Churchill, together with his parents and sisters and brother. They welcomed us with brave smiles, and we settled down to join them for our first night in the deep jungle.

CHAPTER THIRTEEN

UNDER THE BIG TREE

That first night we slept on a plastic sheet on the ground. My mother was very careful about where exactly we should sleep, for the tree above us was as ancient as the hills, and some of the branches looked as if they might fall. We made our bed beneath one of the firmest-looking boughs and tried to get comfortable. Although the days were hot, the nights were cold, but even the dark forest canopy was sprinkled with bright stars high above. It would have been a magical place to sleep had we not been on the run. As I stared up at the starlit heavens, I wondered how such a beautiful land could be full of so much evil. Karen land was named Kaw Thoo Lei, "Land of No Evil." But now the Burmese regime had sent its soldiers to lay waste to our land. Manerplaw lay in ruins, and we were running for our lives. All of our hopes and dreams and visions of the future seemed lost.

Winston Churchill's family had built a temporary shelter under the big tree, and my mother decided that we would do the same with the help of Eh Moo and Tu Chin. We would remain in this place for a few days, she said, resting and rebuilding our strength for the rest of the journey. For two weeks we'd eaten nothing but small portions of rice, salt, and fish paste, but a nearby stream held sweet, fresh water, and the forest was sure to be full of wild foods.

As the adults went about constructing the shelter, Bwa Bwa and I went to the stream to hunt for crabs and prawns. We could not find enough for a proper meal, but we did catch enough for a soup, then foraged for bush food to fill out the meal: wild vegetables and banana pith and shoots (the flesh of the banana trees) to mix with the prawn and crabmeat. The vegetables were not what we'd normally eat, and they contained little nutrition, and banana pith was only ever eaten as a last resort, but at that point even this watery soup seemed like a treat.

We were all physically and emotionally exhausted, but especially my mother. Her exertions at the place with no name had drained her terribly. She needed to rest, and we were happy to let her while we were foraging, protected by the big trees. Moving on was a daunting prospect, and we clung to the sanctuary under the trees.

A week after our arrival, Winston's parents decided that they had recovered their strength enough to continue their journey. It was difficult for them to travel quickly with all of their children, but they planned to follow the river upstream, as had all who had gone before us. None of us had ever been this way before, and we had no way of guessing what lay ahead—safety or even greater uncertainty.

More refugees arrived in the forest around us, and it became harder to find food. So after a week, early one morning we took up our loads and set off walking, leaving the big tree behind us. The path through the forest was very faint, so we followed others' tracks, sometimes down to and along the riverbank, sometimes on the rocky beach right next to the water where there were few visible footsteps, at other times snaking high up the steep valley sides.

As we walked, my mind wandered. I thought about school: I had just been moved up a year at Pway Baw Lu school because I was doing so well. Would I ever be able to restart my studies? Where might we end up, how might we end up living, and how might I finish my education?

Each day we spent struggling through the jungle seemed to take a lot out of my mother. I was beginning to realize that she was not as young or as invincible as she had once seemed. We tried to do extra jobs to take the burden off her, such as carry some of her things and cook or search for food. Every day we saw more and more people, as they, too, fled from the soldiers rampaging through the villages to the north of us. All told the same story of killings and burning and terror. Murder and mayhem were spreading outward from Manerpaw to virtually every village in the area. More often than not, after a few whispered words, people lapsed into a silence of shock and trauma. Mostly, they were caught up in their own trauma: where to run to escape; how to save their families; how to survive the journey that lay ahead.

One morning I plucked up courage to ask my mother the one thing that was preying on my mind.

"Moe, when can we go back to the village?" I asked. "Will it be long?"

Bwa Bwa and Slone pricked up their ears. It was the one question that we had all been dreading to ask but to which we all wanted an answer. *When can we go home?*

My mother looked at me with tired eyes. "I'm sorry, Po Mu Sit, we can't go back. Everyone has left."

I was silent for a moment with the shock of it all. "Never? We'll never go home?"

My mother shook her head. "Po Mu Sit, the Burmese soldiers have taken over our area. We *can't* go home. There's no home to go back to."

I stared at the sand, tears pricking at my eyes. I could hardly believe it, but that was what my mother had said. *We weren't ever going to go home.* Despite everything, I had always believed that we would be able to return to our village and our life when all this was over. It was the first time my mother had told us the grim reality of our situation, and I felt devastated.

"But Moe, we just want to go home," I heard Bwa Bwa whisper. "What's so wrong with that? Why can't we?"

"There's nothing there for us anymore," my mother answered. She was on the brink of tears herself. "I'm sorry, I'm sorry—but the village is gone."

Tears trickled down Bwa Bwa's face. "We'll never see it again? Never?"

My mother gave Bwa Bwa a hug and held out her free arm to me. "We'll have to go to Thailand as refugees and hope for the best. But we'll still be together, we'll still have each other, won't we?"

"But I don't want to be a refugee," I told her. "Refugees are people who need help. People who can't survive on their own. We're not like that, are we?"

"No, Po Mu Sit, we're not like that," my mother agreed. She gazed into my eyes. "But now we have no choice. We have to go to Thailand. There's nowhere else we can go."

At the end of that week we had our first concrete news of what might lie ahead. The Karen National Union had sent people back the way they had come, to tell the people still fleeing that they had found a place where we could stay and that we would be okay. They had reached a place called Mae Ra Moh, where a temporary refugee camp had been established just inside the Thai border, about eight hours' drive from Bangkok. Thousands of Karen were there already, and people were clearing the jungle to build huts for themselves.

The Thai authorities had agreed that this could be a "temporary settlement"—which meant that for now at least people wouldn't be declared illegal immigrants and pushed back into Burma. The Karen Refugee Committee (KRC), a group set up by the KNU to try to deal with the influx of refugees into Thailand, was trying to get the United Nations to recognize Mae Ra Moh as a refugee camp and to give it formal protection. This was the one bright light on an otherwise dark and stormy horizon: We would be in a Karen area, surrounded by Karen people—those who spoke the same language as we did and who shared our traditions and beliefs. All the villages around there were Karen, albeit in Thailand.

And so I began to nurture a new hope—a hope that once we got to Mae Ra Moh we could rebuild our lives to be similar to the ones we'd always known. If we couldn't go back to our village, we would build a new one, as we knew how to do, and we would surround ourselves once more with our neighbors and friends. We would build a new school better than the last, and lessons would start again. We would raise our chickens and pigs, replant our vegetable and flower gardens, and perhaps build a pond where the fish would be safe from the ducks that we raised.

My family decided to spend more time on the banks of the Mu Yu Klo River, as we all needed to rest. But the very process of living consumed our every waking moment. There was so much to do just staying alive. We hunted for *kaw soe dot,* water spinach, which grew by the riverbank. From the shadowy places in the forest we plucked the young shoots of ferns, which we boiled up as a green vegetable. We sought out the distinctive *ka thay kaw may dot,* the horse-hoof plant, whose leaves resemble a shiny, curved hoof. Even the emerald grass that grew on the river—*ta ka dot,* "bitter leaves"—could be boiled up to make a spicy stew. Still fearful that the enemy would track, find, and attack us, my mother urged us every day to be up before dawn, to eat breakfast in the half-light, and to be always on the lookout and ready to run at the first hint of trouble.

"Eat quickly," she urged. "Don't speak—just eat! If the enemy comes and you're in the midst of eating, you'll be left behind. Always be ready to run."

I glanced around at the forest fearfully. We heard no gunfire in the forest, no booming explosions, and no aircraft overhead. It was hard to imagine, in the peace and serenity of this beach by the river in its secret valley, that the war was still going on.

"Are they still after us, Moe?" I asked.

"I don't know. There's no way of telling. But we have to be careful, just in case."

In spite of her physical exhaustion, she was forever listening and trying to sense a threat. She knew that just when the forest was at its most silent might well be when the enemy was near. It was now that I really saw some of the fierce resistance fighter that my mother had once been. She knew so much about the ways of the enemy and of soldiercraft. She knew that darkness was our friend, for it cloaked our presence in shadows. But it was also a potential enemy, for the enemy might creep up on us unnoticed.

My mother taught us how to be cautious in everything we did, especially when preparing meals. Cooked food was vital if we were to rebuild our strength, but we had to be especially aware as we prepared it. Smoke from a cooking fire could put us in danger because it could be seen from a distance, so we did most of our cooking at night. Even then, though, we had to be on guard because a bright moon could reveal the silhouette of the rising smoke and give us away.

After a month in the jungle my mother decided that we were ready to continue the journey. We pushed onward through the forest, following the river toward its source, joining a long line of other villagers all snaking toward safer land, forming a deep groove along the riverbanks where refugees had trudged along the same path before us. Everyone moved slowly, but those who had the hardest time were the families with old people or very young children, who had to be carried piggyback up the steep hills.

As we made our way along the side of a steep gorge, we clung to trees and bushes as we felt our way along the path, our flip-flops trying to find a grip. When the going got most difficult, we were forced to take the path in relays. Bwa Bwa, Slone, and I would wait quietly in the forest, as my mother and the two men went back to fetch one bag at a time. It was too difficult and dangerous to carry more. Once all the bags were with us, we would move on and establish a new muster point for the next stage of the relay. It took much longer, but it was the only way to travel safely.

In this way we neared Mae Ra Moh. Eh Moo and Tu Chin went forward to scout out the ground ahead. This was the first time in four weeks that we would be coming out of hiding, and we had to be careful. They found a place where we could camp and came back to fetch us. They accompanied us into Mae Ra Moh.

It looked nothing like I had hoped, nothing like the old village. There wasn't a single house there, just rice fields, but there was no rice growing because it was February. Thousands of people huddled under plastic sheets strung from trees that they were using for shelter. Others had made temporary shelters, just as we had done in the place with no name and under the big tree. Some families had started to build proper bamboo houses similar to those back in the village—itself an indicator of how long they planned on being here. There were no toilets, and the smell was very bad. It seemed like a vast version of the place with no name. As far as I could see, makeshift shelters were strung out under the trees, and a haze of gray wood smoke hung over everything. Everyone was still tense and scared that we could still be attacked by the Burmese Army.

We made our way through the camp, following the river to the spot Eh Moo and Tu Chin had chosen next to a small stream at the far end of the camp that was not too crowded with other shelters, looking out over an old rice field. The two families closest to us were from our village. My mother knew them by name, and she went and greeted them to find out how they had fared and what news they might have. With Eh Moo and Tu Chin's help, we made the simplest of shelters by stringing up our plastic sheet. By now it was late afternoon. We cooked and ate some rice and got ready for an exhausted sleep.

Our neighbors cautioned us that no one was to show any lights in the camp, which meant no oil lanterns or flashlights. This was a harsh reminder that even though we had reached the refugee camp, we could not count on being protected. Although we were in Thailand, in a semiofficial camp, there was little to stop the enemy from sneaking across the border to attack us. During the first few days in Mae Ra Moh, I noticed groups of Thai soldiers on patrol around the camp. I was amazed at how well equipped they were: each had a pair of shiny leather boots, a smart uniform, and a sleek, modern gun. It made me so sad to think of our own resistance fighters, many of whom wore flip-flops and carried weapons that were decades old and held together in places with wire. I realized then that we Karen were so poor that we couldn't even equip our army properly. We couldn't speak Thai, and it was highly unlikely that any of the Thai soldiers could speak Karen. No one was certain if they were there to protect us or to police the camp boundaries and keep us in. But one thing was clear: they were a very professional army. Our resistance fighters would have fared much better in recent battles if they had had such equipment.

My mother warned us to keep our bags packed in case we suddenly had to run. A camp committee had been established, and the able-bodied men had set up a twenty-four-hour security watch. Volunteers patrolled the camp perimeter, carrying sticks as weapons. There was little chance that they could actually protect us with the tree branches they carried, but the hope was that they could raise the alarm if there was an attack so that we might have the chance to escape.

It wasn't the best of situations in which to prepare for my first night's rest in Mae Ra Moh camp. I couldn't stop thinking about if and when we would be attacked again. Although there was a sense of security in numbers, the very fact that there were so many of us here might draw the enemy to us.

Eventually, my exhaustion got the better of me and I fell asleep. The next morning I awoke feeling rested, so Bwa Bwa and I set off for a walk to the river to see if we could find somewhere to wash. The dirt and grime of the jungle were still thick upon us. We'd barely reached the water's edge when I spotted a familiar form just across the way from us.

"Lily Flower! Lily Flower! Hi! Hi! Over here! It's us! Bwa Bwa and Zoya!"

We ran over and hugged. It was so good to see her! Lily Flower had always been big and solid and strong, and to have such a friendly reminder of home was a comfort I did not realize I was longing for.

She had so many questions for us. "When did you get here? Are you staying nearby? Where?"

"We're just there by the little stream, on the hillside," I said, pointing. "There—that's where we're staying. Where're you?"

"Down by the riverside. Look, you can see our place from here. So we're almost neighbors!"

"And all your family are here?" I asked.

"Everyone's fine."

Lily Flower, Bwa Bwa, and I did our best to avoid talking about the darkness that had engulfed our lives during the past few weeks. In our culture people try to avoid talking about such horrors wherever possible. If we ever did have to mention such sadness and tragedy and loss, we would often do so by trying to make light of it, making jokes to cheer one another up.

Lily Flower's family had constructed a temporary shelter five places away from our own, so she was practically on our doorstep. And it turned out that Moonlight's family was only a few places away from her.

That same day we discovered that Ter Pay Pay and his mother—our grandma—had arrived in the camp. Grandma must have been approaching eighty years old, and it was a miracle that she had made the journey alive. Ter Pay Pay had been a resistance fighter in his youth, and he was still fit and strong. At places on the journey he had had to carry Grandma on his back.

Ter Pay Pay had also managed to bring some chickens with him on his journey. He'd tied them together by the legs and slung them upside down on a pole. We giggled at the thought of how he must have looking lugging the chickens around like that, but we were impressed all the same that he had managed to keep them alive. At times he'd been trekking through the jungle carrying his possessions, his mother on his back, and the chickens. What a journey they must have had! That first day in the camp I made it my job to look after the chickens, making sure they didn't run off.

I was really happy to find them here, especially when they suggested that they come and live with us. Now that we had arrived safely,

Eh Moo and Tu Chin would soon be returning to the resistance. Ter Pay Pay would be a great help to my mother as she set about trying to rebuild our lives. Like Say Say, Ter Pay Pay was a man of the forest. He knew the best bamboo for building, how to cut it and build shelters, and how to survive better than most. He was also a very good cook. And Grandma would be great company as we tried to keep our spirits up in the face of becoming "refugees."

Single and deaf, Ter Pay Pay communicated by using sign language. He would make a sign for my mother by rubbing his cheek in a circular fashion, signifying the *tha na kah* that she wore. He would run his palm over his forehead to signify my balding father. And he would indicate each of us children by showing our height above the ground with his hand. All us children loved him, and he always gave us snacks from what he had foraged for when he went out.

Ter Pay Pay, Eh Moo, and Tu Chin set about building us a proper shelter, of the type we had had at the place with no name and under the big tree. While they cut bamboo in the forest, Bwa Bwa, Slone, and I set about crushing it to make bamboo flats. Together, we constructed two sleeping platforms side by side—a larger one for us and a smaller one for Ter Pay Pay and Grandma. The split bamboo floor and wall gave us a bit of privacy.

Whenever we children had a spare moment, we'd go scavenging for wood in the forest. We'd cut it into short pieces with a machete, tie the pieces into a bundle using vines, and jam the machete in the middle. We'd carry the bundles home on our heads, with a longyi coiled into a doughnut shape cushioning the load. There was a small spring in the undergrowth beside our shelter, and this we decided to make our washroom. We rigged up a split bamboo pipe on stilts that funneled the water downhill. You could crouch under the free end and splash in the falling water. Bwa Bwa and I would go there at dusk and wash in relative privacy. We built a toilet set apart from the house, modeled on the one we had back in the village: a bamboo frame over a deep pit, with a bamboo pipe poking out to let the smelly gases escape.

By the end of the week, our shelter was ready. My mother cooked some rice for everyone who had helped. She wanted to cook something more special to show her gratitude, but we had nothing. I gazed out over the camp. Everywhere there were families doing the same as us—cutting and carrying bamboo and building shelters. As I watched all this activity, I told myself that surely it was only temporary. Surely there had to be a way back to the village. But in my heart I knew that this was it. My mother had told us the truth: there was no going back.

As we reconnected with our old friends, they told us what they had learned about the layout of the camp. Mae Ra Moh had been divided into sections. My family had ended up in Section Seven, which was at the far western end and nearest the border with Burma. We were situated on a hill overlooking the Mu Yu Klo River, which had been our constant companion ever since fleeing the village. At the opposite end were Sections One to Five, situated on a tributary of the Mu Yu Klo.

Once people settled in a section, it was pretty much established that that was where they would stay. That first week I discovered that Sweet Water Flower's and Winston Churchill's families were both living in Section Six. They weren't side-by-side, but there were so many people gathered in each space that they were still fairly close to one another. Nightingale was also living in Section Six, but she was across the river from us. A few days after our arrival she crossed the river on a bamboo raft and came looking for us. It was great to be reunited with her, but it was now a real journey to get to her house. While most of my friends from the village were in the camp, we were spread over a far greater distance.

Within weeks the Karen Refugee Committee helped organize the camps into sections, each with its own committee, and each group of ten households elected a team leader to sit on that committee. My mother was chosen to represent our area. She would go to the committee meetings, raise any concerns that the households she represented might have, and report back to everyone afterward.

During those first months, the camp instituted a strict security regime. By nine in the evening all candles and torches had to be out so that the enemy would find it harder to target us in the darkness. And from then until morning we had to speak in hushed whispers. But the time my mother feared most was daylight, when the enemy could better see to kill us. Often, she sent us off to the farthest end of the camp to hide in the forest. We'd take a packed lunch of rice and we were not to return before dusk. We hated hiding in the forest like that. All we could do was sit still and keep quiet, whereas when we were working in the camp at least we were keeping ourselves occupied.

One morning, a buzz of excitement went around the camp. A group of white people had arrived, and were giving out emergency materials. The elders—Grandma among them—started talking about how this was the "younger brother" coming back to help the Karen, just as our legends predicted. As the old poems foretold, he was coming in our hour of need to make amends for stealing the golden book. It gave some people hope that we hadn't been forgotten.

My mother set off with some of our neighbors to see the white people, and she returned with an enormous, striped, sky blue tarpaulin as roofing material. It was far better than our thin plastic sheet, and Ter Pay Pay soon had it rigged up to cover the entire shelter and cooking area. As we sat beneath out new roof, my mother told us more of what she'd learned. At the far end of the camp, gates opened onto a dirt track that led to the nearest town, Mae Sa Lit. That end of camp was the location of the Karen Refugee Committee office, plus a clinic staffed by Karen nurses.

Another group there—the Thailand Burma Border Consortium, set up by a British man named Jack Dunford—was giving out food rations. But they were limited to those truly in need, which meant families whose own food supplies were exhausted. After four weeks of living in the forest we were pretty much out of rice, so we fit into that category when we first got to the camp. In order to get the rations, we had to register with the Karen Refugee Committee (KRC). Everyone had to go to the office, give his name, and have his picture taken. Once we had done so we could collect a rice ration and a little salt and fish paste. Each person got a daily ration of one small tin of broken rice, plus a monthly ration of a kilogram of fish paste. If you were lucky, the fish paste had big lumps of fish in it. We'd take the pieces of fish out and dry them in the sun so they would keep well, otherwise the fish paste would be all runny goo to be stored in a clay jar and served as a sauce on the rice.

We stuffed the jar with a special leaf that we found in the jungle, which stopped the fish paste from going bad completely. But however careful one might be, flies always seemed to get into the jar and lay their eggs. The eggs would hatch into maggots, and in no time we'd find ourselves with a jar full of maggoty fish paste. If we didn't have anything else to eat, it would be boiled-up maggoty fish paste for lunch or supper. Of course, we did our best to pick out the maggots, but it was not easy.

As a family we had always been so self-reliant. My mother was used to working hard and relying on her own wits to look after her family. Accepting handouts like this felt so abnormal. But we had no choice. In the camp either you took the handouts or you starved. I was starting to get a sense of what it was like living as a refugee.

Life in the camp settled into a rhythm for ourselves, Ter Pay Pay, and Grandma. In the early morning the adults would go to cut bamboo from a nearby grove. By lunchtime they would be back for a snack, usually some rice left over from breakfast. In the afternoon we'd help our mother clear a little land around our plot where we could plant vegetables. Once the cut undergrowth was dry, we would burn it so the ashes would fertilize the soil. Just as soon as we had cleared and burned a patch of land, my mother planted her vegetable garden. She had prepared well before fleeing the village: she'd brought with her chili, aubergine, and bean seeds. Most families had had to flee so suddenly that they had practically nothing with them.

My mother always shared what little she had, and it again struck me how kind and caring she was to others. She even gave away one of

Bwa Bwa's few items of clothing—her favorite pink top. Bwa Bwa loved that top very much, and she was so upset to see it go. But my mother said that we should be happy to give away such things. She'd given it to a young mother who had a tiny baby and whose husband had lost a leg in the war. Their need was greater than ours, she said, and in that she was right.

During the weeks when we were trying to rebuild our shattered lives, we had no time to play. It was so different from life back in the village, yet there was little time to ponder how life had changed. My main responsibilities were looking after the chickens and fetching water from the spring. We tried to drink only boiled water, for there was a risk of catching cholera. I'd keep a pot of Karen tea brewing over the fire, so that those doing the hard work could come and refresh themselves. It made our area a hub where people could talk and exchange information, but it meant I often went down to the spring several times a day. Families lived around the spring, too; I had to traverse a slippery, muddy slope to get there. People washed in the spring, and the water bubbled up into a dirty brown pool.

As our new home became more of a house than a shelter, hope grew in my heart that we might rebuild a village here in Mae Ra Moh. The shelters were crammed far closer together than was normal, but I didn't see why Mae Ra Moh couldn't be made in the image of Per Hee Lu village, only much bigger. But it became clear that we were actually trapped in this camp. As nonofficial refugees, we had no status in Thailand. The Thais would tolerate our presence in their country while we were *inside* the camp, but we could not leave it. This sense of being imprisoned gave us an overwhelming feeling that we had no future, that our lives had come to a dead end.

In summer 1995, a few months after our arrival at Mae Ra Moh, the Thai authorities issued orders that we were to assist with the building of a fence around the entire camp. Each section had to construct its own fence, and barbed wire was provided for the purpose. Those barriers sent a clear message: Don't venture outside Mae Ra Moh. At all times, we were to remain within the confines of the fencing.

Of all the hardships we would suffer in the camps, this was the one we hated most. For a people long accustomed to wandering free, this entrapment was like death to us. The very idea that we couldn't just wander at will in the forest was unbearable. But we had no choice. If the Thai police caught anyone outside the camp, he or she would be treated as a "nonperson." Nonpersons would be either imprisoned or shipped back to where they had come from—which meant Burma—there to be handed into the custody of those from whom we had fled—the junta's border police or security agents. Being handed back to those who had spent decades trying to wipe us off the face of the earth would surely be a death sentence.

CHAPTER FOURTEEN

NO REFUGE

More than two months since the first time that I had run from the enemy aircraft, I still lived with fear as a constant companion. Even after spending so much time making our shelter, the camp didn't seem like a sanctuary. The sudden sound of the wind in the trees was enough to make my heart thump in my chest. Fear began to take over my life. It ate away at me.

Every day we heard rumors that an attack on the camp was imminent; then one day the Karen resistance sent us concrete news of the danger we were in: the enemy had crossed the Moei and Salween Rivers and was heading for the camp. We were all warned to be constantly on the lookout. At night volunteers stood guard at the edge of the camp, and in daylight two volunteers watched for movement, ready to ring a bell if the enemy appeared. If anyone saw the enemy, he was to raise the alarm. Then the camp organizers would tell us in which direction to run.

One bright, sunny day Bwa Bwa, Slone, and I were cutting firewood at the edge of the camp. Slender beams of light streamed down through the leafy bamboo. All of a sudden we heard screams from below us, followed by the pounding of running feet. As we turned to stare in the direction of the camp, we caught sight of a crowd of people charging in our direction, children clutched in the adults' arms.

An instant later my mother was standing outside our hut, crying out to us: "Quick! Quick! The camp is being attacked! Run! Run! Deeper into the forest!"

We darted down to the house and grabbed our bags: our mother had drilled into us that we were *never* to leave without them. Then we helped Grandma to her feet, as she was almost too old to walk, and with Ter Pay Pay hurried her into the forest.

As we ran, we heard that awful, hated sound once again—the crackle of gunfire ringing out from behind us. It was two months since we had last heard that fearful noise, and now it was all happening again. We headed deeper and deeper into the forest, climbing into the high ground. Eventually, the noise of the attack faded away behind us. It seemed that we had escaped, for now at least. We crouched in the dark shadows of the densest bamboo thicket, straining our ears for signs that the enemy were coming after us. We spent the entire day hiding. I felt like a terrified rabbit as a fox stalks it through the trees. Eventually, one of the camp organizers came to find us. The enemy had swept into the camp from the east, attacked Sections One and Two, and completely burned them to the ground. The soldiers had opened fire indiscriminately while people had fled for their lives. Dozens had been captured and marched away into the jungle.

The Thai soldiers had a guard post by the refugee camp's main gate, but when the enemy attacked they were nowhere to be found. The Thai soldiers who had struck me as being so well armed and fierce had run away and stayed away for several hours, giving our enemy time to burn down the camp and kidnap people. My mother was convinced that the Thai soldiers had *allowed* the enemy in to attack us. She was so angry.

When we made our way back to the camp, we didn't go down to Sections One and Two. We were too scared to do so. We didn't want to see the burning remains of the newly built refugee huts, but the plume of white smoke billowing over the camp was enough of a reminder. At any moment there could be another attack, and we wondered if we wouldn't be better off camping out in the forest. As night fell, we bedded down in our hut nonetheless, but used our bags as pillows, while Ter Pay Pay and my mother watched over us.

There were no more scares that night, and the next day we received word that the enemy had withdrawn into Burma. For now at least, the danger seemed to have passed. A week later, some of the women who had been kidnapped found their way back into the camp. The soldiers had taken them to use as human shields. They had also forced them to march ahead, in case there were any minefields. Once the soldiers no longer needed those they had taken, they let them go.

After that attack, life in the camp became much harder. My mother was working so hard that she started having migraines. They would start in the evening and prevent her from sleeping. And with the poor-quality food she started to lose weight. I was a growing teenager with an appetite to match, but I was often hungry, as we rarely had enough to eat. All we could supplement our daily rations with were the few vegetables we could grow around the house. We weren't allowed to leave the camp to search for wild food. Ter Pay Pay's chickens were too valuable to eat, because their eggs were a precious source of extra protein.

Although my mother's garden was turning out a good crop of ladies' fingers (okra), water spinach, and aubergines, we couldn't afford to eat it all. I helped my mother earn a little income selling our produce. With her help I priced a bunch of ten ladies' fingers at 3 baht—around 8 cents. A nice bunch of water spinach was a similar price. And three aubergines were 5 baht. I would go from hut to hut, asking if anyone wanted to buy. It was a hard sell. People had precious little money, and everyone was trying to grow their own food. In a good day I might make 40 to 50 baht. But I was better at making sales than my sister or little brother—I think because I was so utterly determined.

When we had earned enough money, my mother would go to buy

whatever basic essentials we needed. Thai traders had set up a make-shift marketplace at the far end of the camp. There were around fifteen thousand refugees in Mae Ra Moh by now—a big captive population to sell to. Every family had tried to grab what little money they had before fleeing their village, so they could buy cooking pots, plates, clothes, or some extra food. Whenever she could afford it, my mother would buy us a little treat like prawn crackers or a bag of boiled sweets. Or she might buy half a kilogram of sugar, which was a real extravagance. Some of the refugees made rice-flour bread, which was sweetened with sugar and which we'd eat right away when Mother brought it home.

None of us had any idea where our father was at this time, although we constantly worried about him. I missed him so much and told myself that he was still alive, but we had no way of communicating with him.

In my mind my father was off doing heroic work deep inside Burma. He was doing as Zoya the Russian partisan had done, operating behind enemy lines. He was preparing a counterattack by our resistance fighters. And as they had done during World War II, the forces of freedom in Burma would defeat a seemingly invincible enemy. In time we would be able to go back to our land and our homes.

I lived in that hope. It kept me going amid the fear and hopelessness of the camp.

It was my dream of the future.

CHAPTER FIFTEEN

A TIME OF DARKNESS

We had arrived in the refugee camp in February 1995. By April most people had finished building their homes and had turned their minds to other things. "Summer schools" for the children were set up by the Karen Women's Organisation with the help of some non-governmental organizations and were staffed by volunteers. Each camp section had one, with lessons held in the open under the sunshine.

The theme of these schools was simple: how to maintain hygiene in the refugee camp. With thousands of people crammed into such a small area, the potential for disease was high. We had to wash our hands before eating. Before going to bed we were supposed to wash our feet, as invariably they would be covered in mud from the day's activities. Rubbish—plastic bags, paper, food cans—had to be thrown into a pit and burned. One of the NGOs gave us proper toothbrushes and toothpaste, and we were taught how to brush our teeth morning and night. We were given soap and shampoo with which to wash our bodies and hair, and a little bag in which to keep our toiletries. We hung these from the bamboo wall of the bathroom that we had constructed in the back of the house.

My father had been a stickler for cleanliness, so I took all of this very seriously. In addition to the hygiene lessons, we were taught other skills that could make our lives in the camp run more smoothly. A sewing course taught us to repair our clothes, for we wouldn't be getting any new ones anytime soon. We were taught to keep our clothes clean, even if they were old and worn. It was good to be learning again and feeding my head, instead of hiding in the forest or doing the daily grind of the chores.

By June of that year a new secondary school had actually been built in Section Five. I was determined to attend lessons, but the journey across the river was too difficult and dangerous, especially for a bamboo raft in the rainy season. So my mother proposed that a high school be built for our section of the camp.

The Camp Committee called for volunteers to help, and a building was put up, made of a bamboo frame and a roof thatched with leaves. The classroom walls were only of thin bamboo, so we could overhear the goings-on in other lessons. Slone was in year five, and I could listen in on his class if I wanted to.

Our school had opened in the midst of the rainy season; it was only a short walk from our house, but even so we would get soaking wet. So my mother saved up and purchased two umbrellas from the marketplace, one for Bwa Bwa and one for me. She couldn't afford to buy one for Slone, so he had to walk to school wrapped in a plastic sheet—the one that we had used as our makeshift shelter when fleeing from the village. The outer walls of our school were only waist high. During the worst storms, rain would drive through the sides, preventing us from continuing with the lessons. We'd have to huddle together on the far side from the storm until the worst had blown over.

In the refugee school I enrolled in year eight and chose to sit right at the front of class. I volunteered to sit there, for I knew it would prevent me from messing around too much. I wanted to make my parents proud of me, and I knew I'd have to work hard to get good marks. My favorite subjects were English and math, but we had precious few resources with which to learn. We had no textbooks of our own; the teacher would write out the section of the textbook we were to study on the blackboard, and we would copy it down. Often, the entire lesson would consist of little more than this. There would be little or no explanation and discussion, as we concentrated on copying whole sections of textbooks. I often had little real understanding of what I was learning. A young Karen man taught us English; another taught Burmese and Karen languages; there was a math teacher, a geography and science teacher, and another for history. Our geography and science lessons turned into English lessons by default because the textbooks were all in English. The teacher was from Rangoon and spoke English with a Burmese accent that we found hard to understand. One day he was trying to teach us a new word that sounded like "choochooba," which he kept repeating. None of us had heard an English word like that before. Eventually, we realized that he was trying to say "cucumber." We did learn some English in those lessons, but not a lot of geography or science.

Before fleeing to the refugee camp, our teachers had been office workers or housewives. They had volunteered to help and were trying their best. In the refugee camp it was all about making do. In spite of the deficiencies with the school, we weren't ungrateful—far from it. We knew the teachers were giving up much to try to give us an education. We were relieved to be learning; even then I felt that it was important for Karen people to be better educated and informed to help us win our freedom, so that we would not always need to spend our lives in fear or on the run. Whatever the shortcomings of our teaching staff and their facilities, I applied myself 100 percent to my studies. I remembered my dreams of traveling abroad to finish my education and knew that I needed to work harder than ever if I wanted to keep them alive. I also remembered what I had learned about Saw Ba U Gyi, the founder and hero of the Karen resistance. In the years prior to World War II, Saw Ba U Gyi had traveled to Britain to study law at Cambridge University. He had taken law and qualified as a barrister (trial lawyer), practicing in the United Kingdom for eight years before returning to Burma and serving in the government. He had gone on to found the Karen National Union, becoming its first president.

Saw Ba U Gyi's story had in part inspired me with the idea of studying overseas. As he had done, I wanted to go to Britain to take a degree and go on to help my people. But in the refugee camp I wasn't even free to leave the confines of Mae Ra Moh camp. To the gate and the fences was as far as I could go. I worried that my hope would die and that I would never leave.

I had always wanted to be a free person, living freely in my own country and relying on myself. But here in the camp we were helpless and totally reliant upon the charity of others. The start of school gave my spirits a reason to recover. At least this was something we were doing for ourselves. But I worried about the future.

I was not the only one feeling torn. Bwa Bwa had just finished high school and was eager to continue her education. She had been hoping to train to be a doctor; instead, the refugee camp had only a course on palm reading and fortune-telling, a "further study" course set up by one of the refugee volunteers. It was either that or nothing.

The lessons frustrated Bwa Bwa. She would come home and grab my palm and gaze at it, then roll her eyes and tell me that I was going to have two husbands when I grew up, both so ugly! She'd come home with what looked like a map but was actually a star chart and use it to predict what sort of person I would become and what bizarre things the future held in store for me. We would be doubled over with laughter, but I could tell how upset she was that this was the only education available to her now.

It wasn't the fault of the camp organizers that Bwa Bwa couldn't go on to further study. In a camp as large as Mae Ra Moh, where fifteen thousand people sought refuge, there had to have been people qualified to teach her medicine, and the NGOs would have helped us by donating facilities, but the Thai authorities had decreed that no refugees were allowed to leave the camps to seek further educational opportunities in Thailand. All young people were trapped. Slone and I were continuing with our studies as best we could, but Bwa Bwa's life had reached a dead end. Not surprisingly, she was often depressed and confused, as were many of the people her age, and I knew that once my own high school studies were done, I'd be in the same situation.

Occasionally, reports filtered into the camp concerning the resistance, but our best source of news was my mother's tiny radio, our most precious possession. My mother had been determined to salvage it when we fled the village, and she carried it with her wherever she went in a little bag slung over her shoulder. It was tuned to the BBC World Service or Voice of America or Democratic Voice of Burma—a free Burma radio station that broadcast out of Norway but had been based in Manerplaw until the village fell to the Burmese. My mother had worked for it, as had undercover reporters in Burma and on the borders of Burma, who collected news and sent it to the head office in Norway, which then broadcast it back into Burma via shortwave transmitters in Europe.

This was our one link to the world outside the camp, and each evening our camp neighbors would gather at our house to listen to the radio. My understanding of Burmese was still very basic, and all the stations broadcast in Burmese, so I had to keep asking my mother to translate. Although she gave me only snippets of information, I could tell that things were going badly for the resistance. All reports were that, as the military offensive was continuing, tens of thousands of people were fleeing for their lives. We had surmised this as new arrivals streamed into the camp every day, mostly Karen villagers who had been trapped in the jungle for months before getting to Mae Ra Moh. The new arrivals described how the Burmese Army was setting up outposts in the jungle to block the routes leading to the refugee camp, forcing the desperate refugees to make long detours to avoid them.

Five months after our arrival in the camp, we finally had news of our father. Early one morning a friend of the family, Mahn Nyeigh Maung, sneaked into the camp (I couldn't work out how) and asked around until he finally found where we lived. Mahn Nyeigh Maung and my father had been friends since their youth. He told us that our father was fine and that he wanted us to know that he missed us and that we should look after ourselves and especially our mother.

I had so many questions I wanted to ask Mahn Nyeigh Maung. "But where is he?" I blurted out. "And what's he doing?"

Mahn Nyeigh Maung smiled. "He's somewhere safe, so you don't need to worry about him at all."

"When can he come to see us?"

"He'll come as soon as he can. Trust me, he misses you all terribly, and he'll come."

I was beyond thrilled to hear this. Of course, it would have been better to have seen my father in person, but this was the next best thing. My mother supported my father and backed him in what he was doing. No matter how much she worried about him or how heavy her burden was to carry alone, she did not begrudge the fact that he had dedicated his life to the resistance. Without it, there was no hope that any of us could ever go home and live in peace.

Before leaving, Mahn Nyeigh Maung took my mother to one side to have a private word. From where we were sitting we were able to hear most of what was said. My father had been unwell, he explained. Recently, he had addressed a big meeting of the resistance. Halfway through his speech he had collapsed with exhaustion. He was recovering, but he had been pushing himself too hard, and he could come to see us only when he was able.

It was almost impossible to think of my father getting ill. He had always been the picture of good health, and I couldn't imagine what had happened to make him so unwell that he had collapsed. I could tell from my mother's reaction that the relief of hearing that he was alive had been replaced with worry for him. Slone, Bwa Bwa, and I were devastated.

*   *   *

My mother asked Mahn Nyeigh Maung for any news of Say Say, but he knew nothing of my brother. Most likely, he was off fighting with the Karen resistance somewhere toward the front lines. My mother was worried sick for Say Say. She had brought some of his things to the camp—a few clothes and his school photos—as well as my father's most precious possessions. But when she might get to give them to either Say Say or my father was anybody's guess. Attacks on our villages were escalating, and the Karen soldiers were under more pressure than ever.

After two days Mahn Nyeigh Maung had to move on, as he had many other places to visit before he would be able to report back to our father that we were okay.

Several months after our arrival in the camp a young man, Saw Nyi Nyi, "Mr. Younger Brother," came to visit. A close friend of my parents, having known them in Manerplaw, he was one of a number of the younger generation who had left behind their own parents when they joined the resistance, just as my parents had when they were young. My mother and father acted as surrogate parents to many of these young, idealistic people, many of whom looked up to my father.

Saw Nyi Nyi worked for Burma Issues, an NGO that documented human rights abuses in Burma. One night, for our section of the camp, he borrowed a video player and a TV set so he could show a film called *Beyond Rangoon* in the school. Hundreds of people gathered to watch this story of a female American journalist who got caught up in pro-democracy demonstrations on the streets of Rangoon. When the SLORC ordered the soldiers to open fire, she fled with survivors to the border region. Saw Nyi Nyi thought the film would help us understand that other people from Burma were also suffering under dictatorship, but the trouble was that the film was in English. Even those of us who were studying English at secondary school found it hard to follow. For most of the audience, it made no sense at all, and few could see the small TV. Saw Nyi Nyi realized that the showing was a bit of a disaster, so we talked about it afterward and many Karen were surprised to learn that the Burmese Army also killed fellow Burmans. It opened their eyes to see this and to know that the Karen in Manerplaw had taken in Burmans who had also fled the dictatorship.

However, we all agreed that a Rambo film would have been much better. The Karen love Rambo, a tough fighter to whom resistance fighters and their families could relate. To us the Rambo films were inspirational—for the message seemed to be that no matter what the odds, one brave warrior could win the day. When faced as we were with the massive might of the SLORC, whose armed forces outnumbered ours some thirty to one, that was a message we Karen needed to hear.

CHAPTER SIXTEEN

THE JOURNEY HOME

In March 1996, I had my year eight exams. If I passed I would go on to years nine and ten, my final years of high school. I took exams in seven subjects: math, science, English, Karen, history, geography, and Burmese. I had studied as never before that year and had done well on each of the monthly tests. With the school exams finished, it was time for the summer holidays.

The following day, a hot and sunny Saturday, Bwa Bwa and I had just finished lunch, and we were sitting on the bamboo steps of our house, gazing out over the camp. On the bottom step was a scattering of flip-flops, where we left them because we considered it rude to wear our shoes inside the house.

All of a sudden Bwa Bwa let out a cry. "Oh, my God! Pah-Pah! He's back! He's here!"

In a flash she had jumped to her feet and was dancing around on one leg as she shoved on her flip-flops, and then she raced off down the hill toward a figure that was obviously looking for someone. I followed after her as fast as I could, but Bwa Bwa was quicker. She reached our father a little ahead of me and flung herself into his arms, almost knocking him over. An instant later I was upon him, throwing myself into the free arm that he held out to me.

"How are you? How are you?" he said with a smile, as he tried to hug us both tight. "Such big girls! When did you get so big?"

For a few seconds I just buried my head in the warm, familiar smell of my father. I couldn't believe that it was really him, that he had come home to us. I nuzzled into his checked shirt as he hugged us.

He had been walking around for hours trying to find someone who knew us and where we lived.

"Come on, girls! I'm about to collapse!" my father said with a laugh. "So, tell me, how are you?"

"I'm fine, Pah, just fine," I smiled. And then the words started to tumble out. "I'm so happy to see you because we all missed you so much and I've just done my year eight exams but your friend said you were ill—"

My father took us by the hand and led us up to the house, as I burbled away happily. My mother was at the entrance, smiling down at us. She hadn't smiled with such warmth for such a long time; it was so good to see her looking happy again.

We sat in the living room and drank Karen tea, beside ourselves with joy to see Pah. We couldn't go more than a few moments without giving him big hugs. But he had hardly been with us for ten minutes when he went to have a private word with my mother and left us sitting in the living room. Shortly my mother came back in to announce that it was time to leave: we had to pack our things and leave the camp right away in order to go to live with my father in his village.

We barely had time to act on what she had said. A car was waiting for us, she explained, and if we missed it, that was the end of going to my father's village. It was too far and difficult and dangerous to make it on foot. We began throwing things into bags in a fevered rush. As we packed, a crowd gathered at the house. News got around the camp fast, and people were coming from all over to see my father and ask for news of the resistance.

As they chatted to my father, we hurried to finish packing our one bag each. A lot of what we had accumulated in that house we could leave for Ter Pay Pay and Grandma, who would not be coming with us. Grandma was too old and frail to travel anywhere now.

I chose to take my washing things and my precious photos, including some new ones that Saw Nyi Nyi had taken. Each of us had taken a few of the photos to keep for ourselves. If it was chiefly me in the photo, I had claimed it. But if it was me and Bwa Bwa, I'd usually let her have it. A couple of skirts and shorts, a pair of jeans, and a towel, plus my little mirror, and then I was done.

I asked my mother, "Where is Pah's village? And how long will it take to get there?"

"It's not too far," she replied, but her mind seemed elsewhere. "We'll just go and visit, then come back here. A few weeks is all we'll be away."

But I could hear my mother going around to our neighbors in a rush, telling them that we were leaving and saying her farewells. She was wishing people good luck, and it didn't sound like a temporary leaving to me. I was confused.

"Are we really leaving for good?" I asked her. "Or is it just a visit?"

It was important to me to know, for if we were leaving the camp forever I wanted to say good-bye to my friends.

"It's just for a short while, you'll see," my mother tried to reassure me. "It's just to visit the village, that's all."

It seemed strange that my mother thought we could come into and out of that camp at will, because we all knew how difficult it was for refugees to do so. In reality, I realized later, my mother knew we wouldn't be coming back again. She had only said what she had said to make it easier on us and to hurry us in our packing. Every minute counted as we raced to catch that vehicle and get out of there.

As Ter Pay Pay helped my mother parcel up the last of her things, I talked about it in whispers with my big sister.

"If we're leaving for good, we'll lose all of our friends," I said.

Bwa Bwa nodded. "I know. And we don't know what this new place is like. Is there a school there, even?"

"I don't know. Let's try and ask Moe. Pah's too busy with all these people."

My father was surrounded by a crowd of visitors, but the more we tried to ask Mother what was happening, the more she insisted it was just a visit. I noticed then how exhausted and tired Pah looked. He clearly hadn't recovered fully from his illness. At least if we were going to live with him for good, we could cook for him and pamper and properly look after him.

Finally we were ready to go, leaving just about everything with Ter Pay Pay and Grandma—the chickens and pigs we had raised, our pots and pans, our vegetable gardens. Ter Pay Pay and Grandma acted as if they thought we were going away for a short visit and would be back soon, and they promised to keep things in working order until we returned. We said a rushed and confused farewell, lifted our packs, and set off for the far end of the camp.

As we made our way through the camp, people were calling out their good-byes. Some of my friends were there, and they were crying. They knew in their hearts that we were going for good, especially after my mother had said her farewells to their parents. And by now I was more or less convinced myself that we would never be coming back, but I couldn't cry.

Sad to be leaving my friends, I was excited at the thought of getting out of there. Wherever I was going, I would be with my father, and I would no longer be a refugee. I told myself that one day I would come back to find Nightingale, Sweet Water Flower, Lily Flower, and all my other childhood friends. Whatever happened to me now, I wouldn't forget them.

The car had driven as far as Section Five, where the river blocked the way. It was a sleek, open pickup truck, and I had no idea how my father had managed to get the use of it. We climbed into the back and sat wherever we could—either perched on the sides and tailgate or squatting on our bags. Once we were settled, my father got into the front and we were off. A short drive through the camp and we reached the gate, which consisted of two wooden posts with a long pole suspended between.

We pulled to a halt, and I heard the driver speaking with the guards in Thai. The guards glanced at us, asked the driver a few questions, nodded, and then the pole began to rise. My heart was in my mouth. The guards stood back and waved us through. For the first time in more than a year we were leaving Mae Ra Moh camp.

We rumbled through the gate and onto the dirt track. All around us, thick jungle stretched away in every direction. The track snaked through the trees, a thin, red, dusty scar amid the shadowy green of the forest. It was little wonder that so few people knew the camp existed; it was very well hidden. Most Thais—even those local to the area—didn't even know that there was a refugee camp here.

As the pickup bounced and bucked along the rough track, we hung on for dear life. It was too noisy and dusty to talk much, and I reflected on what had happened. We had done our best to rebuild the village in Mae Ra Moh camp, and, in spite of all of the shortcomings and frustrations of being a refugee, in the camp we at least had a small amount of security, as the Thai authorities allowed us to stay in the camps. But now that we had ventured out, we had become a group of illegal immigrants in Thailand.

We had begun another daunting new adventure.

For what seemed like an age we weaved through the dense forest. The jungle gradually gave way to shimmering green rice paddies, which stretched away to the flat horizon. I had never seen a landscape like it. Finally we emerged onto a smooth, black road surface—tarmac—and we were surrounded by honking cars, tall, shiny buildings, and metal lampposts towering over us like animals pouncing to strike. It was the first time in my life that I had seen a "proper" town. I had never imagined that buildings could be so big, or so numerous.

Everywhere I looked, there were crowds of people dressed in clean, smart clothes. We drove past a schoolyard filled with children in neat white-and-blue uniforms. What a contrast it was to our own rickety bamboo school, peopled by malnourished refugee children with no equipment or uniforms. I stared at everything in amazement, as if I were watching a scene from a movie—and one that was better than anything we'd watched on Aung Ba's little television screen.

This was the town of Maesariang. At dusk, streetlamps came on as if by magic, and windows were illuminated by a warm yellow glow. We rattled through the streets to our destination, a house on the far side of the town, whose owner was a friend of my father and a member of the KNU. We were given a delicious dinner of real rice—as opposed to broken rice—and chicken curry. I couldn't remember the last time I'd eaten anything that tasted so wonderful.

That night we bedded down on the floor of my father's friend's house, and in no time at all I had fallen into a deep sleep. It was the first time I had slept in a concrete house, which made no noise as bamboo does when people walk on it. And I slept better knowing that here I was safe from attack. The first thing I thought of when I awoke the following morning was my father. I had fallen asleep without even saying goodnight to him, so I was crushed when my mother told me that he had left again. He had woken early and headed off on some mission connected to his resistance work. He wouldn't be back.

I had wanted to tell him so many things. That I didn't want to be a refugee. How hard things had been in the camp and how much I missed home and how well I was doing in school. But I couldn't tell him any of it.

After a hurried breakfast we set off again in the car—only without my father. Slone and I sat in the front, squeezed onto the seat next to the driver. Our mother had told us we were headed to a place called Mae Sot, another town in Thailand.

The road followed a river that ran through a high-walled gorge, twisting and turning alarmingly, and before long Slone and I were feeling sick. We didn't know what to say to the driver, but luckily he stopped for a rest. We jumped out and ran into the bush, vomiting up our breakfast.

"Oh my Little Son and my Little Daughter—you're sick!" my mother exclaimed. "I'm so sorry."

Neither Slone nor I could respond; we were still heaving into the bushes, although there was nothing left to come out. We'd never been in the hot, airless interior of a vehicle before, and it had made us feel awful.

"Sit in the back," my mother suggested. "That way the air will be in your face, and you'll soon feel better."

She was right. Though far less comfortable, the back of the pickup was the place for us. Bwa Bwa had taken our place in the front, and Slone and I lay down to try to sleep. We were exhausted from all the traveling and the vomiting, and we dozed in the hot sun as it climbed into the sky. We stayed that second night in Mae Sot, a town that seemed even bigger than Maesariang. Again we were put up in a house owned by a friend of my father and given a hot meal.

On the third day we headed out of Mae Sot, on a journey that lasted some five or six hours and went through several Thai police checkpoints. At each the driver spoke a few words in Thai, and we were let through. But at each checkpoint I saw groups of scared Karen sitting by the roadside. The Thai police had arrested them as illegal immigrants, and it seemed that the same might happen to us at any time.

Eventually we left the plains of Thailand and headed into the cover of the forested hills that run along the border with Burma. It had been so new and different to see such open landscape, but with the sight of woods, I began to feel a little more at home again. Finally we reached the border at a place called Klaw Htaw, where we found a Karen vehicle waiting for us. It was such a relief when we discovered that the driver was someone we knew: "Uncle Joe," a friend of the family from our days in the village.

We threw our bags into the back of Uncle Joe's pickup and set off into the deep jungle along a rough and little-used dirt track. And in this way we sneaked our way back into Burma. An hour later we reached Ther Waw Thaw—the New Village. This was where my father had his home. As I looked around, I suddenly spotted a familiar figure. It was Nightingale!

I cried out to her, waving excitedly from the back of the pickup. "Hi! Nightingale! Nightingale! It's me—Zoya!"

She ran over, and we hugged each other tearfully. I'd been unaware of it, but it turned out that she had left Mae Ra Moh camp a few months before. Because she was living in a different section than we were and going to a different school, we'd practically lost touch with each other. We were both so happy to be reunited and to be in a Karen village once again.

Ther Waw Thaw was surrounded by jungle-clad mountains. It could quite easily have been any area around Per Hee Lu village or Manerplaw. As I looked around me, I felt as if we were finally some-where familiar.

I suddenly felt as if I really had come home.

CHAPTER SEVENTEEN

THE NEW VILLAGE

Uncle Joe took us directly to my father's house. The dirt road passed through the village marketplace and petered out at the edge of a beautiful lake. We unloaded our bags and followed a path along the water's edge to the far side. There my father had built a small bamboo-framed house on a vantage point overlooking the waters.

On three sides, the beautiful expanse of the lake was fringed with houses, while the rest was thick forest. The lake was fed by freshwater springs, and one bubbled out next to our house to form a tiny stream. I felt so relaxed and relieved—free, and able to breathe fresh air. For the first time in months I felt more positive about the future.

The lake was the hub of village life. It was where the village elephants would come to bathe and where the village children would swim. From the house we could watch the elephants lumbering in, guided by their mahouts. They'd suck up gallons of water in their trunks and spray it all over themselves. After the elephants had been in the lake it looked like a muddy soup, and it would take an hour before the mud settled and the water was clear again.

At the front of our little bamboo house, running down to the lakeside, my father had planted a flower garden with tiny roses, big purple lily flowers, and bright yellow bushes that he had cut into neat borders. The flower garden was reflected in the placid waters of the lake, and it was magical. My father truly had an eye for what was beautiful and uplifting for the soul. Planting a flower garden wasn't perhaps the most practical way to prepare for our arrival in the village, but it was such a generous expression of his love for us and for his desire to give us a home that reminded us of our happy village life—a home that was more than a shelter—an expression of our spirit and his. My mother had always been the more pragmatic of my parents, and the day after our arrival she set about clearing land above the house, where she could plant her vegetables. She also wanted a duck house and a place to keep pigs. Both the ducks and pigs would love it there, she declared. They could go down to the lake to dabble about in the muddy shallows.

A new energy seemed to come to my mother. It was so good to see her making plans and laughing.

Uncle Joe and Nightingale helped us move in. With its one room, the house was even smaller than what we had been living in at Mae Ra Moh camp, but we didn't mind. It was where my father had lived for the past year, and it instantly felt like home. There, we all felt free and secure. We could go for a walk whenever we wanted, not like in the camp, where we were surrounded by barbed wire.

A week after we arrived my father returned from Thailand, but he went straight to Htee Ker Plur—"Very Muddy Pond"—village, the new headquarters of the Karen resistance, and came to visit us in the New Village when he was free from his work, which was once a month. Even so, we were all pleased to see him, but especially my mother, whose spirits he lifted.

The resistance had moved into more of a guerrilla style of warfare, as it could not match the might of the Burmese Army, which had destroyed village after village and displaced tens of thousands of refugees, many of whom were in Thailand and many more of whom were in hiding in the jungles. The Burmese Army would not stop at bombing a village without warning; they also looted them and raped and killed the villagers. They took thousands of people as slaves, worked them till they fell, exhausted, and left them to die. Reports of similar atrocities were emerging from farther north in Karenni State and Shan State, where the army was attacking the Karenni and Shan ethnic people. There, people were also being relocated by the army, tens of thousands of people at a time being forced to leave their homes and given no aid at the sites to which they were sent. Despite the scale of the abuses, the international community paid no attention.

On the one hand, it made me feel proud that my father was fighting against this evil: I knew that we had to resist.

Yet at the same time part of me resented that the resistance deprived me of my father. I missed him and wanted him to be with us. "Normal" fathers lived at home all the time. Having experienced some of the horrors directly, however, I tried my best to understand my father and why his work always took him away.

In spite of all the uncertainties and fears for our father and Say Say, life in Ther Waw Thaw was like reaching a safe haven for us. After our year in the refugee camp it felt so good to be free. I was happy just to do simple things: to go where we wanted when we wanted and not be fenced in; walk from one village to another; make friends; play the guitar and sing at the tops of our voices; and laugh freely long into the evening. None of that had been possible in the camps. I felt safe where we were. There was no sense of a war going on or of a horrible threat coming closer and closer. It was like a little slice of the paradise we had lived in before the attack.

Shortly after our arrival in the New Village, my mother found out that a summer school program for learning English was taking place in a nearby village. Our teacher was a white Canadian woman called Emma Ghost, though her surname was actually Gorst. Young, tall, pretty, and blond, Emma had volunteered to come to Burma to teach the Karen English, and I thought it was very brave of her to have done so.

Bwa Bwa and I were both in her class. I was very shy with Emma at first, especially as I couldn't speak much English and she had no Karen. We had to communicate in sign language or in broken English. At first she taught us the very basics: my name is Zoya; I am fifteen years old; I have one sister and two brothers. But from the very first lessons I realized she had a different way of teaching from the schools I had been to in the refugee camp or even at home. There was no copying down verbatim in Emma's lessons, and there were to be no tests or exams.

Emma would hand out sheets of paper photocopied from textbooks that had blank spaces that we had to fill in with words. Emma tried to make us understand what a noun, a verb, and a tense were rather than just have us memorize the words. At times she'd divide the class into groups, and we would have to work together on a subject and then present it to the class. Emma wanted us to enjoy ourselves as we learned. She wouldn't tell us answers; she would make us discover them for ourselves. She was the first teacher to really try to make me think, rather than learn by rote.

For the first time I felt a new language really coming alive. We had to learn to reason for ourselves and develop basic critical thinking skills. I loved the way she involved us in the learning process and found her way of teaching captivating and challenging and full of laughter. Over the month of summer school Emma became our friend. She loved to play the guitar and sing, especially romantic songs by musicians like Rod Stewart. She'd strum her guitar, and once we'd learned the words we would sing along with her. It was a novel way to learn English, and often we made the most hilarious mistakes.

One day we were sitting out on the grass singing, and Emma put down her guitar and went to get some photos. First she showed us ones of her family and then of her boyfriend. We giggled shyly at the picture, especially as he had such a funny goatee. No Karen man would ever wear a beard like that; it made him look like my mother's goat.

We told Emma all about life as refugees, and she in turn told us about growing up in Canada. The schools sounded so well equipped, I couldn't imagine them. And people seemed so free to travel in their country, and even around the world! It sounded like a place of such opportunity.

At the end of the summer school there was no formal graduation, but we ate a meal together with a sauce of coconut milk, sugar, and water into which we dunked little balls of boiled rice flour. We call this meal *ko ber baw,* and it is one of my favorites. Then we went to the village water festival, which was as jubilant as any festival I'd been to before. Large groups of young people shouting and laughing and throwing water at one another. It was such fun.

At the end of the day, Emma traveled back with us to the New Village and stayed the night in our little house. We felt special and honored to have her stay with us. My mother spoke hardly any English and my sister and I were not much better, so communication wasn't easy, but we got by. The following morning she went into my father's flower garden and smelled every single flower that was in bloom. Later, Uncle Joe brought the car for her, and Emma left for Thailand and her long journey home to Canada. We had an emotional parting and promised to write to each other if we could. We were very sad to see her go.

The new KNU headquarters, Htee Ker Plur, was still being built, so there was double the work, as they had to keep running the government in KNU-controlled areas but also establish a brand-new HQ.

But the most exciting news was that peace negotiations were taking place between the KNU and the dictatorship. My father had been to Rangoon and met with Lieutenant General Khin Nyunt, a senior regime official, but negotiations were not going well. The regime would not discuss a political settlement. It demanded an unconditional surrender, not even considering any requests from the KNU. It said it would discuss political issues only after the KNU disarmed, but everyone knew that if the KNU disarmed the regime would not keep its word.

Even though my father's negotiations with the dictatorship were of historical significance for our people, Bwa Bwa and I didn't understand that then, and we were eager to tell him what we had been doing at summer school and in our new home. He smiled as he listened to us.

Then he spoke to my mother. "I'm so proud of you," he told her. "You're so strong. You brought them out of the refugee camp, through Thailand, to here. And now you've taken them to the summer camp. And look at all the useful things you've been doing to this house! You are stronger than I ever imagined you could be!"

My mother smiled at him shyly.

Later, she sat us down for a chat. She and my father had decided we were going to stay in the village rather than return to Mae Ra Moh camp. We still felt sad that we would not be seeing our old friends, but we were glad not to have to return to the life of refugees in that prison-like camp.

I really did regret having left my school exercise books behind at the camp, but my mother told me that there was an excellent missionary school in the New Village that was far better than those at Mae Ra Moh. As soon as the holidays were over, we would enroll.

Sadly, my father was home for one day only and would be leaving for work the following morning. We sat in the front of the house at a low bamboo tea table my father had built where we had a view over his flower garden down to the lake. For a while we chatted and laughed—a happy family back together again at home.

I sat on my father's lap and intended to stay right where I was. My sister and little brother felt they were too grown up to sit on his lap, but not me. My father put his arms around me and hugged me tight.

"Little Daughter, you're too big to sit on Daddy's lap," my mother objected. "You're a big girl now. Don't you feel embarrassed?"

"No," I replied. "I like it this way. I like it just the way it is!"

My father laughed. He knew there was no embarrassing me where he was concerned.

After a while my father declared; "Okay, who's going to help me in my flower garden?"

I jumped to my feet. "I will! I will!"

Slone and Bwa Bwa followed suit. "We'll help too!"

My mother rolled her eyes in mock annoyance. "You just got home, and all you want to do is tend to your flowers! Well, then—you can go and eat your flowers too!" We could tell that in spite of her words, she was happy to see him back to his old routine.

Bwa Bwa, Slone, and I began to clear the vines and weeds that were choking my father's flowers. As we worked, he seemed happy and relaxed as he told us the name of each and what made it unique. It was amazing how his garden took all the stress and strain from him.

Helping my father in his flower garden was the best way to spend time with him. Now and then he would break off from his weeding and give me an affectionate kiss. He would announce what a great job I had done arranging some stones to make a little wall or pulling up vines to clear the path.

That day in the flower garden flew by. In no time the sun was dipping behind the mountains, and our little house was thrown into cold shadow.

My mother had prepared an evening feast with chicken and vegetable soup, followed by yellow bean curry with rice and the obligatory fish paste pounded with chili. We didn't eat this well often, but what a change it was from the refugee camp's rancid, maggoty fish paste.

My father took the ladle and spooned out some chicken soup for Slone, Bwa Bwa, and me. But he stopped short of my mother's bowl, teasing her.

"This is ridiculous!" she announced. "You serve all the children but not your wife!"

We laughed and laughed at Mum as she acted all annoyed. Everyone was happy that evening. We were back together as a family, and we cherished those few precious hours. My mother seemed especially happy, as if a radiant light were shining out of her.

After dinner my father drank green tea and listened to the BBC Burmese Service on my mother's tiny radio. We gathered around, but I couldn't understand much of what was said. My parents spoke in Burmese for a while, discussing the news. Eventually my father snapped off the radio and announced that there was no major news about the Karen situation. The misery in Burma ground on. Aung San Suu Kyi, who had been released from house arrest in 1995, was being stopped from traveling freely around the country. The generals had released her, hoping to avoid international sanctions, but she was mobilizing the people and the generals were becoming more afraid of her. Political activists were still being arrested, and more Burmese Army soldiers were being sent to Shan State, where more forced relocations were reported to be imminent.

We talked for a while longer about family matters, schooling in particular, and then we began to drift to bed, our stomachs full of that good food, and hugged each other for warmth.

In the morning my father was gone. But a letter delivered care of Nightingale cheered our spirits. We had mail from Mae Ra Moh camp, letters from just about all of my friends. They hoped that I was happy and that life in the village was good. Things in the refugee camp were as bad as ever. There was still the constant danger of attack, and no one was allowed to leave the camp. Though they were grateful for aid, Karen people are used to being independent, and it was difficult to be completely dependent on aid, not able to farm their own food, not allowed to work and to have a feeling of independence. People were sad and depressed, feeling trapped in the crowded camp, eating the same rice and fish paste for every meal, day after day after day.

I became tearful as I read their letters, each of which was scribbled on the old pages of an exercise book. I wanted to write and let them know how sweet and good it was to be free and to urge them to try to get out of the camp. Bwa Bwa and I desperately wanted to visit our friends, but Mother told us it was impossible. We had no transportation; it was a long way and dangerous, and we might get trapped there. Bwa Bwa and my mother had huge fights over it, Bwa Bwa insisting that we needed a chance to say a real good-bye, to gather the things we'd left behind. Our mother told us to stop being so stupid. Here we were in a village with food, shelter, space, and freedom, living on our own land in our own home, not forced to beg and take charity from others. Slone backed my mother. He told her that wherever she was, that was where he wanted to be. I was disappointed but had to accept my parents' decision.

I wrote a letter to each of my friends, telling them how much I had loved getting word from them. I told them that I wanted to see them but that it was impossible. I told them how we couldn't risk traveling through Thailand with its dozens of checkpoints. I also told them that people, including my father, were working so that we could all be free someday soon. Seeing their letters reminded me of how important my father's work really was; I was glad that he was contributing to the efforts that could reunite us all someday.

Not long after we sent our letters back to the camp, my father sent a messenger with exhilarating news, inviting us to visit him in his workplace. Uncle Joe volunteered to drive us.

It was a two-hour drive to Htee Ker Plur, which I had thought would be like Manerplaw, with a big parade and training ground, and houses and offices like in the New Village. And a beautiful flower garden. But it was nothing like I had expected. Htee Ker Plur was a place for soldiers, democratic opposition leaders, and administrators. It was also plagued by mosquitoes, which screamed around our heads all night long. The only way to deal with them was to build a fire, throw green leaves onto it, and sleep the night in a smoky fog.

I felt sorry for my father, having to stay here. In this place his priorities were different: food came before flowers. His hut was on a hilltop, and he had to carry water from a stream below—but he was doing so to water the vegetables he needed to grow to survive. There was no time or energy for flowers, and I could tell that it saddened him beyond measure.

My father took us to visit friends and to see the local base of the Karen National Liberation Army (KNLA), the armed wing of the Karen resistance. The soldiers seemed relaxed and easygoing, as there was little sign of the ongoing war here. It was the rainy season, when there wasn't much fighting because roads and rivers were impassable and the SLORC could not resupply its troops.

Even though I have seen firsthand the horrific things that the Burmese Army has done, I thought of many of the Burmese Army soldiers as victims of the dictatorship. They are poor and uneducated and have been fed propaganda all their lives. Many were forced as children to join, were beaten and made to take drugs. Few people know that, in the 1990 elections, the townships where Burmese Army soldiers and their families were based voted for Aung San Suu Kyi's party, the National League for Democracy.

The SLORC troops would normally use the rainy season as an excuse to rest. Many of the lower-ranking soldiers were poorly paid conscripts and children. Their morale was low, and they suffered high casualties when they fought the KNLA. They knew they were safe from attacks by the KNLA, as by now the KNLA was mainly a defensive organization, protecting villages from attacks and helping to get aid to people. They didn't often launch military attacks.

In spite of this change in mission, the base buzzed with energy and determination. There was activity everywhere, new buildings being put up, people rushing around carry out their duties. It was encouraging and inspiring, and I wanted to become part of it.

CHAPTER EIGHTEEN

THE MISSION SONG

Mother took us to the village market to buy some school things. Bwa Bwa and I each got a brand-new white blouse and blue skirt, and Slone got the boy's version of the uniform. It was the first time we had been bought any new clothes since fleeing our village.

Near the market was a Buddhist monastery perched atop a hill. It was built of a rich, dark red wood, and it exuded warmth and a deep peacefulness. I'd been up to that monastery a few times for the monthly Lah Pweh—"Full Moon"—ceremony. In the middle of each month, the village would gather at the monastery under the full moon for chanting, prayers, and lovely food: delicious rice porridge, spicy chicken curry, and sticky rice with fresh coconut. I loved Lah Pweh, for then the whole village would be bathed in silvery moonlight. Sometimes the dogs would be barking at the moon. We would tease each other that they had been spooked by ghosts, and we'd often end up scaring ourselves.

Each morning the monks of Lah Pweh would walk around the village with their clay begging bowls. A novice monk would walk ahead, ringing a flat little bell suspended on a string. Whenever we heard that sound, we knew the monks were coming to seek alms.

Recently, my parents had started to encourage Slone to become a novice monk and Bwa Bwa and me to become nuns. It wasn't uncommon for Karen children to serve a short period as an initiate, usually for a few months during the summer holiday, after which they would return to their studies. Because Bwa Bwa and I knew that nuns had to shave their heads, we refused point-blank. Slone also refused to become a monk.

As in our old village, the New Village contained a mix of Buddhists, Christians, and animists, although Buddhism was the predominant religion. Our school was a Christian mission school, one of the best in the area, and no one seemed to mind its religious affiliation. The day I started at the new school, I had to explain to the headmaster, Thera Tha Wah—"Teacher White Heart"—why I didn't have my last year's exam results; I had left the refugee camp before they were released. After he checked with my mother, who told him that I was very dedicated to my studies and had always done well, I was accepted into year nine on her word. Bwa Bwa was accepted into a course of further education in English and Bible study.

From Per Hee Lu village, I recognized a girl named Mular Moo, "Hope Life," and a boy from Pway Baw Lu village named Sah Moo Daw, "Star in the Sky." We introduced ourselves to the other pupils, telling them where we were from and who our family was. I felt embarrassed to say that I came from a refugee camp, so I thought about telling them I'd come from Per Hee Lu village only. But I had to say where I'd done my year eight, which meant that I had to talk about the camp. I felt like a second-class citizen admitting that I had been a refugee. No one seemed to mind, though, and I quickly made friends.

One of the most beautiful girls in the whole school was named Eh Phyo Paw, "Collective Love Flower." Eh Phyo Paw is considered a very lovely name in Karen, for it means you are loved by everyone and as beautiful as a flower. Collective Love Flower was in my class, and we quickly became very close. We both loved sports and played volleyball together; we loved pop music and Bollywood movies. Another thing we had in common was that both our parents were in the resistance, and we both knew what it was like to have parents who were taken away from us a lot.

It was a big school compared to the one I had attended in the refugee camp, with some thirty teachers. There was an unbelievably tall teacher from England, called Thera Tom, "Teacher Tom." We nicknamed him Grandfather Long Legs, after Major Seagrim, but not to his face of course. There was also James, another tall teacher from England, and an Australian named Jacob who turned out to be my English teacher. Fairly quickly Jacob proved himself to be a disciplinarian and introduced a new way of marking us, called "continuous assessment." Under this system exams were replaced by the marks we got in our course work. It seemed like a good idea to me, and I redoubled my efforts in English. Our first continuous assessment task involved filling in the blanks in English sentences and marking certain phrases as "true" or "false." I handed in my homework certain that I had done well.

I couldn't believe it when our marks were handed out, and I had been given zero out of one hundred. I sat at my desk, stunned. Zero? How could I possibly have got zero? Something had to be wrong. Other students had got over ninety, and they were beaming happily. As I sat there staring at that zero, I felt tears trickling down my face.

My tutor was a kind and gentle Karen woman named Theramu Paw Lah Soe.

"Zoya, what's wrong?" she asked me.

"Well, I did my homework very well and I expected to get a high mark," I blurted out. "But instead Thera Jacob gave me a zero."

My emotions were all mixed up. Half of me was upset, the other half angry. I couldn't have gotten zero. There had to be a mistake. She said she would go and check and was back a few minutes later. Teacher Jacob had told her that he hadn't seen any homework from me. That wasn't possible, I objected. I had put my name on my work, and he had given it a zero. How could he have given it a zero if I hadn't done any?

My tutor didn't know what to say. "Well, I'm going to see Thera Jacob myself," I announced.

It was unheard of for a pupil to challenge a teacher, especially a foreigner. But I was so annoyed that I marched over to his office. The door was half open, and I could see him sitting by his desk. He looked up and didn't appear surprised to see me. I was tearful and flushed. He, on the other hand, looked completely unperturbed.

"Thera Jacob, you told my tutor I didn't do my homework," I announced. "But you know I did. You marked it. You gave it a zero."

He shook his head. "I didn't see any homework by you."

"But how could you mark it if I didn't do any?" I persisted.

"All I said was I *didn't see anything done by you*."

"But why not? I submitted it with my name clearly written on it. How could you not see it?"

"I'm just saying I didn't see any work done by *you*."

I couldn't for the life of me grasp what he was driving at. "Look, I'm not happy. You gave me a zero. How can you give someone a zero if you didn't see their homework?"

That night I couldn't sleep properly, I was so angry. The next day Teacher Jacob explained that he had found my homework after all. He handed it to me with a mark of 96 percent. I didn't say anything, but even though I was happy that I had gone from zero to the highest mark in the class, I didn't like Thera Jacob. He had hurt my feelings and undermined my confidence, yet he didn't seem overly bothered. It wasn't a nice way for a teacher to behave.

But I had learned something important from the exchange. In spite of the odds, in spite of tradition and in spite of power, if I believed something was wrong or right and pushed for the truth, I would eventually get it. If someone is trying to put you down, you just have to redouble your efforts to make things right. No matter how hard or embarrassing or even frightening it might be, you will win in the end if you fight for what is true.

Another school friend named Moo Moo, "Life Life," was in the year above and was always first in her class. Her house was on the lakeside, and her brother had a guitar. In the evenings we'd gather at Moo Moo's place and sing along at the tops of our voices as the boys strummed.

Moo Moo's brother's favorite Karen song was "Ta Eh Hsoe," "First Love," often sung by a famous Karen pop star named Naw Ler Htoo, "Miss Golden Stone." It went like this:

> *Oh, my very first love,*
> *Whom I love the most,*
> *I would like to be with you.*
> *You are my only hope,*
> *Higher than the sky,*
> *Deeper than the ocean.*
> *I love you more than anyone.*

> *Oh, my very first love,*
> *Whom I love the most,*
> *Please come and rest in my heart,*
> *You are my only hope,*
> *And you are my strength.*
> *I open my love door for you,*
> *Come, come into my heart,*
> *I'll keep all my love for you.*

I was happy to enjoy the singing and the company of friends, laughing together—that's how we spent our evenings at Moo Moo's house. We sang long into the night, gazing out over the starlit lake. No one told us to shut up. People enjoyed hearing our happy songs. After we'd sung our hearts out, we'd cook some food and eat and then wander home in the velvety darkness.

More often than not Collective Love Flower was with us, for she was going out with Moo Moo's brother. He was named Eh Ker Ter, "Loved the Most." All the boys were after her, but she only had eyes for Loved the Most.

When Loved the Most sang that song, "First Love," Collective Love Flower gazed into his eyes. I had no one's eyes to gaze into, but I didn't feel left out. There was one guy who liked me, who was in the same class as my sister. One day he wrote me a letter asking if I felt the same for him and had one of his friends deliver the letter, as he'd been too shy to bring it himself.

I wrote back saying that I wouldn't mind being his friend, but at the moment I didn't want a boyfriend. In my letter I mentioned the fact that his father had a garden full of durian, a foul-smelling but delicious fruit that I adored. I told him that I would like to visit him to get some of his father's durian, but not to go out with him.

After that love letter I received ones from other boys, but I just wasn't interested in having a boyfriend. Collective Love Flower supported me wholeheartedly in this, agreeing that if I didn't like anyone, I should stay single. It was my choice.

In our age group everyone wanted to marry freely, for love, although in the past parents had chosen who their children should marry. A girl still wasn't supposed to say that she liked a boy, for then she would be looked upon as being "easy." A boy could tell a girl he liked her, via a letter, but if a girl did that it would be seen as forward and wrong. Back in Per Hee Lu village a girl in Bwa Bwa's class had gotten into trouble at around sixteen years of age. After a week of her skipping school, the teacher had decided to investigate. It turned out that the girl was pregnant. She was instantly expelled from school and had to marry the boy who had made her pregnant, but even then the burden of shame fell on her far more than on him. She didn't go out of her house until the baby was born, and it took her years to live down the scandal.

A new subject at my new school was Bible study. Thera Doh Moo, "Teacher Big Life," was our Bible teacher, educated at a Bible school somewhere in Burma. He had a fuzz of dark curly hair, which was unusual for a Karen, who mostly have straight hair like my own. We had to memorize verses from the Bible and the stories of the different characters. I particularly liked the story of Queen Esther, who was married to a king who kept many slaves. Queen Esther's cousin was arrested and accused of being a rebel, and was about to be executed when she learned of his fate and leaped into action. She organized a great feast for the king, during which she asked him to release her cousin. Wise rulers always showed leniency, she counseled. Moved by what Esther said, the king freed her cousin and the slaves.

I saw Esther as another model, a woman relying on the courage of her convictions to help her people. I hoped that, like Queen Esther, I would have the courage to help my people someday when the opportunity arose. I also liked the story of Joseph, who went from being a house slave in Egypt to being the adviser to the king, and who saved the Egyptian nation from famine. The lesson I took from that story was that if you behaved in a good, honest way, your life would be happier and more fulfilled.

Those Bible stories inspired me, giving me ideas that I could use in the struggle for freedom for my people. Thinking this way started to become a habit. When I read a novel, I would try to apply it to the Karen situation: what could I learn? The same with movies or learning the history of other countries. Always I was seeking an answer for solving the problems Karen people faced, even though I didn't know yet how I could use what I learned.

Halfway through that first year at the new school, I became very ill. It might have been due to bad food or water, but my stomach was in agony. I couldn't eat anything. I couldn't go to the toilet properly. I could barely walk. I started to get weaker and weaker. Next to the school was a clinic set up by Dr. Cynthia Maung, a Karen doctor who had fled the August 1988 military crackdown in Rangoon.

Dr. Cynthia had set up a series of clinics in the border region. She also ran mobile "backpack" clinics similar to that which the French couple had brought to our village when I was little. She was a humble, gentle person but projected a real presence. As I grew weaker and weaker, my mother finally decided I had to go to Dr. Cynthia's clinic.

I was immediately put on a drip, which contained a clear liquid. It had some writing on it in English, but I was too ill to pay much attention to it. Day after day I was kept on that drip. After school Collective Love Flower, Moo Moo, and Nightingale would come to visit me, to see if I was okay. And Bwa Bwa and Slone looked after me as best they could. As I couldn't eat solid foods I was given rice and chicken soup, but even that often caused me to vomit.

It was only the drip that was keeping me alive. I had no idea just how sick I was until I was all but recovered. Dr. Cynthia's clinic—one that is funded by charities and foundations from all over the world—saved me from almost certain death.

That would not be the last time Dr. Cynthia's clinic would save me.

CHAPTER NINETEEN

RUNNING FROM BULLETS

O ne evening, when my father had come home for his monthly weekend's leave, he told us that he was holding a big press conference in the village the following day about a new buildup of Burmese Army soldiers and the human rights abuses they were committing.

Early the following morning we set out together for the village green. Every few moments someone would stop to greet our father.

"Padoh, good morning," they'd say. *Padoh* means "respected leader" in Karen.

Mostly, he'd never met those people before. They knew him from hearing him on the BBC World Service or Voice of America or reading his articles. But my father would graciously return the greeting and ask them how they were and how their children and families were. I felt proud to walk beside him and to be his Little Daughter.

When we arrived at the village green, hundreds of people had already gathered. My father joined some speakers on the stage, and we sat on the ground in the audience. There were several video journalists there, mostly from the Thai and Burmese media. General Saw Bo Mya, the leader of the KNU, said a few words, explaining that the Burmese Army was continuing to wage war against the resistance, Karen villages, and civilians. The KNU was trying to solve the problem by political means, while doing its best to defend the people. The KNU had called for genuine talks about a cease-fire, but the dictatorship had ignored it. It had asked the international community for support, for aid to help the Karen people forced to flee their homes, but the United Nations and others refused to work with the KNU to deliver aid in KNU areas, even though they worked with the dictatorship to deliver aid in areas it controlled. The Karen soldiers did their best to protect Karen villages against attacks by the Burmese Army, but they were outnumbered, and unlike the Burmese Army, which thanks to foreign trade and investment had lots of money for new weapons, the KNU got no support internationally.

One of the leaders of the democracy movement, who was also a good friend of my father's, spoke next in Burmese, which I couldn't understand, but people clapped, so I presumed it was good stuff.

My father spoke last. This was the first time that I had ever seen him speaking in public, and I was suddenly seeing what a great orator he was and that he really knew how to engage his audience. He talked about a recent peace delegation that he had led to the capital, Rangoon. Its aim was to speak directly with the SLORC generals and try to negotiate peace with them. Four times they had traveled for talks, and each time the generals had demanded what amounted to an unconditional surrender.

He made two main points, and each really touched my heart. The first was that we had to defend our people by force of arms, for the SLORC was waging a brutal war against us. We didn't want to have to fight. We were a peace-loving people and just wanted to be left alone to bring up our families, to farm in peace. But we had no choice, we had to defend ourselves; the alternative was death or slavery. The second was that we had to work with everyone in the country who believed in democracy, no matter what their ethnic background. We had to be united against a common enemy—the military dictatorship. The regime tried to divide and rule, and we must not let them succeed. He warned against nationalism going too far, saying that just because we love our Karen people, that doesn't mean we have to hate other people. We wanted a peaceful federal Burma, where we would live side by side, with guaranteed rights.

My father had gone to the SLORC with a few requests: that it remove its troops from Karen areas, stop burning our villages, and stop raping our women and killing our children. That was the minimum required from our side to reach a cease-fire. But the generals had demanded that the resistance first give up its arms. This would have amounted to de facto surrender, my father told the crowd, and it would have left us at their mercy. The SLORC had no interest in dialogue. It refused to discuss a political solution, a federal Burma with protection for ethnic cultures, or any form of compromise.

"How can we have genuine dialogue with the generals when they refuse to stop shooting our farmers and raping and killing innocents?" my father said. "How can we lay down our arms, to allow them to continue to burn our villages? How can there be genuine negotiations when they even refuse to stop doing these things?"

People were clapping and cheering at what my father said. After the conference my father was mobbed for interviews.

I turned to my sister. We were both amazed by our father. We had always known that he did important work, but now we knew exactly what that was. He had gone to Rangoon to risk meeting the generals face-to-face, and he had refused to be bullied or back down.

That evening I wanted to tell my father how proud I was of him. I wanted to tell him that he was my hero. But there were too many visitors for me to do so. I never got the chance to sit with him for a few minutes alone and to speak with him, and the next day he was gone. I knew I wanted eventually to do what he was doing.

It had been two years since we had been forced to flee Manerplaw, and now that we had been in the New Village for a few months, I felt like things were getting back to normal. Some things were even better. There was a market, a movie theater (a small room with a normal-sized TV), and a sports playing ground. I was very happy.

A few days after the speeches, Bwa Bwa and I were coming home from school when I spotted a familiar figure coming along the path toward me. My heart missed a beat. I couldn't believe it! It was Say Say!

I rushed up and jumped on him, almost knocking him over. I was so happy. Bwa Bwa was crying with happiness at Say Say's return. My mother was beside herself when we got home. We'd had no idea he would be coming to see us. She declared that she would cook a special feast of welcome. But Say Say said he couldn't wait. There was some cold leftover rice, and he just took it and started to wolf it down.

"How did you find us?" my mother asked him. "How did you know where we were?"

"It was Pah," Say Say answered. "He sent a message to the commander of my unit. It took me a whole month to find my way here."

Poor Say Say was practically starving. He ate every last grain of that leftover rice, and then he licked the bowl clean. He placed it on the bamboo floor and glanced up at us.

"You should never waste any food. *Never*," he said. "I've learned never to throw even a grain of rice away."

Over the years that he'd been away, Say Say had changed enormously. The war had aged him way beyond his years. He was so thin and pale. But his voice was the biggest difference: it was the voice of an older man, not the young soldier who had left. Say Say had been stationed in Papun, an area far to the north of us, where he had seen untold horrors on the front line. At first he had been fighting the enemy, but increasingly he had been tasked with helping the victims escape from the Burmese Army and the Democratic Karen Buddhist Army. Thousands of civilians had fled, and Say Say had guided them through the jungle so that they might reach safety.

So many of those people had been starving, he told us, and he had not been able to save them. Men, women, and children went for days with nothing to eat. In desperation they ate plants and roots from the jungle that were not safe to eat and provided no nutrition but stopped the hunger pangs for a short time anyway. If they were lucky they would find a banana tree, and even though it had no fruit, they would eat the pith of the tree. He'd watched people die even as he tried to save them. Mostly, it was the old and young who perished, for they were always the most vulnerable. My mother told him that she was sorry for what he had been through, but Say Say insisted he was better off knowing the truth of what was happening.

That evening we sat down to a proper meal. Say Say hadn't eaten like that for a very, very long time. In Papun he had been forever on the move. If he and those he was protecting stayed in one place for any time, the SLORC soldiers would find them and attack. He told us about such terrible things: Karen women who had been gang-raped and killed in the most disgusting ways imaginable; farmers shot in the stomach for no reason in their own fields; villagers worked as porter-slaves and left to die a slow, lingering death; whole villages set on fire, and whole families burned alive in their houses. Children died of malaria, cholera, or hunger—if the enemy soldiers didn't kill them first. His was a vision from Hell.

I was so relieved when he told us that Papun was a long way away. We were safe for now, he said. The village wasn't in any immediate danger.

Say Say stayed with us for a week. He spent his time helping my mother in the garden and eating the hearty meals she prepared. He was so thin he was like a skeleton. His stomach had shrunk to nothing after so many months of not having enough food to put in it. In the past he had always been healthy and strong. I couldn't believe what those years on the front line of the war had done to him. He had changed so much, become quiet and subdued, no doubt traumatized by what he had been through. My father came home at the end of that week and told us that Say Say would be returning with him to his place of work. For now, at least, he wouldn't be going back to the front line. They would work together in Htee Ker Plur and return home to us each month.

* * *

By February 1997 we had settled into a new and comfortable rhythm in the New Village. We had arrived there the previous March, so we had been there almost a year. In the New Village all seemed peaceful and well. I hoped it would remain like that, and that I could concentrate on my studies and on having fun with my friends. The visits from my father and Say Say lifted all of our spirits, but Say Say's stories were a horrible reminder of the darkness that was out there.

On February 11 we didn't have school, because it was Karen National Day. There were speeches in the village square, and everyone shouted the popular rallying cries of the Karen resistance. We felt a new spirit of strength and hope.

After the ceremony one of my school friends insisted on coming home with me, as she wanted some help with her math. I was annoyed, because the math exam was the following day and I needed to study myself. We spent an hour or so going over my friend's math problems and I was just about ready to turn my focus to my own work, when suddenly I heard a voice crying out from below.

"Little Daughter! Little Daughter! Come quick! Come quick!"

It was my mother. We rushed down the hill to find her frantically stuffing possessions into bags.

"We're under attack!" she cried. "Quickly! Pack your bag! We have to run!"

Immediately after she said that I heard a horrible screaming whine from the far side of the village, and a mortar shell crashed into the forest. My friend stood staring, frozen in panic.

"Quick! Run! Run!" my mother shouted at her. "Find your family! *Run!*"

Without another word my friend rushed off down the path along the lake. I was shocked and confused. How could the enemy be here? Now? What should I do? What should I pack?

"Don't just stand there!" my mother yelled. "Where's your bag? Get packing! Get packing!"

My mother's harsh words shocked me into action. With the crash of the mortar shells growing louder and louder, I started throwing things frantically into my black backpack. There was the crackle of gunfire now, a noise that I had wished never to hear again. It was coming closer and closer, and I could hear voices from the far side of the lake crying out in terror.

I glanced up to see a crowd of people surging through the village. Men, women, and children were running for their lives toward the Thai border. Children were crying and wailing as some of them stumbled and fell. Parents screamed at them and dragged them to their feet, the little ones sobbing in bewilderment. How could this be happening? I wondered. How could it be happening again?

The noise of the fighting drew closer still. I heaved up my bag and slung it onto my shoulders. Oh, my God, I told myself, if they catch me my life will be over. Say Say had told us what had happened to the women at Papun who were captured. The SLORC soldiers would rape us all. I was rooted to the spot with terror.

"Are you ready?" my mother yelled. *"Are you ready? Let's go!"*

She grabbed a cooking pot and stuffed some cold rice into Bwa Bwa's, Slone's, and my mouths to give us some energy. Then she shoved me out the door.

"Everyone—*go!*" my mum yelled, as if she were commanding a military unit. "*Go!* No stopping until we reach the border!"

Slone, Bwa Bwa, my mother, and I ran from the house and into chaos. There were almost a thousand people in the village, and they were all running to find their families or grab their possessions. People were running in every direction, shouting and screaming. Animals were bellowing or squealing in panic. Children were crying, the crackle of gunfire rose above the uproar, and then there would come the *boom!* of the mortar bombs landing, as if every glass window in the world had shattered at once. Sometimes there was just one explosion, sometimes three—one after another. With everyone running, they turned the dry earth into a suffocating dust that I could barely see through. I was terrified.

Bwa Bwa and Slone were in front of me, Aunty Black (who had recently joined our family) behind me, and my mother last, pushing us ahead. Another mortar bomb landed, so close and loud that I fell to the ground. *"Up! Move!"* ordered my mother, and I climbed to my feet and ran on.

Every now and then I lost sight of Bwa Bwa, and I was scared I would never see her again. The dust got so bad it was almost like night. I couldn't breathe, I couldn't see, my legs ached with running, my lungs burned, my whole body shook with fear. I just knew I had to keep going or I'd be killed. If we slowed down my mother would yell *"Move!"* and we'd run faster again.

Another mortar bomb landed, scaring me so much I fell to the ground again. It was so loud my ears popped and then I could not hear properly. *"Move!"* yelled my mother, and again I was up and running. I wanted to cry but knew I couldn't. I had to keep running.

All around us were people running, but many families had several small children with them. The parents could not carry them all. Tiny children were stumbling through the dust, screaming with fear, pushed on by their parents who had babies or younger children in their arms. I wanted to help but I couldn't. I was too weak to carry them, and my mother wouldn't have let me. She had her own children to protect, and she was determined to save us.

My bag was so heavy I took it off my back and rested it on my head as I ran. My whole body ached. I wanted desperately to rest but knew I couldn't. I knew if the Burmese Army caught me I would be raped. I knew I would be tortured. I could imagine the soldiers beating me. I kept running. Another mortar exploded with a *boom!* and I was on the ground once more. I scrabbled around in the dust trying to find my bag. *"Move!"* yelled my mother again, and I ran on.

We were lucky our family members stayed together. We passed men desperately shouting the names of their wives and children. Old people were separated from their families, crying out for help. And still there was the dust, the explosions, the gunfire, animals and people screaming. I couldn't believe it was happening. Just one hour earlier, everything had been peaceful.

Finally we reached the edge of the jungle and the road that would lead us to safety in Thailand. It could have taken only thirty minutes by car to get there, but it had seemed like forever. We stopped running and stumbled onto the dirt road. Everyone was jammed together into the small space. The air was still full of dust.

There were more explosions and gunfire in the village now. KNLA soldiers had rushed to the village to stop the Burmese Army and give us time to escape. But we knew the KNLA were outnumbered, and we were still scared the Burmese Army would come after us.

It started to get dark as we walked down the road, which was uneven and rutted from cars and carts. I kept stumbling and falling, hurting my knees. One time I tripped and twisted my ankle, making every step painful. But every time my mother was there, urging us on, and on we went.

Hundreds of us walked in the darkness hoping to reach safety. No one spoke. We were too shocked, too exhausted, and too scared to make a sound in case it brought the Burmese Army to us. We could not use flashlights either, for fear they would alert our attackers. The only noise was of people's feet on the road and the crying of children and babies. The crying never stopped.

Keep walking, keep walking, I thought to myself. The world seemed to shrink around me as I focused only on walking. My legs ached so much it was as if they were burning. Keep walking, keep walking.

The night seemed to go on forever. At last the first light appeared in the sky. And in that light we saw a soldier on the road ahead. Bwa Bwa and I froze in fear, but my mother told us to keep going. "It's okay, they are Thai," she said. The soldier waved us forward with a flashlight, and once again I was a refugee in Thailand.

Just over the border there was a small camp where there were Karen refugees. Frightened and exhausted, we entered it.

Bwa Bwa, Slone, Aunty Black, and I collapsed, exhausted, to the ground, but straightaway my mother started cooking rice for us. She had saved our lives, and as tired as she was, her first priority was to take care of us.

As far as the eye could see were the humped, shadowy forms of people slumped among the trees. Old people, children, breast-feeding mothers—all around us were the dirty, frightened inhabitants of the New Village. Some had crudely bandaged injuries. Piles of salvaged possessions lay everywhere. Each and every person had the same vacant stare. Yesterday these had been our neighbors and friends. Today we were the haunted and dispossessed.

On the flight through the forest, huge leeches had sucked our blood and mosquitoes had eaten us alive. Conditions here were little better, for whole families were squatting down on the jungle floor. But at least we had made it to Thailand, which might offer us a little sanctuary and security.

Despite my exhaustion, I tried to ask around and find news of my friends. One of my fellow students, Star in the Sky, had volunteered to stay behind and fight in order to help buy the women and children time to escape. I learned that it had cost him his life. One of the first mortar shells that had crashed into our village had torn Star in the Sky to pieces.

As for my other friends, I could see no sign of Nightingale, Moo Moo, or Collective Love Flower. I searched everywhere among the shifting mass of traumatized humanity, but they were nowhere to be seen. I hoped and prayed that they had escaped. It didn't bear thinking about if any one of them had been captured.

Among the shapes humped beneath the trees I did notice the unmistakable forms of teachers Tom and James. The white foreigners had been forced to flee the enemy, along with the rest of us. The difference was that they had their passports and the ability to travel home to their countries of freedom. Once we had stepped across the border into Thailand, we became nonpersons again.

Once again we were illegal immigrants in a foreign land.

CHAPTER TWENTY

REFUGEES AGAIN

Tens of thousands of refugees were created by this new wave of attacks on the Karen, and we converged on a patch of land near a Thai-Karen village called Noh Poe. In contrast to the first refugee camp that we had lived in, this one was quickly granted official UN recognition.

Once again, my mother set about building us a temporary bamboo shelter. We registered with the United Nations and received our first rations of food and medical supplies. After that, we followed the same regimen as at Mae Ra Moh camp: no lights after dark; no singing or loud noises; and no one allowed to go beyond the camp boundary. And that was it: we were back in refugee hell.

There were no grown men to help us this time—no Ter Pay Pay or the two young Karen soldiers who'd led us to Mae Ra Moh. It was only us now. We had to cut the bamboo and build the hut frame, make the split bamboo walls and floor, and thatch the roof with leaves. I think this was the seventh or eighth house and shelter we had built in two years. But no one was counting anymore.

A couple of weeks after our arrival I woke with a start in the middle of the night to the staccato bark of gunfire. *Oh, my God, not again. Not again.* My mother yelled for us to take cover under the floor of the shelter. We squeezed ourselves in there in a frantic rush, terrorized. For hours we sat cowering in the cramped darkness, until one of the camp organizers came to speak with us. It turned out that it had been just a drunken Thai soldier getting off some gunshots.

We climbed out and found our beds once again. But I was so scared I just couldn't get back to sleep. I lay there thinking about what my life had become. I did not want to be here. I wracked my brain, trying to think about how we could get out. But what could we do? There was nothing. This was our life now. Welcome to Hell.

The terror and trauma of the flight from the New Village had been hardest on my mother. She was depressed and weak and was not rebounding as she had after our first escape. I kept asking her to go to the clinic, and eventually she agreed to. But the medics couldn't work out what was the matter with her. They told her to try to rest and relax, which was impossible in the refugee camp. My mother's condition steadily worsened.

Over the coming weeks, I was reunited with Nightingale and Collective Love Flower. We missed Moo Moo hugely, but no one knew where she, or many others, might be: killed or captured in the attack on the village, hiding deep in the jungle, or picked up by the Thai police and deported to Burma.

I was sixteen years old now, and the harshness of my last three years had made me into an adult. Life in this refugee camp was worse than before because not only were we exhausted and traumatized, we had lost all hope for the future. We went through the rituals of living, but with little thought now about trying to make plans for the future.

In each place where we had tried to build a future, we had ended up fleeing for our lives. The suffering was so widespread. Where in the Karen areas was anyone safe now? Where was anyone free from attack? The killing and burning and raping and horror were on a shockingly massive scale. Why did the United Nations and the international community allow this to happen? And where especially were the British? We had been their allies. We had fought and died beside them in World War II. Why had they abandoned us? I dreamed that they would come and rescue us. But they did not.

I had thought our own escape traumatic enough, but others had worse stories to tell. One evening our neighbor in the camp Nant Than Htay told us what had happened to her. When her village had been attacked, she had fled with her three young children, a five-year-old, a three-year-old, and a little one-year-old baby, and somehow they had all made it into the safety of the deep forest. They had hidden there for days, surviving on what little food they had managed to carry with them.

One day they were resting in an open area, before continuing to try to make their way to Thailand and safety. All of a sudden the grassland all around them burst into a massive wall of flame. Nant Than Htay didn't know what had caused the burning, but they had to run for their lives. She put her smallest child on her back, and, holding the other two tightly by the hand, she started to run, away from the place where the blaze was at its fiercest. But within minutes the fire seemed all around them. Vegetation turned into a roaring mass of flames as thick, acrid smoke filled their nostrils and choked them. Nant Than Htay was totally disoriented and terrified. All around her fallen leaves and grass roared and crackled, her terrified children screaming with fear. She was certain she was going to faint with suffocation and be consumed by the flames.

She didn't know how they had made it out of the inferno alive. Afterward, she forced herself to continue the epic trek to the refugee camp. It had taken several weeks. Hearing her story made me admire her as I admired my own mother and her drive to get us to Thailand.

In Noh Poe camp, my mother was plagued by a fear of losing us. At all times she wanted us within her sight, and after six o'clock we had to stay inside the hut. It was at a high altitude, and it was the coldest it had ever been. During the day we didn't have enough clothes to keep warm. And at night the two blankets the Thailand Burma Border Consortium had issued to us weren't enough to keep out the cold. My mother's health worsened. Her skin dried and cracked. She developed a painful, wracking cough, and her night fevers worsened.

Despite it all, life somehow went on. I enrolled in year ten, my final year before graduating from high school, at Noh Poe camp school, the highest level of schooling available to refugees there. The school was very similar to the one at Mae Ra Moh: it was run by Karen Refugee Committee volunteers, with basic educational supplies provided by NGOs. I was determined to do well in my exams. Studying was the only thing that gave me any kind of hope. I nurtured that spark of hope, telling myself that if I believed in something strongly enough, it had to be possible.

There was a new threat in this camp, one that menaced us everywhere. The Thai soldiers who were supposed to provide camp security were sexually aggressive and harassed Karen girls. We were warned to be always vigilant.

One day I went to get some water from the camp well. There was one water point per camp section and about three hundred people per section. In the rainy season it wasn't so bad; people could store rainwater using a bamboo gutter that ran into a big pot. But in the dry season the line of people for water was interminable, and I often daydreamed as I shuffled forward closer to the single tap.

On this day, though, I became aware of a presence off to one side. A Thai soldier was staring at me. He was just staring and staring, not even trying to hide his interest in me. He was thin and wiry and not the slightest bit handsome. He didn't have his gun with him, which was a small relief, and was dressed in a mixture of uniform and civilian clothes, so I guessed it had to be his day off.

He was muttering to himself in Thai, and I guessed quickly that he was most likely drunk. I was scared.

Eventually I reached the front of the line, filled my plastic bucket as quickly as I could, and turned away from the tap, hoisting the bucket onto my head. Then I hurried up the empty path to our hut, marching ahead as fast as I could and trying to resist the temptation to glance behind me. Doing so would only betray my fear. By the time I'd reached our hut, I was sure I had lost him.

As I climbed the stairs, however, I glanced behind and almost fainted. There he was, right on my heels. I raced inside, spilling some of the water as I did so, but he followed me straight through the doorway. Luckily, my mother was home. She ordered me into the bedroom. I ran inside, closed the door, and crouched down with my back to it, my body shaking.

The soldier argued with my mother in Thai. She just kept telling him that she didn't understand a word and that he should leave the house immediately. He had no right coming in, she told him bravely.

Just as his voice was becoming more and more insistent, I heard footsteps on the stairs and then my mother yelling at Bwa Bwa to get into the bedroom with me. My fifteen-year-old brother, Slone, had returned with Bwa Bwa and must have looked daunting. The soldier must have been hoping to catch me in the hut alone. After a few further menacing-sounding utterances he turned on his heel and left.

My mother was so upset. The Thai soldiers had all the power, of course, and we refugees had none. If we reported him to the camp authorities, it was far more likely that we could be punished, not him. After that my mother became even more protective of us. Now more than ever, I longed for my father's presence.

One day a friend of my father came to visit. He told us that our father was well but busy with his resistance work and not able to join us in the near future. It was then that my resentment really flared up. The visitor would be seeing my father soon, and I asked him to take a letter. I wrote:

> Dear Pah, Well, I think you must have completely forgotten us—especially your Little Daughter. Well, it's okay, I suppose. . . . But I don't want to be a refugee anymore. Life in the refugee camp is so horrible. Do you know what it's like? What it feels like to be a refugee? The Thai soldiers are so horrible to us.

I was angry that the Thai soldiers could treat Karen girls so badly. We were trying our best to avoid them, but harassment was commonplace. I didn't want to blame my father, but I did want to get it out of my system. I wanted to let my father know the reality of our lives, even though he was never with us.

My father wrote back, but he addressed the letter to my mother, who read it out to us. He wrote that he trusted in our mother to look after us and to care for us all. He wrote words of encouragement, about how much he missed us but also how important his work was for all Karen people, so he must continue it. He wrote that there was suffering all around and that it was the same for all the Karen. The only option was to be strong in the face of such adversity.

By now some people had been living in the camps for a decade. Babies had been born and grown up never knowing life outside the camps. Hope had long passed that we would be able to return home to Burma soon. A few families had managed to get permission to settle in a new country, and this increasingly became a hope and dream for people in the camps. A chance to start a new life.

We had been in that refugee camp for ten months when my mother decided that Bwa Bwa and I had to leave. The harassment by the Thai soldiers had worsened. It seemed as if it were only a matter of time before a soldier cornered us somewhere where we had no one to defend us and no room to escape. Bwa Bwa and I were so scared.

Mahn Chit Sein, a longtime friend of the family who had also arrived in the camp, came to talk to us. He was trying to find a way to get his family out of the refugee camps and into Australia. He had relatives in Australia who, through a UN program, might be able to get permission for his family to join them.

Knowing how much we loved education and that there was no opportunity for further education in the camp, Mahn Chit Sein offered to try to take Bwa Bwa and me with him. He wanted us to have a chance to go to university. We were so thrilled and talked excitedly about what it would be like. We knew very little about Australia but had heard that the people there had an advanced way of living, with lots of schools and hospitals, and that they spoke English. We had no chance of returning to Burma as long as the military regime was in power and the international community did nothing to stop the attacks. There was no hope of a proper education or any future in the camps and no other way to escape. Australia sounded like Heaven.

It took some time before it sank in that we would be leaving our mother and Slone behind. Suddenly I was torn. On the one hand, I didn't want to leave them. On the other, I wanted to complete my year ten free of harassment and danger. We discussed it over and over again. It was my mother's concern for us that clinched it: she was convinced that we were in serious danger in the camp and wanted us to have the opportunity of a good education.

But getting to Australia was not going to be easy. Mahn Chit Sein said he would take care of the paperwork as well as the pass out of the camp that would allow us to pursue permission to leave Thailand. We would have to apply for overseas resettlement in person at a UN office in Bangkok, but first we would have to go to Mae Sot to get the official letter that we needed from the Thai authorities to travel to Bangkok. My father was staying for a while at a friend's house in Mae Sot, and we would go to stay with him there while we waited for our papers.

It was an emotional parting. I had just turned seventeen, and I had never lived apart from my mother for more than a few weeks. But now we were leaving her and Slone behind with no certainty of being able to see them again.

As we sat down for a final breakfast together, we were silent, all of us lost in our own thoughts about what would happen. We had to walk from our home to a camp entrance, where a truck would be waiting for us. As we left the house, Bwa Bwa started to cry, and Mother hugged her.

As we reached the car, I saw that lots of my friends were waiting there. We hugged, and some cried. That was it, I couldn't hold back the tears anymore. I had been trying to be brave and strong, but when they cried I couldn't hold back my own tears any longer. Bwa Bwa and I left the camp in the back of the pickup truck. As we drove away, we watched the camp until the last possible moment when the road curved away. Both of our cheeks were wet with tears.

The trip took five hours and we passed beautiful mountains, but I still wasn't used to traveling by car and got very motion sick. Despite what had just happened, all I could think of was trying not to be sick.

Finally we arrived in Mae Sot and met up with our father, who was both pleased to see us and very sad that we would be leaving. As usual, he had lots to tell us about how the struggle was going, stories of the horrors across the border, of civilians being killed, and of the SLORC's military machine continuing to steamroll onward. The Karen resistance had taken a battering, and the enemy had seized the new headquarters. Life in the villages sounded hellish, and we felt lucky to have escaped as we had done. The Karen resistance was being pushed farther east, along the border with Thailand. Those Karen now living under military rule were being used as slave labor, and some were being rounded up into relocation sites that were fenced off, like a giant prison or concentration camp.

Young Karen girls who had fled the horror ended up in Thailand on the streets of Mae Sot, working in the sex industry because they had no other options. Young Karen men were laboring on building sites for long hours with almost no pay. As illegal nonpersons, they were treated almost as slaves. When not "working," they were restricted to their rooms, for on the streets they could be arrested and deported. Father pointed out the truckloads of young men and women being shunted back across the border by the Thai authorities.

One evening after dinner, my father told us that he had received a message that the Burmese Army had launched a new offensive in Kler Lwee Htu district, two weeks' walk away, in the far north of Karen State. This area had seen little fighting until now, but Karen villages had been shelled and burned and survivors were hiding in the jungle, starving. When they became too ill to run anymore, they were caught and used as forced labor until they collapsed. Then they were killed.

My father was outraged and arranged a press conference for a few days later to explain to the media what was going on in Karen lands. It was inspiring to hear him speak passionately about how we needed to unite more than ever, but he looked tired. When he was young my father had had a dream of joining the resistance and winning freedom for all peoples of Burma, but he had now spent most of his life working to make his dream a reality, and its possibility seemed even more remote. He was deeply troubled by what was happening now and sometimes became short-tempered, but he still hadn't give up hope that the resistance would ultimately prevail.

I thought about the letter I had written in the refugee camp, complaining to my father that he had forgotten us. When I saw what he was dealing with on a daily basis—the annihilation of our villages and the despoliation of our homeland—I let go of the resentment I'd had at him for leaving us. Not that there was anything to forgive. He had sacrificed his family life for the bigger cause, even though worrying about us drained him immeasurably. The torment and horror in Kler Lwee Htu district made me understand this. He had made a choice to stand beside those at the sharpest end of the suffering. A deeply humane man, he couldn't turn away from all that.

Not long after his speech, I was sitting outside in the garden and I noticed something odd in the trees. Something with a body of fiery red light and a burning tail was flitting from tree to tree. It was the size of a small kite, but the ghostly light made it seem far bigger. It made me shudder in horror, and a cold chill went up my spine. Many Karen believe demons appear as a sign that something bad is about to happen. I could sense its evil, and I was terrified.

I called out to Bwa Bwa in fear, and she came running. But by the time she reached me it had gone, flying off behind a coconut tree. Bwa Bwa could tell that I was scared. I explained to her what I had seen. Bwa Bwa didn't say whether she believed me or not; she just told me to come inside.

We just didn't need any more misfortune.

CHAPTER TWENTY-ONE

MAE LA CAMP: TWO TESTS

After three months in Mae Sot, we were no closer to leaving Thailand than we had been in Noh Poe camp. We had known it might take some time to get the permissions we needed to travel to Bangkok and then on to Australia, but as the weeks turned into months our dreams began to fade. We discussed over and over again what we should do: keep waiting, or give up and go back to the camp? Eventually, we heard that a new school had been set up in Mae La camp. Classes would begin soon, so we made up our minds to go to Mae La and enroll at the school. The decision turned out to be a wise one, as it would be several years before Mahn Chit Sein and his family got permission to resettle in Australia.

We were anxious on the hourlong journey from Mae Sot to Mae La camp. My sister and I were not supposed to be outside the camps and had no papers. If we were stopped we could be deported back to Burma, but we crouched inside the back of a covered pickup truck and made it there safely.

Just five miles from the border with Burma, Mae La camp had been in existence for more than twenty years, itself testimony to the duration of the Karen struggle. Well established, with bamboo houses, schools, and clinics and a greater level of support from the NGOs and the United Nations, it had a boarding school called the Mae La Further Studies Program, where Bwa Bwa and I lived. The headmaster, Pu Taw—"Grandfather Honest"—told us that the Burmese Army had attacked Mae La camp twice before, so we had to be careful. In the time away from my mother I had become a little more confident, but I still worried what would happen in an emergency without her there to help us. At least in the boarding school we were safe from the Thai soldiers.

Because this was a further studies school and the Thais would allow no formal study in the refugee camps after high school, the only subjects on offer were mushroom cultivation and vegetable farming. With no land to call our own, the subjects were strikingly inappropriate. Where would we establish mushroom or vegetable farms anytime soon? I quickly proved not to have inherited my father's green thumb, as every plant I took care of fared poorly or died. But the further studies school opened up other exciting opportunities for us. One day, an American lady visited to talk about something called the OSI Scholarship Program. The OSI is the Open Society Institute, a charity that gives grants to support human rights and democracy work, set up by the international investor George Soros.

The American lady told us that scholarships were available to refugees like us who wanted to study for a degree. Anyone over a certain age could apply, and if successful we would go to a university in Bangkok. We had to pass an entrance exam to show we could satisfy university-level requirements, and we had to write three essays, one on how we would use our education to help our country. Bwa Bwa and I had to apply!

It was April 1999 when we took the OSI scholarship exam. Dozens of hopeful students did so in our camp alone, and it was anyone's guess how many other eager applicants there were in all the camps. I was desperate to do well. Competition for places was fierce, and only five people from our camp were accepted. Bwa Bwa was one of them, but I was not. I had passed the exam, but there just weren't enough places for everyone. I knew it was right that Bwa Bwa go ahead of me—she had been sitting around for months with little to do—but even so, I was bitterly disappointed. It looked as if I would be stuck in the camp for at least another year.

I had hung all of my hopes on getting a scholarship, so when I heard that I had failed, my spirits plummeted. I was inconsolable. Bwa Bwa tried to comfort me, telling me not to worry, for I was still young. I was sure to get one the following year.

In September Bwa Bwa left to begin her studies at a university in Bangkok. The day she drove out of the camp I was so happy for her, yet desperately sad for myself. I stood at the gates and watched her drive away, waving at my big sister until her hand was lost in the dust and shadows. And then she was gone.

I went back to the school dormitory feeling alone and disappointed. I had always relied on having Bwa Bwa around me. For the first time in my life I had no family with me. I felt as if a great void had opened up in my life. My spirits were at a real low, and all I was living for was next year's OSI exams.

A school motto painted on the wall became an enormous source of strength and comfort for me during this dark time. It read:

1. To learn
2. To live
3. To serve

To me, the motto meant that we could endure in spite of all the odds against us. And if we endured, we could learn. And if we could learn, we could still hope to do good in the world. This became my compass through the unfamiliar territory of life alone.

A few months before Bwa Bwa left, my mother had written us a letter. I was missing her more than ever now and felt that I really needed her, so I would reread that letter to hear her voice. "My lovely daughters," it said, "look after yourself, take care of your health. I am sorry you didn't get the chance to go to Australia and hope your education in Mae La is going well."

Reading the letter always made me feel a bit happier because she had also let me know that she and Slone were well. I wrote her telling her that I was happy, I had made lots of new friends in the camp, and I would apply again for an OSI Scholarship next year. I didn't want to worry her by telling her how I really felt, because when Bwa Bwa and I had left her she had been depressed and ill and I didn't want to make things any worse or make her wonder if she had made the right decision in sending us off.

But I did feel I could be honest with my father. I wrote to him about my failure to get accepted by OSI and that I was disappointed and cast down, as if all my hopes had been dashed. He wrote back telling me not to be so hard on myself and to consider the first OSI exam as a dress rehearsal. A few weeks after she had left, I also received a letter from Bwa Bwa, who wrote me that everything was going well. She was so impressed by the university facilities—the lecturers, the computers, the literature. It was like being in another world, especially with its space-age escalators and elevators with glass doors. As much as I appreciated hearing from my sister, her letter made me feel all the more left behind and abandoned.

In a strange way, however, although I missed Bwa Bwa, I also felt it was good for me to be alone. I had to learn how to become strong and independent. Life was harder, but I liked learning to do everything for myself, not always depending on other people. I wanted to be strong and capable in order to be able to help my people when I got older.

Not long afterward, I became ill. At first I felt as if I had a cold, but it soon became a very high fever. I was shaking so much that by the time I was taken to Dr. Cynthia's clinic I was unable to stand. I had never in my life felt so cold. I lay on the bed covered with blankets and shivering uncontrollably, the headboard knocking against the wall as my whole body shook. It was frightening.

The medics diagnosed me with cerebral malaria—the type that can and does kill. My doctor said that I had reached the clinic only just in time. Any longer, and it would have inflamed my brain to such an extent that I would have died. I lay in bed for two weeks on a quinine drip, and I could keep little solid food down. It took me months to recover my strength. That was the second time that Dr. Cynthia's clinics saved my life.

Outside the camp, things were not getting any better. The Thai government was very unhappy about having hundreds of thousands of Karen refugees in the country. It did allow the refugees in Mae La camp to register formally with the United Nations, but it refused to formally recognize us as refugees. This was a huge blow; only registered refugees were eligible for rations. The Thais did this to discourage more refugees from coming to the camps, but of course people kept coming because the Burmese Army kept attacking them.

By 1999 the Karen Refugee Committee estimated that there were around five thousand "ghost refugees" in Mae La—ones who might be physically present but who officially didn't exist. This meant that the fifteen thousand official refugees were sharing their rations with the five thousand "ghosts," so there was never enough food to go around. Because of all we had been through, we had a strong community spirit in the camp and no one was left out.

One week, we had an influx of students from Huay Kaloke refugee camp. The Burmese Army had attacked their camp and burned it down. Many had been burned to death in their huts, and others had had to flee. As with most of the camps, Thai soldiers had been paid by the United Nations to protect it, but they had run away, again.

I knew the United Nations had money and resources. I knew it represented all nations on earth. I knew it was aware of how bad things were for us. So why didn't it stand up to the Thai government or the military junta in Burma? What excuses were there for the United Nations' failings? My father had often talked about the United Nations as the one organization that could really affect our lives for the better. But it seemed useless to me. If even the United Nations wouldn't stand up for our rights, who would?

A year passed in Mae La camp as I studied agriculture and basic English and kept myself as busy as possible. I played volleyball and had a large group of friends who gathered to sing, talk, and study together. But really I was just waiting for the time when I could apply for a scholarship again. Getting a scholarship was the main focus of my life, my only hope of a future and escape from the camp.

In June 2000 my mother and Slone made it to Mae La camp. I hadn't seen them for almost two years and was beside myself with joy when they arrived. Officially they didn't exist; they joined the ranks of the ghost refugees. Slone was allowed to enroll in school, but neither he nor my mother was entitled to any rations.

It was amazing how much had changed since we'd parted in Noh Poe camp. Slone was now a handsome young man, with thick eyebrows like our father and a strong body. But Mum had aged so much. Her arms and legs had swollen up, and if you pushed her skin it would stay in the shape it had been pushed into. Her ankles and wrists were the worst. Only her hair had retained its rich, lustrous shine. It struck me that she was looking like an old woman long before her time. She was such a wonderful mother, and I longed to be able to provide for her the way she had for us for so many years.

She was ill when she arrived, and the camp clinic could do only so much. They told us she had liver and heart problems and that the swelling was a result of water retention. Within a matter of weeks, she was seriously ill. Her arms and legs were heavy, her joints painful. The pills from the clinic were not doing her any good, so she asked a traditional healer to come see her. He gave my mother a bottle of the medicine that he'd prepared for her using herbs from the forest and other traditional remedies. It looked like homemade lemonade, and she had to drink a capful every day. One night I dipped my finger in and tasted it, and it was so bitter that I was surprised that my mother could even drink it. It was a diuretic, with which at first she did seem to get better. She seemed somewhat recovered for a little while, but she still needed more help than Slone and I could give her while we were also trying to go to school and make sure there was enough food to go around.

Luckily, a little help was at hand. A fourteen-year-old girl, Thu Ray Paw, a relative of Say Say's, and a teenage boy, Saw Nu, whose relatives were friends of my mother's, came to stay with us. Both were alone and in need of parents. and my mother was happy to take them in. She "adopted" two other homeless boys, one of whom was Say Say's ten-year-old nephew, Poe Thay Doh, "Baby Big Tree." He was the youngest, and my mother adored him. He was treated like the new baby of the family. My mother was a matriarch to whom the lost were drawn. They helped her in her day-to-day living, and she in turn gave them much-needed love and security.

A few months earlier, in March 2000, I had sat my second OSI exam. I had studied hard to prepare myself. I had to write essays in English about myself, what I would like to do in the future, and why I wanted to study for a degree. I wrote that I was a refugee from Burma but that I would like to become educated so that I could fulfill my potential and help my people in any way that I could. Some sixty students from our school took the exam. Hundreds more were doing so all along the border. Overall there were nine refugee camps, housing more than a hundred thousand refugees, and the OSI could offer only a handful of scholarships. I didn't want to build my hopes up too much, but I was more desperate than ever before.

The results came two months later in a sealed letter. I ripped mine open, barely daring to hope for a place. But I had passed! I had been accepted for an OSI scholarship. My results meant that I would also qualify for a scholarship from Prospect Burma, a British charity set up by friends and relatives of Aung San Suu Kyi. I was ecstatic; having two scholarships was very important, as the OSI scholarship alone was not enough to cover the costs of going to university.

I finally had a route out of the camp. That afternoon the headmaster, Grandfather Honest, took me to one side to have a private word. He was very proud of me, he said. In all, five from our school had gotten through. The other fifty-five had failed. Of the hundreds of students who had applied for an OSI scholarship, I had scored the highest mark of all.

A few months later, I said good-bye to my mother and Slone with mixed emotions. On the one hand, I was so excited at what lay ahead, but on the other, I felt guilty to be leaving my mother. She looked so ill. She was trying to be happy for me, but she couldn't shake off her depression. Slone was overjoyed that I was getting this opportunity. He planned to follow in the footsteps of his big sisters to escape from the camp.

I had known that leaving my mother would be tough—now, when she needed me most. But she didn't complain. She wanted us all to find a way to escape, for she knew the desperation of being trapped in the camp. On September 27, 2000, as I approached my twentieth birthday, I hugged my mother and my little brother one last time, jumped into the truck, and left Mae La camp. I was heading to Bangkok to join Bwa Bwa at the same university she had been attending for the last year, but I still had to be smuggled out of the camp, because I was still a refugee with no formal ID. I existed only as a name on a UN list in the refugee camp. I had no idea if I might be back again.

CHAPTER TWENTY-TWO

BANGKOK DAZE

After my life in the Karen jungles and the refugee camps, Bangkok was like another planet. It was my first time in a big city. I was in awe of the tall, beautiful buildings, all sheets of concrete and stone. As I was riding through the streets on my way to our apartment I thought to myself, if only my country could find peace, my people might leave the squalor of the refugee camps and live in places like this.

At first I didn't really notice the noise and the smell and the car fumes, and how busy everyone was. I was blind to the Bangkok traffic jams and the dark underbelly of the city. All I saw was the development all around me; the smooth, mirrored glass, the shiny vehicles gliding through the streets on tarmac roads, and everywhere people buzzing about on motorbikes and scooters.

Life in this huge, chaotic city was going to be a challenge for a girl from the jungle. Luckily, Bwa Bwa was there to help me. She had rented an apartment in a complex populated largely by students, situated in an area called Ratchda Piseit, a business and banking district that was about a ten-minute walk from the college. My sister had decorated the apartment by hanging a photo on the wall of my father, herself, and me taken on Karen Resistance Day. There wasn't much room for anything else. The apartment consisted of one small room with a shower and toilet, and one bed to share. We had to cook with an electric coil—a portable ring that we plugged into the wall. Bwa Bwa and I had some friends nearby, though. Nightingale lived in a neighboring apartment block, along with her sister, Paw Wah, "White Flower." They had both won OSI scholarships, although White Flower had done so from a different refugee camp. And Moo Moo, my friend from the New Village, was living in that same building, with her sister, Khu Khu. We had all chosen to live as close as possible to each other, partly out of friendship and partly for security.

The money Bwa Bwa and I got from the OSI scholarship was barely enough to go around. It paid for our university fees, with 5,000 baht—less than $100—left over each month to cover our living expenses. With that we had to buy our food, clothes, and books and pay the rent. We hoped that we would be able to send some money back to my mother and Slone; by sharing an apartment we might just be able to afford to do so. This was the first time in my life that I'd lived in a concrete box as opposed to a house made of bamboo and leaves. Even with the window open it was stale and airless. Our tiny apartment had to be locked every time we went out, in case of burglary, whereas even in the refugee camps we'd not even had doors or windows. I had no idea how to use an escalator or an elevator; there was no electricity in the jungle or the refugee camps. Crossing a busy road was a real trial, and it took me an age to learn to recognize window and door glass. If it was see-through, my brain told me it had to be air. On several occasions I walked right into a glass door. It was very embarrassing.

Though this unfamiliar life had a funny side, it was also worrying. I was living in Bangkok without legal papers, and the more I stood out as a misfit, the greater the chance that I might attract the attention of the Thai authorities. Even with my scholarship, I was an illegal alien.

If I were stopped by the police, I would be in big trouble. The Thai police set up roadblocks and roamed the streets on foot, stopping anyone who looked out of place. Not being able to speak Thai or wearing scruffy, "rural" clothes was a dead giveaway. At first I couldn't speak any Thai, so I couldn't communicate on the streets, but even as I began to learn the language, I felt scared whenever I saw a policeman. I tried to make myself look "Thai." I wore trousers, not the traditional Karen longyi that I was used to. I cut my hair in a short, Thai-style bob. On the streets I spoke the few words of Thai that I had mastered or not at all. I did everything I could to stay under the radar.

Most Burmese in Bangkok had no papers, so I was living a life similar to an awful lot of others. There were millions of illegal immigrants in Thailand, and every day they lived in fear. The Thai police stopped people all the time to demand papers and invariably deported them if they had none, although those with money could bribe the police into letting them stay. Bwa Bwa and I had to hide, even as we went about our daily studies. I tried to spend as much time as I could on the college campus or at home studying, for there I was safe. Bwa Bwa and I had gone from living in a camp with ghost refugees to being ghost citizens ourselves.

Of course, Thai people could be good or bad, just like any other people. A few of them were openly racist, but most were just getting on with their lives. None was ever racist to me, but most thought I was Thai. My friends called me by my nickname, "Poezo," which means "baby Zoya" and could just as well have been Thai, as could my appearance. My fears were fueled by a Thai neighbor of ours named Pi Dao. She and I had become good friends, and it was through her that I learned about the fate of many of the Burmese illegal immigrants in Bangkok. Pi knew of a Burmese refugee who had worked for years for a Thai family as a domestic but who was virtually a slave. She was never allowed out of the house and never paid. Eventually, that girl had killed herself. Pi said it was terrible what was going on. Every Thai person knew of a Burmese who was living in the city as a slave, yet most Thais acted as if they didn't care. In the city, people lived and slaved away and suffered and died, unnoticed. Burmese girls were vulnerable to being abused by the Thai police. Men were savagely beaten, sometimes half to death. That was the normal way to treat "illegals."

An underground support organization called the Overseas Karen Refugee and Social Organization (OKRSO) had been formed to help us illegals. It helped illegals find proper work, tried to get them released from police custody, and even paid the necessary bribes to free them. It had an office in someone's house, but it worked in constant fear of the Thai police because it was illegal under Thai law to run an organization that helped illegal immigrants—or so the Thai police argued. So the relief office also had to carry on in secret.

There were ten OSI scholarship students in my year coming from the main ethnic groups in Burma—Karen, Mon, Karenni, Arakan, and Burman. We were all victims of the Burmese military regime and opponents of the generals who had seized power illegally in our country. We weren't able to choose our degree subjects; if I had been able to choose, I would have opted to do Southeast Asian studies, but the scholarship was available in one subject only: business administration. Business administration was my least favorite subject, for it was so alien to me and I didn't understand many of the most basic concepts. I had no idea about the practices of international business, let alone the relative benefits of Kimberly-Clark's logo versus that of Toyota or Tesco, and at first I was completely lost. What was a logo? What was a superstore? Who were Tesco, Toyota, and the rest?

Our college was called the St. Theresa Institute of Technology (later changed to Bradford Business School Bangkok), an international school affiliated with Bradford University in Great Britain. The majority of the students were either the children of affluent Thai families or foreign students—from China, Taiwan, Cambodia, Sri Lanka, India, the United States, Canada, and the United Kingdom. At the start of term we were all given a schedule of classes, which was confusing—finding where a class was for each subject. In the camp, we had sat in the same class all day, and teachers had come to us. Classes were in English, and they used lots of new words we Karen didn't understand. In addition, our teachers came from all over Asia and so spoke English with many different accents, which made it even harder. In that first term I had little time to make friends, for I had to spend every waking hour studying if I was to have any hope catching up with their level of education.

My biggest challenge was learning how to use a computer. I had to study late into the evening to master those skills. Everything at the college was done with computers, so we were lost if we couldn't use one. The teachers would send their lecture notes by e-mail. Our research was to be done via the Internet. Our essays were supposed to be typed, printed out, and handed to our tutors. I was on a very steep learning curve, with masses of catching up to do. Here we had an hour lecture on a subject and then were supposed to spend time in the library or on the Internet doing our own research. This kind of individual study was a real challenge at first, and although I was frustrated by the huge amount of catching up that I faced, I soon discovered that I liked developing my own thinking in this way. The friends I did make were invariably other OSI scholarship students, and we bonded over frustrating evenings spent in the computer studies hall trying to master the use of a PC.

My favorite subject was ASEAN Studies. ASEAN is the Association of Southeast Asian Nations, an alliance of nations similar to the European Union that consists of Thailand, Laos, Cambodia, Vietnam, Singapore, Malaysia, the Philippines, Indonesia, Brunei, and Burma. We were asked to pick one country for an essay. In theory, we were free to focus on the economy of any ASEAN country. No one chose Burma, for there wasn't a single textbook in the library on the economy of Burma; for decades the dictatorship had run the country for its own benefit under a chaotic and corrupt rule. I chose instead to study Thailand—and that's how I found out that you can run a nation's economy so that anyone can benefit—as opposed to making a handful of military leaders obscenely rich.

Once I had been in Bangkok a few weeks, I began to see its flaws. It was all tall buildings and neon lights. Cars, trucks, and swarms of motorbikes clogged the streets, spewing out a choking cloud of pollution. Dirt, crowds of people, snarling traffic, locked doors—I began to realize that life in the village had its own benefits.

I also realized how different the other OSI students and I were from the rest of our class: We had lived through hell, while the rest of the students had comfortable lives. The students from wealthy backgrounds would turn up at college driving their own cars and often talked about going to expensive restaurants and the movies and playing golf. They wore trendy designer clothes. Their parents were businesspeople, doctors, and diplomats. They had enjoyed freedom and privilege all their lives, while we had been in the jungle running from bullets. I wondered why people were so different in their life experience and how it could be just an accident of their birth.

I had been born a Karen and had faced fear, persecution, and oppression. By accident of their birth, those students at the St. Theresa Institute of Technology had never faced one fraction of the hardship that we Karen had experienced, yet they complained about the fact that they'd ripped their designer jeans or their parents wouldn't buy them the newest cell phone or their car had been bumped on the street.

I had been driven out of my homeland and shunted from refugee camp to refugee camp, places where I had had nothing—not even a future. And here I was among people who seemed to have everything, yet they complained about trivial things. In fact, they seemed unable to appreciate the life of privilege with which they had been blessed. Sometimes they'd skip class or turn up late, or they'd miss study deadlines and not even seem to care. And I would think, This is nothing. What are you complaining about?

I was amazed that people could treat education with such a lack of respect. We OSI scholars had fought so hard to be there. *I* had fought so hard to be there. This education, this degree course—*this was my dream*. But to them it was just another chapter in their lives. So many thousands in the refugee camps would have given anything for their place in the university. These students had access to the Internet and the global media, and there was no excuse for them not to know what was going on just inside and over their borders. My country wasn't far away, and it was in the newspapers and on the TV news. But it was never once a topic of conversation at college among the nonrefugee students.

At times I did feel inferior, and the only way I had to combat such feeling was to try to succeed in the exams. I had to prove that in spite of being a Karen "jungle girl" and refugee, I could be the equal of anyone.

Whenever we felt as if our lives of study, study, study were getting on top of us, Bwa Bwa, Nightingale, Moo Moo, and I would find ways to treat ourselves. If we could afford it, we would go to the movies. The first film I saw in Bangkok was *Black Hawk Down*. I thought to myself, if the United Nations can send peacekeepers to Africa, why can't we have them in Burma? Why won't the United Nations do the same for us?

Aside from that, all we learned from that was that war was hell, and we knew that anyway. The movie was so graphic and so realistic that it brought back dark emotions and memories—from Manerplaw, from Per Hee Lu village, from the refugee camps, and of fleeing from bullets and bombs. At one point I almost walked out, but I told myself that I had paid for it, so I would see it through to the end.

During that first year of college I missed my parents and brothers enormously. My one link to home was my father's phone. He split his time between Burma and Thailand now, and if he was on the Thai side of the border Bwa Bwa and I could often reach him on his cell phone. It was the most contact I'd had with him for years; we were farther away physically than ever but united by this phone link.

The news from "home" was often mixed. Slone was doing well, coming in first in his class in Mae La camp, and Say Say had given up the life of a soldier to help my father with his work. But Mother still wasn't well, and my father wanted to get her into Dr. Cynthia's clinic in Mae Sot. He needed a car to carry her there, as she was too ill to make it any other way, and money to hire a car and buy gas. He also had to pay off the refugee camp guards to let her leave. I told him that Bwa Bwa and I could save some money and help, but he said that he would manage.

I desperately wanted to visit my mother, but I couldn't take the risk of traveling all that way and getting caught.

During that first year I studied as I never had before. I was giving up so much to be studying in Bangkok: my family, my home country, the environment I had grown up in. I knew I had to make this work. In the end of year exams I scored 60 percent, which put me about average in the class. My biggest failing had been Information Technology. But bearing in mind that I'd learned to use a computer only that year, it was a miracle that I hadn't failed.

The girl from the jungle and the refugee camps was holding her own.

CHAPTER TWENTY-THREE

CITY GIRLS

During my second year, Bwa Bwa, Khu Khu, and I decided we had to do more to help our people along the Thailand-Burma border. Together with other Karen students, we set up the Karen University Student Group (KUSG). Our aim was to use the skills that we had learned in school to help those trapped in the limbo of the refugee camps. We knew from personal experience being at the university how empowering it is to have an education and to understand the world better. We wanted other young Karen people to have the same opportunity. At our first KUSG meeting, some twenty Karen students attended. We charged a membership fee of 500 baht; the money would fund a prize for the top student in the refugee camps. Of course, this was all done in secret, because the Thai government would not allow us to organize.

We decided to create a medal that would display the KUSG logo of a book, a candle, and a Karen drum. One of our members, Saw Eh Tha Shee, "Mr. Clear Love Heart," drew up the design in gold, silver, and bronze, and some Thai metalworkers made three of them up for us. Our aim was to give a medal to each of the top three pupils graduating from the refugee camp high schools, plus a Karen-English dictionary. We couldn't give the prizes in person but would send them to the schools for the head teacher to officiate. The first year we ran the KUSG prize-giving program, we had such positive feedback. It had really motivated the students in the camps to know that there were people outside thinking of them and encouraging them to keep up their studies. They wanted to follow in our footsteps, which meant that the OSI scholarships would be in even greater demand. It was good to give something back, even just a little.

That September—of 2002—Bwa Bwa left Bangkok to finish her final year of study in the United Kingdom, at Bradford University. It was hard to see her leave, but I was happy that she could continue to follow her dream and took encouragement from her example that eventually I might leave behind the fear of arrest and my illegal status, too.

With Bwa Bwa gone, a Karen girl named Tha Say, "Miss Silver," moved in to share the apartment with me. Tha Say was another OSI scholar who had won her scholarship from the refugee camp. She was a couple of years older than me, and one evening she told me her tragic story.

Tha Say was born and brought up in a village in Du Pla Ya district, far to the south of Manerplaw. There was no school in the village, and Burmese soldiers were forever coming and demanding money from people. Those who couldn't pay were forced to do hard labor, such as carrying weapons and food for the army. Those who weakened or faltered were beaten and killed.

When Tha Say was thirteen, a Karen lady had adopted her. As with my elder brother, Say Say, her impoverished parents had given her up in an effort to secure her a better future. Tha Say's adopted mother had treated her as a much-loved child and put Tha Say into a school in a village near the border, where she could get educated along with the rest of the village children. But the village had been attacked, and they

191

had had to flee through the jungle to the refugee camps. Like me, Tha Say had been driven out of her homeland.

Shortly after Tha Say moved in with me, I began an internship that was a required part of my course: I would be spending three months working in the consumer department of Telecoms Asia, which was based in a gigantic glass tower block not far from the college. I could hardly believe that I would be working in such a place. Hordes of people passed in and out, each dressed in a smart business suit. Since this was the uniform of those who worked there, I set about making myself resemble them in keeping with my general strategy—*do not stand out*. Tha Say and Nightingale offered to take me shopping. I needed to buy myself a professional-looking jacket, skirt, blouse, and *high heels*.

I tried on several pairs of shoes, but they hurt my feet and I couldn't for the life of me imagine how anyone could walk in them—especially the stilettos! I had broad, flexible feet more used to jumping rivers, sliding down mudslides, or gripping bamboo. After much searching, I found a pair of platform shoes that gave me extra height but didn't threaten to kill me.

Luckily, Tha Say knew how to do makeup and taught me how to apply foundation cream, rouge, lipstick, and eyeliner so that it didn't look overdone. She was also great at helping me choose my outfits and telling me which colors went with which.

The first day of my work placement I checked myself in the mirror before leaving the apartment. I barely recognized the person I had become. I felt a shiver of excitement. I looked so professional, like someone I had never imagined myself becoming. It was a long journey for the girl from the jungle to where I was now. It was as if I had grown a new skin, which was exciting, even though it felt somehow unnatural.

But as soon as I was out the door I realized how difficult it was to walk in those silly shoes. I had to fight my way onto a crowded Bangkok bus, where for the forty-minute journey to Telecoms Asia, I was crammed in like a sardine, breathing in car fumes. Most Thai bus drivers seemed to have a death wish, and this one was no different. I arrived at the office at 8:30 A.M. sharp—the time to start work—but feeling frazzled.

I had a desk on the twenty-second floor, right in the middle of the steel-and-glass building, which was fully air-conditioned. I couldn't see much from my desk, but I could go to the windows whenever I needed a break, where as far as the eye could see, the view was of the city. There wasn't a mountain or a river or a patch of forest in sight. I could hardly believe that so many people could live in such a vast area of concrete and glass and tarmac.

One of my Thai managers, Pi Mao, received me in her office on the twenty-eighth floor of the Telecoms Asia building. Perusing my CV, she seemed pleased by how well I spoke English, for that would help with the company's international clientele. She was friendly and help-ful as she showed me to my desk and explained what was expected of me. Most of the time I would be in the office, where I had to enter in-formation into a database and register returned phones that had faults with them. The rest of the time I worked in one of the shops, selling phone lines to customers.

Pi Mao was patient with me and very supportive as I learned the ropes of the telecom business, how to sell telecommunications services and how to enter customer details onto spreadsheets. Then I was sent out to the shopping malls to sell six-month contracts for landlines. Because cell phones were hugely popular in Thailand, selling landline services was a real challenge.

People at the company were friendly, but the job wasn't exactly fun. Everyone worked too hard to have much fun—that was the corporate work ethic. The highlight of the workweek was when Pi Mao took me out to lunch at a Thai restaurant just around the corner. Usually I would have fried rice with egg and she would eat noodles. She would drink iced coffee, and I would have iced tea. I had never been taken out to eat in a proper restaurant, so this was a real treat.

Over lunch, Pi Mao would outline for me the challenges and opportunities facing Telecoms Asia. At the time, it had a virtual monopoly on landline sales. But in 2006 the telecom market in Thailand was going to open up to global companies. Orange was already investing heavily in Thailand, and there would be more and more competition. Telecoms Asia needed people with language skills, especially English, as the market for supplying foreign customers was very lucrative. After my placement exam, there might well be a job for me.

I learned a lot from working at Telecoms Asia. While the direct sales side was boring, I liked learning about different marketing strategies and enjoyed meeting people who worked in the industry and hearing them discuss their international strategies. At the end of my internship, the head of the department called me into his office. I had done very well, he told me, and everyone at the company was very pleased with my work.

"You should feel very proud of yourself, Zoya," he said. "And if you would like to come back and work for us, we would be happy to have you. Let us know."

I couldn't believe it; he was offering me a job! I thought to myself, wow, what an opportunity! I could work here and learn the ins and outs of the telecom industry, knowledge that I could then take into Burma. There was no better place in which to learn, and I would be ideally placed to start a Burmese telecom company when freedom came to our country. We would need a telecom industry.

I allowed myself to imagine what it would be like to have a normal life with a proper job, security, and a bright future. I would have money, and I would live in peace. I could build my life, support my family, and even look to have my own children in time. I could invest in my own future. And when Burma was free, as surely one day it would be, I would be ideally placed to help build the new country. Every way I looked at it, it really wasn't such a bad idea.

At the end of 2003, my father phoned with some worrying news. My mother's condition had worsened, and she had been admitted to Dr.

Cynthia's clinic, her entire body horribly swollen. The medics had diagnosed her as having liver failure, compounded by a heart condition. My father sounded really worried, which was unusual for him, as he normally took every adversity in stride.

A week later my father phoned again: My mother had been admitted to a Thai hospital, and he was visiting her every day and praying that she might recover. I was devastated. I so wanted to go and see her, but the risks of making that journey back to the border were too great.

Thankfully, two weeks later, I had another call from my father and he sounded relieved. My mother had responded well to treatment and the swelling had gone down so much that the Thai doctors had discharged her. She would stay for a short while with my father, in Mae Sot, to recuperate, and then go back to the camp to be with the others, who could look after her daily needs. Over the coming months this would become the pattern of my mother's health: Once she was out of the hospital, the swelling would slowly build up again, and eventually she would go back in again. It was so hard to be cut off from the rest of my family when I knew how much easier things would be for my mother if I could be there to help her.

Now that I was in my final year at university, my biggest challenge was studying for my final exams while coping with the worry over my mother. My biggest fear was that she would die before I could get back to the border to see her. When I wasn't occupied by study, that fear played on my mind. I saw two options ahead of me once I had finished my degree.

The first option was to take the job with Telecoms Asia. That would mean a life of luxury and freedom, of good food, money, and fine clothes. I would have status, and no Thai policeman would ever think of arresting a smart "Thai" Telecoms employee. I could turn my back on poverty, death, suffering, and the indignity of life as a refugee. I could turn away from the struggle, the never-ending path of resistance, and I could enjoy life. I could earn good money and send it to my parents, and get them out of the camps. The second option was to go back to the border, to work with the Karen community in and around the refugee camps, to become a stateless person based in the camps again, but at least it would mean that I would be near my ailing mother. It was a difficult decision.

In March 2003, almost three years after I had first arrived in Bangkok, I took my final exams. I had worked and studied very hard and desperately hoped I had done well. The day the results were issued, I rushed over to check on the college notice board, excited and worried. When I found my mark on the list, I practically jumped up and hugged the board: I had scored high enough to continue my education and do a master's degree! Tha Say and Nightingale had also scored well. I phoned my father with the news, and he told me that he was proud of his Little Daughter.

There was no formal degree ceremony. Instead, the dean of the college handed us each our degree certificate, which displayed the name and logo of Bradford University, plus the words "Bachelor of Arts in Business Administration."

And now I had to choose. My OSI grant was finished, and living in Bangkok was expensive; I would have to take the job with Telecoms Asia if I were to keep my little apartment. But first I had to get to the border to see my mother. I couldn't wait any longer.

I traveled back to the border region by bus, dressed in my best clothes and having donned my armor of makeup and platform shoes in order to look like a Thai city girl. When the bus was stopped at the first checkpoint, a Thai policeman came on.

"Get out! Get out! Karen and Burmese—out!" he ordered, fiercely.

I stayed where I was, but I was practically shaking with fear, knowing what awaited those people forced off the bus. Many were probably making their first journey "home" in many years, with whatever money they had saved from the pittance they earned in Bangkok, and now the Thai police were about to fleece them. Most would pay the bribe and be allowed back on the bus. An unlucky few wouldn't have enough money, and they would be sent back to Burma. I waited breathlessly while the people outside negotiated and breathed a sigh of relief when many reboarded and the bus started moving again.

We finally reached Mae Sot after running the gauntlet of several further checkpoints, at each of which I had bluffed my way through in the same manner as before.

My father had rented a house in Mae Sot for himself and my ailing mother. Whenever her health deteriorated, she had to go on oxygen in order to keep breathing, and she needed to be somewhere outside the refugee camp where she could have access to such treatment. The house doubled as his office, and there he briefed the media on what was happening across the border and met politicians and others of influence.

In spite of my father's warnings, I was shocked at my mother's appearance. She was so very, very thin. The swelling had gone away except for her stomach, which was distended like a hard drum. Her face was wrinkled, and for the first time in her life, her hair was cut short. When I realized that she didn't even have the energy to care for her beautiful hair, I knew she had become gravely sick.

Mother could still walk in the garden, but only slowly and with help. Because she couldn't cook anymore, her food was prepared by Say Say and Poe Hser Gay, a Karen woman who combined working in my father's office with looking after my mother. She could still read, so she was able to lose herself in books, about the only joy left her now. She had no vegetable patch, no chickens, pigs, or ducks. She was so unhappy.

After a few weeks of my being home and caring for her, her spirits seemed to improve a little. She told me how proud she was of my degree and high marks, and now and then I even managed to make her laugh. I would tell her stories about my life in Bangkok: how I used to walk into glass doors; how I got stuck on the escalators; and how I got crammed into those buses with the mad Thai drivers. My mother smiled. She said Bangkok sounded like a madhouse. After talking for a while I'd get up and make some lemonade, my mother's favorite treat. I'd squeeze fresh lemons into a jug, add a little sugar and a pinch of salt, and top it up with water. I'd take the jug out to her in the garden and maybe a glass to my father in his office. Before bed I'd massage my mother's shoulders and stroke her back, but I had to be gentle with her, for she was as thin and delicate as a little bird. I'd light a candle in her room, tuck in the mosquito net, and leave her to sleep.

In the morning I'd prepare a pot of water over the fire. I'd take her to the bathroom and bathe her with warm water and a sponge. After that my mother would insist on my plucking out the gray hairs from her thick black mane. We'd do it in the privacy of her room, and it would take an hour, during which she would drop off to sleep. As I plucked out the gray hairs, I thought about when I had done so as a child. Back then, she'd had very few gray hairs and they were hard to find. When I did pull out a gray one I'd show it to her, and then I'd pluck out a black one a few minutes later, and show her the same gray one again. Eventually, I'd tell her that all the gray ones were gone to cut down on the time it took.

I'd been home about a month when it came time for the Karen University Student Group prize-giving in the refugee camps, which we had not been able to do in person in the previous years. This time, however, we wanted to do more than just give the prizes. A number of us wanted to go across the border to lead a fact-finding mission into the areas where the refugees were coming from.

Over the past few weeks I had been shocked to hear from my father just how bad things were across the border in Burma. I had first fled my country when I was fourteen years old and then again when I was sixteen. I was twenty-two years old now. Yet nothing seemed to have changed. Those three years in Bangkok had put a distance between me and the reality of what was happening across the border.

Some of my fellow students' parents banned them from going.

They said it was too dangerous. My father dug out his mosquito net and his hammock, which he used on his regular journeys inside, to lend me. The hammock was particularly precious, he explained, as he had carried it with him for decades on his travels. He advised me on what to wear and which medicines to take. And then he gave me his blessing for the journey ahead. In a way I was surprised that my father supported me. We were going to Papun district, far inside, and would be dodging enemy soldiers the whole time and passing through great swaths of their territory. But he backed me in my desire to go, and in spite of the risks, we went.

CHAPTER TWENTY-FOUR

BACK INTO THE LAND OF EVIL

I n the jargon of the aid industry, the people we were going to visit were called internally displaced persons (IDPs)—people who had been driven from their homes without a permanent place to resettle. If they had crossed an international border, they would have been called refugees, but as long as they were trapped inside Burma they were IDPs. Mostly, they were ignored by the world. At our KUSG meetings in Bangkok we discussed what we could do to change this. Our aim was to learn the current situation they faced, to see what they most needed, and how we might be able to help them.

Eventually, thirteen students in the group signed up for the mission going over the border, including my friends Khu Khu and Nightingale. Another KUSG member, Hsa Pwe Moo, "Full Star Life," was originally from Papun district—the area we were going into—so he would know the lay of the land. He had also come from an OSI scholarship but at a different university, where he had been able to study ecology. He became our informal leader, for he knew the area well.

It wasn't easy to get back into Burma. We had to travel several hours by foot, car, and boat, with the risk of being stopped by Thai soldiers or police at any time. Eventually we made it to the Salween River, which marks the border of Thailand and Burma. For the first time in years I could see my homeland. But we couldn't just cross the river to get there. This part of Karen State was under the control of the Burmese Army. We had to take a long-tail boat and travel for sixty miles and four hours, until we reached an area under KNU control, through several Burmese Army checkpoints. Full Star Life told the Karen boat driver not to stop for anything—and especially not those checkpoints. If they tried to flag us down, he was to outrun them. The boatman agreed to run the checkpoints, in spite of the risk of being chased or shot at or worse, because he believed in the mission and because we paid him well to do so. On the advice of Full Star Life we had all dressed like local villagers to blend in with the rest of the traffic on this busy river. Our cameras and recording equipment were hidden out of sight in the bottom of the boat.

After the boat journey, we would have to walk for two days in the jungle, during which we could be in danger from the enemy. We could have chosen to head for an area where the Karen resistance fighters were still firmly in control, but our aim was to get into the areas that the media and human rights workers could seldom visit; we wanted to go to the places most in need.

We had been on the river for half an hour or so when we were waved into a Thai checkpoint. The boatman went to sign his name in the register. Other boats had pulled in to do the same. One was a huge craft that was transporting a herd of water buffalo, with a hut built on it for the boatman to shelter in. A few of us wanted to take a closer look and had only a few moments, so we jumped from boat to boat to inspect the water buffalo and then hurried back before our expedition left without us. I jumped from the last boat into our own, and Khu Khu went to follow me, but my leap was already forcing the two boats apart. Khu Khu landed with a splash behind me. Only her arms had made contact with our boat, and she was hanging on for dear life.

The sight of her head peering above the side of the boat and her thrashing legs was just too funny. Everyone cracked up laughing, but an instant later we heard Khu Khu's terrified cries: she couldn't swim! The boys raced to her rescue and hauled her out of the water. She lay in the bottom of the boat gasping for breath and dripping water.

"I'm soaked and terrified!" she shouted. "I was that close to getting swept away or forced beneath the boat, and all you could do was laugh!"

Khu Khu declared that I was the worst of all, for I had forced the boats apart. She was most annoyed at me. I didn't know what to say; it's a fact of life that Karen people look for humor in uncomfortable situations. If I had fallen in, everyone would have laughed at me. The moment we realize that a situation is serious, however, everyone turns to helping. We wrapped Khu Khu in the towels that we had with us and tried to convince her that we really did care.

We set off again and a half hour later approached our first Burmese Army checkpoint. We lowered our heads and stared at the bottom of the boat, no one saying a word, as our driver stuck to the far bank on dead slow. He hoped that the soldiers wouldn't even hear us. The tension was unbearable, but little by little we inched along and finally made it past the checkpoint.

The driver gunned the engine, and as we picked up speed the tension and fear evaporated. If we could make it through one checkpoint, we should be able to do the same at those that lay ahead. Approaching the second one, we found the enemy soldiers stripped to their shorts and taking a bath in the river. It was such a stroke of luck. Preoccupied with their washing, none of them thought to stop us. I began to really believe that we could make it without any problems.

By the time we reached the third checkpoint, the river had widened to some five hundred yards across. We sneaked past on the far side, where it was all but impossible for the enemy to intercept us. The soldiers stared, but even if they were to open fire, it was an awfully long way to try to hit a long-tail boat bobbing on the water. They had no vessel that we could see to chase us.

A half hour later we reached a fourth checkpoint, which was flying the Karen flag. We all breathed huge sighs of relief. Full Star Life announced that this marked our entry into safe Karen territory, so we pulled in, but we were told worrying news. The Karen soldiers had just received a warning by radio that the enemy was launching an attack on a nearby village. We were free to continue our journey, but we might run into fighting ahead.

There was no question in any of our minds of not continuing. This is why we had come: to witness for ourselves the plight of the villagers deep inside our land. A few minutes later a hilltop village came into view, where Karen soldiers were leading women and children down to the river. A long-tail boat was pulled up at the riverbank, ready to ferry them to safety on the far side of the Salween. We altered course and came to a halt at the riverside, a scene of panic and chaos. Women clutched babies in their arms and balanced bundles of possessions on their heads. Little children wept and stumbled as they tried to reach the river. Karen soldiers frantically passed children into the waiting boat, helping the mothers aboard with their heavy loads.

It broke my heart to see this. It was exactly the same thing that had happened to me eight years before. Part of me wanted to do as my mother had done, and pick up a gun and fight. The desire to fight and to kill those who were doing this to my people was powerful, but at the same time I knew the power of bearing witness and communicating that to the outside world. I knew I could achieve more that way than by becoming a resistance fighter. Surely if the world knew what was going on it would step in and help us, if they saw how innocent people were being killed and driven from their homes. I wanted to stay and help them, but we were told we had to leave now.

I recognized one of the Karen soldiers, Saw Lah Doh, "Mr. Big Moon." I grabbed him by the arm, and he knew me right away. As hurriedly as I could, I explained why we had come.

"Great!" he enthused. "It's great what you're doing. Thank you for coming to witness this. You must go and tell the world what is happening to our people, right here and right now."

Saw Lah Doh put his radio to his ear to listen to an incoming message. He looked stressed and exhausted beyond words. The three years since I had last seen him seemed to have aged him a dozen or more. He issued various instructions, ordering his men to round up the villagers and bring them to the riverside while other units protected the beachhead from the advancing enemy. The soldiers would buy the villagers time to escape, which had been the main task of the KNLA for many years now.

He turned away from his radio, and his eyes met mine. "You must go. There's no time to lose. The enemy are very close. It's time to leave."

We said our farewells. "You're doing great things," I called to him. "You are my hero, Saw Lah Doh. I'll keep you in my thoughts."

And then we were hurrying down to the riverside and our boat. The boatman gunned the engine, set the prow upstream, and we thundered onward into Burma, pressing on through the gathering darkness. Eventually, we arrived at another Karen village, where people made us welcome as best they could. Exhausted by the day's events, I quickly fell asleep.

Awake at five o'clock the following morning, we cooked food and prepared for the long day's journey ahead, up a high mountain to reach the next village. It was too early for me to eat, so I decided to carry my rice breakfast with me. Within minutes I realized that I'd forgotten how to walk in the jungle. After three years of life as a city girl, I was unfit and unsteady on my legs. I had to wrap a towel around my neck to soak up the sweat, which was pouring off me. Others were slower and tripped even more than I. My pack, which contained some rice, water, and extra clothes, felt like a dead weight on my back. Luckily, one of the male students offered to carry it for me, and I accepted.

Two Karen resistance fighters acted as our guides, but we all knew that they would not be able to defend us. All they could do was try to show us where to run if we came under attack. At first we chatted and admired the beautiful forest, and Full Star Life consulted a nature guide to plants and birds. Our route took us within a mile of a Burmese Army post, but we had no choice as it was the only passable way. As we drew closer the resistance fighters told us to keep quiet, and we had to walk in single file with at least fifteen feet between us, so that we did not present an easy target to the enemy. We did not stray from the path, in case there were land mines.

As we crept past that army post soundlessly, every now and then the resistance fighters signaled for us to stop and crouch in the undergrowth. We would remain like that for a minute or more as they listened for danger, then signaled us to move quietly forward. We pressed ahead fearfully, casting furtive glances into the shadows beside the path with every step.

Once we were over the mountain summit, we entered an incredibly beautiful land that had nonetheless seen some of the worst fighting as the Burmese Army attacked the Karen, a lost world of tall forests and plunging mountain valleys. Few people lived here now, for most had been hounded out by the enemy. We were going to visit some of the stubborn few who remained.

At the foot of the mountain we stopped to refill our water bottles from a sparkling stream. One of the male students climbed a tree and threw down the fruit, which had a sour-sweet flavor and was hugely refreshing.

That night we stayed in a tiny village deep in the jungle. Again we were warmly welcomed by the villagers, who wanted to make us comfortable and tell us their stories. They had so little, but they shared everything with us. We had brought a little food with us, but they insisted on feeding us themselves. It would be the same everywhere we went.

They told us how they wanted to educate their children but couldn't because they had no teachers. They were in constant danger but determined to try to stay. They didn't want to go to a refugee camp in Thailand and were afraid that the Burmese Army would attack just after harvest, stealing all their food as it had before. Occasionally local backpack teams with food or medicine would bring them help, carrying the aid across the border from Thailand, but it wasn't enough. They got no help from the United Nations or aid agencies but lived day to day, hoping for a miracle that would bring them peace.

On the evening of the third day we reached our destination, Village Three. The villagers hadn't known we were coming but were delighted to see us and, the following morning, invited us to a celebratory feast. They told us that some months back, their village had been attacked for the fourth time. The Burmese Army had rampaged through it, burning down many of the huts. The villagers had fled into the jungle, where they had remained until the danger was past, returning to rebuild their homes. No one knew how long it would be before the enemy returned and attacked again.

It was the same story for most of the area's villages. Recently, a neighboring settlement had also been burned down, and the villagers there had had to rebuild. Village Three was special, however, because it had a school. Each time it was attacked they rebuilt the school anew, and it drew students from all the local villages from miles around because it was the only one available. I marveled that they had found the strength to rebuild their village *four times,* never knowing when it was next going to be burned to the ground.

A ten-room building made of a bamboo frame and a leaf roof, the school had an old, battered blackboard and a couple of dog-eared textbooks. Even though they were in a difficult situation, everyone was passionate about the cause; the teachers had little more than a stubborn determination to teach and the students an insatiable hunger to learn. We gave a workshop at the school in which we sang and playacted and did our best to lift the children's spirits. They seemed to enjoy it, and my heart warmed at the thought that we were able to brighten their days just a little.

Then we asked them to share some of their stories with us, and the happy atmosphere that had resulted from our "show" evaporated. Just about every child had survived an attack on his or her village, some several times over. There were dozens of orphans and even more who had lost one or more family members. It was impossible for them to hide their trauma. Listening to their tiny, faint voices telling their stories of horror, one after another after another, broke my heart.

The headmaster said that he expected that they would never complete a whole school year, for the enemy always found the school and destroyed it. Often, the soldiers planted land mines before leaving an area, which made it incredibly hazardous to ever return. If anyone ventured back into the village—to try to retrieve a blackboard, maybe, or some textbooks that had survived the burning—he risked having his legs blown off by a mine.

He chose a handful of students to talk to us privately. One was a ten-year-old boy who came from a poor farming family. His family's supply of rice was exhausted, and they had been reduced to eating the green shoots of the rice plants growing in the fields. Sometimes he went without food altogether, and the pain of the hunger gnawing at his stomach was unbearable. His family was charged a nominal school fee of 5 Thai baht, or less than 15 cents a year. But this coming year his parents would struggle to pay even that.

As I listened to his story, I felt myself close to tears. He spoke in a soft, quiet voice, without a hint of self-pity or a trace of hatred or anger—matter-of-factly, as if there were nothing exceptional about his story. Life had always been thus for him and his family; wasn't this what happened to every child? The tragedy was that, here in Papun district, his was every child's life. His story was normal. *Normal.*

Here, normal life for every child was like his, poor, starving, fearful—or worse.

CHAPTER TWENTY-FIVE

THE REAWAKENING

A few days after our sojourn at Village Three, we set off on a triangular walk that would take us back to our starting point on the Salween. We prepared to leave in the early bitter cold of dawn. The villagers had few clothes or blankets and only the heat of the fire to keep them warm. They couldn't afford candles or oil lamps and so lived in darkness until the sun lit their world.

On our march through the forested mountains, we came across a family hiding in the middle of nowhere. Having fled from a village farther inside Burma, which had been attacked and burned down, they had been on the move for weeks now, spending each night in a different makeshift shelter, terrified of being caught by the enemy. The poor, frightened mother gestured to her two little girls—indistinct bundles wrapped in rags. One was on her lap, the other lying on a bed of leaves. One had the high fever typical of malaria, and the other had chronic diarrhea, which was most likely cholera. They had no medicine and no means of getting any treatment, other than reaching a refugee camp in Thailand. They were so poor that even the clothes on their backs were in shreds. The man of the family tried to maintain his dignity while holding up a pair of threadbare shorts with one hand, as his wife talked to us.

At the pace they were able to move, carrying their meager possessions and dying children, Thailand was still weeks away. It was unspoken, but I read the pleading in the mother's eyes: would they make it before one or both of her little girls died?

I gave them all the medicines I had. My friends and I pooled our money, which came to only 100 baht—two dollars—but for them it was a fortune. We gave them what clothing we could spare and left them building a temporary shelter next to a little stream. I glanced back once and saw the mother squatting by the water. In the shadows under the forest she produced a withered breast and tried to get her youngest to feed—the little girl who was dying of cholera.

I felt something change within me then. Tears poured down my face. This was a turning point; I couldn't go back to the good life and work for Telecoms Asia, not when my people were suffering and dying like this—like animals hunted in the jungle, bereft of all dignity and comfort. This family's bitter tragedy turned my mind away from a soft, moneyed, and easy future—and brought me back to my people, to the struggle, to the resistance.

There was no end to the need. The next village was full of families in similar circumstances to the one we had just left. In one hut, they had nothing. *Nothing.* No pots and pans; no blankets; precious little to eat; no medicines. Their little children were sickly and ill fed. Their eyes had a listless, hollow look. How could they live? I wondered. How could they survive this?

I gave them my father's hammock, one of the last possessions I had. I wanted to give everything away to each family that I met. I wanted to give something to each of them, just to ease their pain a little. There were hundreds of families like this—maybe three hundred in this village alone. Each had the same chilling story of running from the Burmese Army, of hiding in the jungle, of darkness and terror.

It was all so hopeless here in our homeland. In the refugee camps we'd at least had the basic requirements to sustain life: food rations, clean water, shelter, a little medical care. Here there was nothing. They died from hunger; from simple, curable diseases; or from the bullets or the bayonets of the soldiers who hunted them.

Occasionally a team of backpack medics would make its way through this area, but the last had been a year ago and they didn't expect another one anytime soon. This was their only contact with the outside world. The villagers had thought at first that we were a backpack relief team. They were so disappointed when they discovered that we weren't and that we'd come only to *record information*. Of course they didn't tell us as much, but we knew it for sure, for we could read it in the hopelessness in their eyes.

There was one woman whom I shall never forget, a young mother with three small children who was trying to build a life for her family in the midst of such despair. Still beautiful, she was aging fast, her skin cracking in the sun because she had to work so hard. She was just three years older than I, the same age as my sister. I couldn't even begin to imagine her life.

"My husband spends most of his time on the farm," she told me. "In the rainy season we feel a little more secure. But come the dry season, we live in fear every minute of the day."

I took her hand and held it tightly in my own. What could I say?

"We really need your help," she continued. "Please do something about the suffering here. Go and tell the world."

Where was the United Nations? It was operating in Burma. But not here. The regime told the United Nations it could not come here, and it just accepted that. The denial of aid to these people was part of the Burmese dictatorship's ethnic cleansing policy and was as effective at killing them as bullets.

On the final leg of our journey, the return to the Salween, we came across even more families trying to make a break for Thailand. Each was like a blow to my heart. And with each I felt my anger and the spirit of resistance rising within me.

Before reaching the Salween River we had to scale a high mountain. It would be three hours up and two down. By now we had learned that the Burmese Army was after us. We started the climb in the dark. A handful of Karen resistance fighters scouted the way ahead, searching for the enemy. We reached the summit without incident, although I was dripping with sweat, my legs shaking with exhaustion.

We began our descent keen to reach the comparative safety of the Salween, but after just a few minutes the scouts reported that they had spotted Burmese Army troops to the rear and urged us to hurry. Suddenly we blundered into a wall of flame that completely blocked our path. A Karen farmer had set alight a patch of dry, cleared forest to prepare an area to plant rice.

With the enemy at our backs we had no choice but to push on through the burning, smoking heat, dodging the flames. We forged ahead, Full Star Life and some of the others beating a path through the withering heat. Halfway across the flaming hillside we realized we had to make a dash for the far side. If we delayed, we could collapse from the suffocating fumes and it was even more likely that we would get caught by the enemy. I ran ahead with the rest, through the smoke and sparks.

We reached the far side and collapsed on the ground to catch our breath. From there we stumbled and staggered the final few miles to the foot of the mountain. I had never felt so relieved to see the wide expanse of the Salween River stretching before us. Once we had reached its shores, we would be comparatively safe. From here the village at which we had commenced our journey was only a short stroll away. Our whole time in Papun district had lasted less than a fortnight, but to me it had felt like a lifetime. No matter how much preparation we'd thought we had, none of us had been prepared for it.

Horrific memories of that journey will live with me forever, and I vowed that I would return to this place, to this land of suffering, to help. That journey was my awakening.

* * *

The boat ride back to Thailand began as a repeat of the journey in. We sneaked past the first two checkpoints without incident, but as we approached the third we spotted soldiers waving us down. Expecting our boatman to gun his engine and force a way through on the far side as he had before, we were alarmed when instead he slowed and turned the prow of the long-tail toward the shore where the soldiers stood waiting.

Full Star Life let out a strangled hiss of alarm, but by then it was too late—we were too close to the shore and within easy range of their guns. I was terrified. What on earth was going on? Full Star Life issued some hurried instructions. If anything happened, we were to jump into the river and swim for our lives. Whatever else, we mustn't let ourselves be captured.

The boat hit the riverbank with a soft crunch. Not a word was spoken as we waited in trepidation for whatever was coming. The nearest soldier spoke to the boatman. It seemed that they needed a lift downriver. They came on board and sat in the prow of the craft facing backward—*toward us*—with their assault rifles clutched between their knees. The boatman backed the craft out into the river, and we set off downstream.

The two soldiers sat quietly, their eyes expressionless and their bush hats buffeted by the boat's slipstream. Surely it was only a matter of time before they started to question us? Though we outnumbered them, they were armed and we were not. Fear gnawed at me as I tried to avoid looking in their direction or showing any interest.

All of a sudden Full Star Life turned to face me and burst out laughing. Why was he drawing attention to us like this? Laughing in the face of the Burmese soldiers! Surely he of all people should know better?

"Why're you looking so worried?" he asked as he tried to contain his laughter. "Check out their sleeve badges. They're ABSDF. *ABSDF!*"

The ABSDF is the All Burma Students' Democratic Front—a group of students who had taken up arms after the 8/8/88 uprisings. They were Burmese soldiers, all right, but they were *on our side*—they were part of the resistance! In our unreasoning fear we'd missed all of the obvious signs, such as the ABSDF flashes—a yellow fighting peacock and white star over a red background—on their sleeves. They were sharing our same struggle, to liberate our suffering land. The two ABSDF soldiers sat there chatting away in Burmese, completely oblivious to how our fear had transformed itself into relief and joy.

We reached the Thai border without further incident, but bad news was waiting for us on the other side. Burmese soldiers had followed in our wake and were now hunting us; they didn't want anyone to do as we had done—to witness the horrors that they were perpetrating in our homeland. And so I left my country as I had always done, being hunted by the enemy.

My two weeks back in my country had left me angry and determined. I didn't know how, but I was going to make sure the international community knew about what was happening and did something to stop it. I promised myself that I would work harder, that I wouldn't accept being stuck in a refugee camp unable to do anything. I decided that as soon as I got home I would go to my father and tell him I was going to dedicate my life to the struggle for our people. He would advise me what to do.

CHAPTER TWENTY-SIX

CHILDREN OF DARKNESS

When I got home, I told my parents and Say Say about everything that I had seen and experienced across the border. When I told my father about giving away his hammock, he was really annoyed. He'd had that hammock for ten years and had never lost it or given it away. I tried telling him how I had been compelled to give everything away in the face of so much suffering. Then I had to confess that I'd also given away his blanket and all the medicine that he'd loaned me!

I tried to impress upon them the horrors of what I had seen, but they were hardly surprised. That was the daily reality of life beyond the border, as it had been for many years. Why would it have changed? Despite my parents' attitude, I knew that I had been changed forever; my priorities had changed, and I felt the fire of rebellion running through my veins as never before.

My parents were pleased that I had learned the situation of ordinary people and was now determined to try to do something about it, but they were also practical. They told me I must keep studying in order to get the best education possible. At the moment the Karen struggle was waged mainly through military means, defending our people, but things would not always be like that, and the Karen would need an educated leader who understood how the world worked and could fight on the political battlefield as well.

I had been offered a place at Bradford University for the 2003–2004 university year, studying for a Master of Arts in marketing. But my mother was deteriorating fast, and I couldn't leave her. As much as I wanted to pursue my higher education, I moved in with her and my father, in the house in Mae Sot. I would pursue my studies at some future date, if possible.

My parents had two more adopted boys living with them then, in the summer of 2003. They had spent their lives taking in the children of suffering, but these two were very different: they were ex–child soldiers with the Burmese Army. The Burmese Army has the greatest number of child soldiers of any military in the world. Each had been seized when he was just eleven years old; one had been on his way to the movies when he was taken from the streets and bundled into a military vehicle. Some child soldiers in their unit had tried to run away but had blundered into the minefields that surrounded the camp or been shot by the sentries.

The Burmese Army gave child soldiers barely any training before sending them to the front lines. They were made to carry guns that were as tall as they were and, if they refused to fight, were threatened with being shot. When they weren't fighting, they were used as forced labor. They were given amphetamines and other drugs to raise their aggression levels. They were ordered to rape and kill ethnic women— Karen, Shan, and others—wherever they found them. Although the two boys hadn't done this, one of them had seen soldiers doing this and had heard the Karen women crying desperately for help: "Please help me! Please help me!"

One day the two boys had decided to try to escape. They had sneaked out of camp and found their way across the jungle to a Karen military base. Eventually, the Karen soldiers had managed to get them to my father, who had taken them in and given them a home. He treated them like his own grandchildren, and they in turn called him "Grandfather."

There were dangers in taking ex–child soldiers into his home. My father knew the enemy plotted to assassinate him, although he never talked about it to us. Friends had warned him that the Burmese intelligence services might try to use the boys against him, but he also knew what danger the boys would be in if they were forced to return to Burma. They would try to find their families and were sure to be picked up by the police or the intelligence services, tortured into revealing their story—how they had escaped, who had helped them—and likely forced back into the army. His worry for them weighed on him, but he was able to keep it from the boys.

One morning as we prepared for breakfast, however, the two boys had disappeared. My father was worried, and together we set out to search the town but couldn't find them. Convinced that they had left to try to find a way back into Burma and to their families, my father believed that the pull of their real families had been too much to resist. Two weeks later he had a telephone call from one of the two boys.

He said, "Grandfather, I've come back. I'm sorry I ran away. Will you let me come stay with you again?"

"Of course," my father replied without hesitation. "You know you're welcome."

Yet the rest of us were worried. Father suspected that Burmese intelligence had picked the boy up and sent him back into Thailand to cause trouble. Why else would he have returned? Nonetheless I supported his decision to allow the boy back. My father was very smart, and I knew he must have a plan to find out the truth.

Three days later the boy sat down in front of my father and confessed all that had happened. He and the other boy had crossed the border to try to find their families but in no time had been picked up by Burmese intelligence and taken into separate interrogation rooms, where each could hear the other cry out as the beatings began.

The interrogators had pulled out two photo albums. First they had shown the boy lots of pictures of my father: in his car around Mae Sot, speaking at official functions. Then they had shown him the second album, full of photos of . . . *me*. They showed him close-ups of me in my father's car, me on the streets of Mae Sot. The interrogators asked the boy, Did he knew this woman? He told them he did not. So they beat him around the head. Who is this woman? they asked again. He confessed that he had seen me at my father's house. They asked him again, Who is this woman? He refused to answer, and so they pulled out a set of crocodile clips connected to electricity and clipped them onto his bare arm.

They demanded that he answer their question: *Who is she?* If he refused to answer, they would give him electric shocks. He refused to speak, so they turned on the power. The boy confessed to my father that getting shocked was such a horrible, unbearable agony that he couldn't remain silent anymore. Tearfully, he recounted that he had identified me as my father's daughter and told them that I was staying in his house.

The Burmese intelligence said that they wanted both my father and me "dealt with" and gave the boy an ultimatum: he could either return to Thailand to assassinate my father or go to prison for deserting the army. He wasn't just to deal with my father; he was to kill me, too. If he refused, they would not only imprison him, they would ensure that his family was made to suffer.

When faced with the threat to his family, the boy had made his decision: he would return to Thailand to kill us. Burmese intelligence had offered him a bayonet or a pistol, but he had refused to take the pistol because it was too obviously a weapon, and if he were stopped by the Thai police he would be in serious trouble. The knife he might get away with. And so the Burmese intelligence officers drove him back across the border into Mae Sot.

Before dispatching this boy, they instructed him to kill my father over breakfast, when the two of them normally ate together. He was to do so by driving the bayonet up under his rib cage and into his heart. Then he was to kill me. If he couldn't kill me, he was to rape me. And if he couldn't manage to kill my father, he was to rape me and leave me alive. I was my father's "heart," they told him. If I were raped, my father's heart would break, which would be almost as good as killing him.

After showing him where they would be hiding so that they could observe my father picking him up, they dropped the boy in the center of Mae Sot. The boy had made the phone call but had been unable to carry through his terrible mission. He loved my father dearly.

My father could only treat the boy with compassion now that he had failed in his mission, for the Burmese intelligence would want their revenge on either him, his family, or both.

Nothing that this boy had told my father had come as a shock to him, except for the revelations about the plot to kill *me*. By now my father was the secretary-general of the Karen National Union, which meant he was highly placed in the resistance, and, of course, his position made him an obvious target. But it had never crossed my mind that the junta would have his family in their sights. Yet what the boy had told us made perfect sense. If they managed to kill one of us—Bwa Bwa, Slone, Say Say, or me—it would cause my father untold pain.

My father found a way for the boy to be looked after, and he improved security at home.

I was used to living in fear, but this event left me feeling very scared. As an ethnic Karen I had had to flee for my life more than once, but I had never been a specific target before. Now it was personal. They were out to get *me*. I was no longer able to leave the house at night or even sit in the garden during the day. Again I felt imprisoned, but I trusted my father to keep me safe.

Even if I had been free to leave the house, I wouldn't have done so often. My mother's health continued to get worse, and I spent almost all of my time looking after her. In the spring of 2004 she was again admitted to Mae Sot hospital, where the doctors told us again that she had both liver and heart problems. They made it clear that she had to remain in the hospital on oxygen, and she lay there for a month. This time she developed bedsores on her back, and once again her body became horribly swollen. Every waking hour she was in terrible pain.

Each night I slept in her hospital room on a roll-up mattress that I carried with me. I'd spend half the night massaging her back to try to relieve the pain of the bedsores. As I did, she told me stories of her time as a Karen soldier in the jungle. She had felt guilty about not being able to spend time with her parents and look after them in their old age. I told her not to worry; even though she had been unable to do so, she should be proud that she had achieved so much in her life. And I reassured her that my sister and brothers and I would always look after her.

Sometimes Say Say or friends would visit and even stay the night at the hospital. My father came every day but couldn't stay overnight because of the threats to his life. The nurses tried to get my mother to eat and take her medicine, but she could hardly keep anything down. She was putting so much effort into trying to live. Seeing her wracked with pain and suffering tore me up inside.

Eventually a nurse put a pipe into her nose to feed her food and medicine directly. My mother hated it and kept pulling it out. I tried to explain to her how important it was, but sometimes she was unconscious and she pulled it out without realizing. The doctors put drips into her arms and then her legs as well.

Finally, one of them asked to have a private word. "I don't know quite how to tell you this, but your mother is very ill now. There is no more treatment that we can give her. If there are family members who need to see her . . . you should call them home now."

The doctor told me that my mother was alive only because of the drips and the oxygen mask—that her body had already died. I felt as if my heart were breaking. I went outside the hospital and cried. I called Slone, who was studying in Bangkok on an OSI scholarship, and Bwa Bwa in England. They both said they would drop everything and come. I went back inside and told my mother that Bwa Bwa and Slone were coming to see her soon, and to hold on.

I could tell that she was happy at the news, even though she was too weak to speak. I asked the doctor if he could keep her alive long enough for her children to see her. He agreed to give her two more weeks. But after that there was nothing more they could do; the life support machines would have to be switched off. I hoped that would be enough time for Bwa Bwa to get a visa to return to Thailand and for my brother to return from university in Bangkok.

Now my mother—who had fought and survived so many battles—had only days left to live. I told her to be strong and to hold on for my sister and little brother, but I knew that she was leaving us. Her mind was still working, but only just. She was unconscious a lot of the time, but she was holding on so my sister and little brother could get to see her.

About a week after I phoned, both Bwa Bwa and Slone made it back to her. Slone got there first and my mother smiled her love at him, but she was too weak to speak. And two days later, Bwa Bwa made it to my mother's bedside.

She called out to my mother, gently, "Mum, Mum—it's me."

My mother opened her eyes and saw my sister. She knew that she had come.

"I've come back to be with you," Bwa Bwa whispered. "So don't worry. Don't worry."

My mother just smiled and nodded.

The doctor gave me a document to discuss and sign that would give him clearance to turn off the life support machines so my mother could die. I talked to everyone, and we decided it was the right decision to let her go. Even so, my father and Bwa Bwa couldn't bring themselves to sign the consent form. My father was in tears; losing my mother was the greatest blow any of us had suffered. Neither he nor Bwa Bwa had it in them to sign her life away. Say Say and I signed the form to let our mother die.

They turned off the life support machines on July 31, 2004. My brothers held her hands as she faded before our eyes. Just before she breathed her last breath she called out a name: "Say Say!" It was Say Say, her adopted child, who had stayed with her all through the time when she was really ill, when the rest of us had run off to chase our dreams.

Even though she had been suffering, I had never wanted to lose my mother. Now that she was gone, I felt guilty I hadn't spent enough time with her. I hadn't had the chance to return all the love that she had given me. Her last few years had been ones of suffering, poverty, indignity, and illness. Even in her old age her life had remained difficult. I felt as if I had not had the chance to try to make her well and her life easier and happier. We held the funeral in a Buddhist monastery on the Thailand-Burma border. Buddhist monks prayed in the morning and Christian priests in the afternoon. The way animists mark a loved one's passage into the spirit world is by calling out a message: "You do not belong to the human world anymore, so you must now find your own way." And that is what was done for my mother.

A massive crowd of mourners gathered to pay their last respects. Thousands turned up, mostly Karen refugees and orphans, illegal immigrants, and the dispossessed—those whom my mother and father had spent their lives trying to help. They had come to mourn her passing.

Two weeks after my mother's death we commemorated Karen Martyrs' Day. On August 12 each year, it is a day for remembering all those who have died during the decades of resistance. As a family we went to the Moei River, a river my mother loved so much, where we scattered her ashes under a spreading tree and into the river itself.

Animists believe that a person's spirit endures in the world after his or her death. We knew that my mother's spirit would be happy residing in such a beautiful place—by the banks of the Moei.

The same month we scattered my mother's ashes, Slone won a scholarship with the World University Service of Canada. He would leave for

Canada at the same time that Bwa Bwa returned to the United Kingdom. I had also accepted an offer to study for an MA at the University of East Anglia in the United Kingdom.

But with Bwa Bwa and Slone already leaving the country, I faced a quandary. My father needed me to stay longer, to help him cope with his loss, but if I didn't get to the University of East Anglia by September—the start date of my course—I would miss my chance.

As usual, my father put me and my education first. "Go," he said. "Get your education, and when you return you can help me with my work."

So I made up my mind to take up the offer and head for the United Kingdom.

Chapter Twenty-Seven

London, with Bwa Bwa

Two weeks after Mother's funeral, I arrived at Bwa Bwa's tiny London apartment. My journey from Bangkok to London had been difficult. I had traveled to the United Kingdom on false papers, the only way for a stateless "nonperson" like me to do so. But the details of my story have to remain untold for many reasons—not least to protect those who helped me.

Bwa Bwa was working in a pharmacy to help pay her way through college. That first day she went off to work and left me in the house to get settled, which turned out to be harder than I expected. I couldn't get the complicated tap contraption on the shower to turn on or remain at the right temperature, and the electric tea kettle proved beyond me. I didn't understand buttons and lids and what to do with them. Worst of all was trying to work the washing machine. I put in my dirty clothes, twisted some dials, and pushed some buttons. There was a satisfying hum, followed by the hiss of incoming water, and the drum started to turn. It seemed to be working. An hour later the machine stopped making its noises, and I opened the door. But when I reached in, the first item came out baby-sized. I had shrunk and ruined most of my wardrobe. When Bwa Bwa came home from work, she had a good laugh at me. As she inspected each of my tiny items of clothing, you'd have thought she had never seen anything so funny before. I thought that the adjustment from life in a camp to Bangkok had been difficult, but it was nothing compared to the foreignness of Bwa Bwa's apartment that first day. When she recovered from her merriment, she explained that I had pressed the button for the very high temperature setting and gave me some of her own clothes to wear until I was able to replace my wardrobe.

After a week Bwa Bwa put me on a train for Norwich, where I would be studying, and arranged for a Burmese friend to meet me at the other end and see me safely to my university accommodation.

Again, two scholarships were paying for my studies: One was from Prospect Burma, the other from the Burma Educational Scholarship Trust. But they weren't enough to cover all of my fees and living expenses. Bwa Bwa had suggested I try to find work waitressing in a Thai restaurant. So I went around the nearby city of Norwich asking at all the Thai restaurants if they had any work. Several of the restaurant managers took my phone number, and the very next day I had a phone call.

I went for an interview at a restaurant called Sugar Hut. The manager asked if I had worked as a waitress before. I told him I had not but was willing to learn. I told him I would make a good waitress, because I liked talking to people. They said they'd give me a try, but first I had to learn how to open a bottle of wine and pour it properly, so that a diner could taste it and declare it good to drink.

That first evening I tried to open a bottle but managed to knock it over and break a wine glass. I was embarrassed, but the customers were really nice to me and the restaurant owner told me there was no need to apologize so much, for everyone makes mistakes. I had to try to memorize the wine list, but I couldn't even pronounce most of the names. But I liked talking and joking with the customers, and they were forgiving of my mistakes and generous with their tips.

I had chosen to do an MA in Politics and Development, a subject that was truly close to my heart. I wanted to understand what was happening in my country, and to learn skills that could help people like those I had met on my recent journey into Papun district. And I wanted to learn to communicate to the world the horror, as that young mother I had met on that trip had asked me to.

In the university halls of residence, I had a small, clean, neat room that looked out over a beautiful green lawn running down to a lake. It had a little bed, sink, and desk, which I positioned by the window to take advantage of the wonderful view. There were also a shared bathroom and shared kitchen.

Things were completely different in England. I had had to be so careful at college in Bangkok, but here I could talk openly about the story of my life. I shared my stories about fleeing my village, the refugee camps, the ongoing crisis, and the lives of those affected by it. I had brought with me newspaper articles and reports about the situation in Karen State, and I was determined to talk to as many students as I could about it.

From the very start, I loved my courses. In one class, "Government, Democracy and Development," I learned the basic tenets of good governance: transparency; accountability; the rule of law; the will of the people (one person, one vote); provision of the means of survival (clean drinking water, health care, education); respect for human rights and religious freedom; and freedom of expression. I was moved by what I learned in the university, which was exactly what I had hoped for.

I began to make friends who were helpful and supportive. I became close to the people in study group: a Canadian named Hugh, a German named Mike, and a girl from Cyprus, Rana. Before meeting me, they had known next to nothing about Burma; none of them even knew who the Karen were, let alone that we were suffering. I had to explain our history to them from scratch, up through the destruction and enslavement of my country, and it shocked them. For them, it was a unique experience to be studying a country together with a victim of a nation's oppression.

It sounds strange, but not until I escaped from Burma and came to the United Kingdom did I actually have the chance to learn the full truth of what was happening in my own country. In Burma, all news is controlled by the regime. Education is limited, there is no freedom of speech, even poets and comedians are jailed if they say something negative about the government. Ethnic areas are also cut off from news, not just by the government but also by poverty and geography. We were able to get some information from the radios that were smuggled in, but the news was always fairly local. Even the information that came to my father because of his position in the resistance was limited. Learning about the history of my country and the enormous extent of the human rights abuses—of which I had witnessed only a fraction— was a revelation to me.

I learned that they use torture in Burma's jails. In one method, an iron rod is rubbed up and down on a person's shins until the skin and flesh wear off and the rod scrapes directly on bone. I learned that rape is used as a deliberate policy by the regime, even against girls as young as five. I learned more about Aung San Suu Kyi, the leader of the democracy movement, who had spent so many years under house arrest, and her sacrifice and determination never to give up. I was proud that our country had such a leader, and she inspired me. I learned of the cruelty of the regime that had refused to allow her English husband to visit her for one last time before he died of cancer.

All of this also shocked and angered me. British, European, and other companies had been doing business with the generals of the regime for years. Even as the Burmese Army attacked my village, a British trade delegation was dining in Rangoon with the regime that had ordered our slaughter. And although Britain was now a strong critic of the regime, many other countries were turning a blind eye.

Clearly, the increase in trade and investment has enabled the generals to buy more weapons and double the size of the army. I was disgusted with the European Union and United Nations for failing to act. How could there not be an UN arms embargo against my country? Year after year the United Nations seemed to send envoys to Burma that made no difference. Why couldn't they understand that the generals were brutal killers? They would not listen to polite requests from the United Nations. Tough action was needed. At times the United Nations seemed to take sides, making excuses for the generals, always putting the best spin on what the generals were doing. Some humanitarian organizations were just as bad, delivering aid only in cooperation with the generals, meekly accepting restrictions on where aid could be delivered, which was often ethnic areas, and refusing to work with pro-democracy groups, such as the KNU, to deliver aid in areas under their control.

I wished all the people in Burma could have the chance to learn the truth as I had. It was hard to believe that I had had to leave my country and travel thousands of miles to learn the full truth about it.

Ten months into my MA course, Bwa Bwa called to invite me to go to a march in London. On June 19, 2005, people would gather to celebrate the sixtieth birthday of Aung San Suu Kyi, the leader of the National League for Democracy. Dr. Win Naing, one of the pro-democracy leaders in exile in London, had asked Bwa Bwa to attend the demonstration and to bring me along.

I was really excited at the idea of going. I had no idea what a demonstration was exactly, as I'd never been on one. All I could imagine was the 1988 uprising on the streets of Rangoon. I pictured students and monks marching in the streets of London, calling for an end to the dictatorship. I knew we would be gathering outside the Burmese Embassy in London, but what would we do and how would the British police react? In Burma, they would shoot and beat such protestors.

When I reached London, I headed to 10 Downing Street, where the prime minister lived and the march would start. There was a crowd with banners displaying Aung San Suu Kyi's photo. Bwa Bwa had been unable to get away from work, so when I found Dr. Win Naing, he explained to me what was happening.

Wow, I thought to myself, we're making a show of force right outside the British prime minister's house!

It struck me as being a funny little place for Prime Minister Tony Blair to live in. I had seen images of the White House on TV, a suitably grand, impressive residence for the U.S. president. But here the prime minister seemed to live in a house like any other, in a row of similar houses. I took out my cell phone and dialed my father's number, to see if I could reach him in Thailand.

"Pah! Pah!" I cried when he answered. "You're never going to believe this, but I'm at a demo for Aung San Suu Kyi's birthday, and we're trying to tell Tony Blair all about the problems in Burma! We're right outside his house!"

"My Little Daughter!" my father exclaimed, with laughter in his voice. He was so happy. "That's my Little Daughter."

We started the march from there to Green Park, the location of the "Embassy of Myanmar," as the junta calls it. In 1989 the military dictatorship renamed Burma Myanmar. However, the name isn't recognized by most countries of the world, including the United States and the European Union, which continue to use the name "Burma." None of the pro-democracy resistance groups has recognized the name change, either.

As we walked, a couple of policemen placed themselves at the front and rear of the column of marchers. At first I watched what they were doing a little nervously, but their main concern seemed to be stopping the traffic at various points so we could march safely onward. It was amazing. No one was arrested. No one was carted away. This is what a free country ruled by democracy must be like, I told myself.

As we marched through the streets, more and more people joined us: Burmans, Karen, and people from other ethnic groups, but also a lot of white people. I was really touched; I hadn't realized that white Europeans cared so much for our country. It was so gratifying to see them demonstrating alongside us.

I was wearing a traditional Karen dress, hand-woven in a refugee camp, sky blue, with red and white tassels hanging off it. It dropped from my shoulders to my ankles. I'd decided to wear it because that's what I would have worn to an event back home, but now that I was here I realized I was the only Karen person dressed in traditional clothes, and it did rather make me stand out. I was proud to be there representing the Karen people.

As we marched, a young white guy approached me, dressed in smart casual clothes, with cameras slung around his neck.

He smiled at me. "Hi. I'm a freelance photographer. And who might you be?"

"My name is Zoya, and I am a Karen refugee from Burma."

"Great. Mind if I take your picture? And ask you a few questions?"

I told him a little of my story, and as I did so he started snapping some photos. It felt a little odd at first, especially as people in the crowd began staring at me. But I tried to act natural and keep walking straight ahead.

We reached the embassy, which had the Burmese flag flying from the roof—a simple slab of red with a square of blue in one corner, within which are fourteen white stars (representing the seven divisions and seven states of Burma). The last time I had seen that flag, it had been flying from a Burmese Army checkpoint on the Salween River.

I felt a tap on my shoulder. It was Dr. Win Naing. "Zoya, would you like to be the MC?" he asked me.

"The MC?"

"Master of ceremonies," he explained.

I had no idea what an MC did, but I said I'd be honored to. "Can you just explain to me what an MC does?" I asked him.

"Well, it's just introducing the speakers, that sort of thing. Plus saying a few words about Daw Aung San Suu Kyi's birthday. Okay?"

"Fine," I said.

He handed me a heavy, funnel-shaped device.

"It's a megaphone," he explained. "Press that button and speak into this end, and everyone will be able to hear you—even the people inside the embassy!"

I had never done anything like this before, and his request had come completely out of the blue. But instead of feeling nervous, I felt quite excited. He knew my father, of course, so maybe he just assumed that I, too, would be good at public gatherings. I put the megaphone's thin end to my mouth and pulled the trigger.

"Ladies and gentlemen," I began—that was how my father had always begun such things. "Ladies and gentlemen, today is the sixtieth birthday of Daw Aung San Suu Kyi. We are here because we care about her and what she stood for. We are here because she is not free and is under house arrest. We are here because she cannot be here herself. And I know you are all here because you care about Burma, democracy, and human rights. Now, our first speaker is U Uttara, a Buddhist monk and a leader of the monks in the U.K."

U Uttara stepped forward to speak. I handed him the megaphone. He looked superb in his rich saffron robes, with his shaven head bathed in the summer light.

"Today is a very important day," he began, in his soft, gentle voice. "It is important because we are here to remember . . ."

As he spoke, I gazed around. We were surrounded by a crush of photographers, video journalists, and people scribbling into reporters' notebooks. I thought to myself then, Wow! This is great! This is democracy and free speech and a free press in action—all of the things that we do not have in Burma.

As U Uttara finished speaking, I took back the megaphone. "What do we want?" I shouted. "De-mo-cracy! De-mo-cracy!"

"Democracy! Democracy! Democracy!" the crowd thundered back at me.

"When do we want it?" I shouted.

"Now! Now!" the crowd cheered.

I didn't find it at all nerve-wracking to MC the rest of the event. In fact, I found myself enjoying my job as MC. As the chanting thundered around the streets, I saw the curtains on the upper floor of the embassy building twitch. All of a sudden people were in the window with cameras snapping photographs and videoing the crowd. But no one seemed the least bit scared, and the crowd continued chanting. So I thought to myself, Well, let's shout and chant as loud as we can, because we certainly can't do anything like this is Burma—or Thailand, for that matter!

Afterward, I was surrounded by a crowd of journalists, all of them asking the same questions: How long have you been here? What happened to you in Burma? Why did you come to the United Kingdom? What is your birthday message for Aung San Suu Kyi? And what is your message for the Burmese junta?

As I answered their questions, the words and gestures just seemed to come naturally. It struck me that perhaps they were a gift from my father. It reminded me of the first time I had ever heard my father speak, at the rally in the New Village. And now I was here, following after him.

At the end of the interviews, a white man in a business suit approached me. He had chosen a quiet moment in which to speak with me. I instinctively liked him, for he had smiling eyes and a friendly face. He introduced himself as Mark Farmaner, from an organization called the Burma Campaign UK, based in London.

"You did a great job today," he said. "We don't know a lot about the current situation with the Karen. Would you come into the office to brief us?"

"I'm studying for an MA at the University of East Anglia," I replied. "So I'm really busy, and it's hard to get to London. But I'll try."

That evening I settled back into my seat on the train and thought about the day's events. It was one of the most empowering and exciting things that I had ever done. I called my sister and told her every detail I could remember. Then I phoned my father again and told him what I'd been up to.

"Oh, my Little Daughter!" he exclaimed. I could hear the pride in his voice. "Now, that's my Little Daughter—following in the footsteps of your old dad . . ."

I didn't know then how true his words were. This would be a life-changing day for me, setting me on a new path that would fulfill my ambitions to help my people, but also put me in a new kind of danger.

For the first time in my life I had been able to stand up to those who had ravaged my country, murdered my people, and driven me out of my homeland. All my life I had been a victim, but today I had felt what it was like to fight back.

And it was the most amazing feeling in the world.

Chapter Twenty-eight

In the Footsteps of My Father

A week after the rally in London, I was in my little room at college working on an essay when Mark, the man from the Burma Campaign UK, called my cell phone. A British human rights researcher, Guy Horton, had produced a new report, *Dying Alive,* detailing the genocide of the Karen people. BBC *Newsnight* was preparing a story based on that report.

"They'd like someone from the Karen to do an interview," Mark said. "Someone who can speak from personal experience about what is going on. Is that something you'd be willing to do?"

"Yes," I said, without even thinking about it. "Of course. What do I need to do?"

I didn't know who or what *Newsnight* was, but of course I recognized the name of the BBC, an institution from my childhood, and remembered my mother's evenings spent listening to the World Service on her tiny long-wave radio. This was a chance to speak out. Shortly, I received a call from the BBC and gave an outline of my life: my parents, the refugee camps, my experience with the Thai soldiers and in Karen State. At the time I had no idea that this was such an influential program, watched by millions.

"Right, well, if you're happy to do the interview, we need you on tonight, okay?"

"Okay. But how do I get there?"

A few hours later I was in a taxi that took me to the BBC's offices in White City in London, where I met Tim, who took me outside to film the interview on the grounds.

A couple of days later I received another call from Mark. I had missed the program's broadcast as I had no TV in my dorm room, but he had seen it.

"Congratulations, Zoya!" he told me. "Well done. We'd like you to work with the Burma Campaign UK. Would you be interested in meeting to discuss it?"

I had to finish my MA first but agreed to meet Mark for lunch so we could talk about it some more.

It was now July 2005. I had six months left on my visa, and then I was facing another momentous life decision. My scholarship money was all but exhausted. Sometime soon it would be time for me to return home. But the question was—*where exactly was home?* Where did home exist for me? It wasn't Burma. Was it Thailand? The refugee camps? Bangkok?

Toward the end of the month I received some news from Thailand. The Mae La refugee camp was holding a second UN registration program; if I was not there when the UN came around, I would not be registered. Officially, my refugee status relied upon my registration in that camp. If I remained in the United Kingdom, I would be struck off the camp's list of refugees. Yet I couldn't go back if I wanted to complete my MA. Even if I could somehow scrape together the money for the flights, I had only a single-entry visa for the United Kingdom. If I flew to Thailand to register, I wouldn't be allowed back into the United Kingdom. I had no choice but to allow my UN refugee registration to lapse.

All this was on my mind when I met Mark in London. We went to a pub, and he passed me a big menu. I ordered sausage and mashed potatoes. My English friends thought that this was my favorite food, but in reality I always ordered it because it was the only thing I felt comfortable eating. I didn't know what any of the other foods were, and I still hadn't learned how to use a knife and fork properly. Sausages were easy to cut, and mashed potatoes didn't need cutting at all.

I picked at my food as Mark explained the work of the Burma Campaign UK. He was the director but had started as a volunteer many years before. The Burma Campaign UK had been set up to support the democracy movement, promote human rights, and raise awareness about what was going on in the country. It wanted to train and support people from Burma to campaign and raise awareness internationally. He was eager for me to join it, and it seemed like a dream come true. Finally I could tell the world what was happening to my people. Mark said the organization would give me training, but when he talked about the kind of things he wanted me to do—meet MPs, organize campaigns, speak at public meetings, and do media interviews—I couldn't believe I would be able to do those things. How awful it would be if I finally had the chance to tell the world what was going on but turned out not to be good at it and failed?

I had never really thought about doing this kind of thing in a country so far from Burma. I always thought I would be doing it on the Thailand-Burma border, among my people, thinking that, in order to help them, of course I had to be with them and I would have to return. I explained this to Mark, and without hesitation he told me I could do more to help them in London than I ever could on the border.

This white man is crazy, I thought. How can I help them when I'm thousands of miles away? I left the meeting with my mind swirling. I had new options I had never even dreamed of and so much to think about.

Soon after meeting Mark, I received a phone call from my father. The KNU had intercepted a Burmese Army radio message. It was a hit list with my name on it.

I discussed it with Bwa Bwa, and she told me that there was no way I could risk going back to live in Thailand. I should make a claim for refugee status here in the United Kingdom. She had done so, and she had already been issued official papers recognizing her as a genuine refugee in Britain. That meant that she was able to stay in the United Kingdom until it was safe to return to Burma. The United Kingdom is a signatory to the 1951 Convention Relating to the Status of Refugees and so obliged to give sanctuary to those who face persecution in their home countries. Even so, immigration into and asylum in the United Kingdom had become a hot political issue, and the government was making it harder and harder for people to claim asylum. From my sister and others, I knew that the system was underresourced and the process could be difficult.

But with my UN refugee status in Thailand about to expire and the Burmese regime planning to kill me, I felt I had little choice. On July 7 I tried to go to the Refugee Legal Centre to lodge my claim, but the entire city was paralyzed by a terrorist plot to blow up the London Underground. I tried again on July 21, but there was another terrorist scare and the subway was closed. I tried again on August 5 and managed to speak to a Refugee Legal Centre lawyer, but she told me that I needed to speak with someone in the Home Office in Croydon to submit the paperwork for my claim. It was a two-hour journey, and when I got there I was amazed at the length of the line. People of all nationalities and religions were claiming a right to remain in Britain on the ground of fear of persecution. It said a great deal about the tolerance of the British nation and people that they extended their kindness to so many from all corners of the world. It opened my eyes to how much suffering there was in other countries that so many people had been forced to flee.

As I went to lodge my claim, I was a bundle of nerves. I feared the Home Office people might arrest or detain me because of my false papers. If it did so, all it had to do was deport me to Burma, and then I would be finished. I was known to the regime; I had openly criticized it; *I was on its hit list.* I had little doubt that it would show me no mercy.

I took my numbered ticket and waited to be called for more than six hours. Finally, at around 6:30 P.M., an officer summoned me to one of the booths. I was asked a few questions relating to my Refugee Legal Centre forms, and then I was told to come back on Monday; it was Friday evening, and things were closing down for the weekend.

I spent the entire weekend worrying about what would happen when I went back again on Monday. I returned to the Home Office at seven in the morning, was fingerprinted and photographed and given an asylum seeker ID card, but by the end of the day I still hadn't seen anyone and was asked to come back again the following day.

I was staying with Bwa Bwa on the outskirts of London, and the journey to Croydon took hours and the train fare cost a fortune. When I returned for the third day, the line had to have been several hundred strong.

At lunchtime I was called into an interview room. I sat on one side of the table, facing my interviewer. He asked me how I had gotten my passport. I explained it was a false one and pointed out that all of this was detailed on my form, as completed by my lawyer at the Refugee Legal Centre. The man warned me that procuring a false passport was a very serious offense.

"Don't you know what trouble you're in?" he said. "You can be imprisoned for twenty years for doing what you've done. Don't you know that?"

"No, I didn't know that," was all I could think to say.

He scribbled a few notes on the interview form, and then he got up as if to leave. I asked him for a copy of what he had written. It was what my Refugee Legal Centre lawyer had advised me to do.

He shook his head. "You don't need a copy."

He left the room. I had expected sympathy, but he had been so rude. I imagined him returning with two policemen, that I was going to spend twenty years in jail. I tried to hold back the tears. Had everything I had struggled for been for nothing?

All of a sudden the door swung open and a new man walked in, accompanied by a worried-looking lady whom I guessed to be Burmese. Without any introduction he started to fire questions at me. He spoke in English, and before I could answer, the Burmese-looking woman began translating into Burmese. I don't speak Burmese and could follow only half of what she said. I could understand his English but became confused by the two streams of questions.

"Look, I've already said I don't need interpretation," I objected in English. "I don't speak Burmese. I'm *Karen*. We have our own Karen language."

The woman repeated the question in Burmese. "Look," I said to her, "I've already told you, I do not speak Burmese."

I turned back to the guy. "I don't need an interpreter. I don't speak Burmese. She doesn't speak Karen. So let's do this in English."

He snorted derisively. "So you're from Burma but you don't speak Burmese. How d'you explain that one?"

"As I have already explained and written clearly on my form, I am from a separate ethnic group," I said. "I am a Karen. We have our own traditions, culture, and language that is not the same as the Burmese language. That is why we are unable to understand each other. There are several dozen separate ethnic groups in Burma, many of whom also speak . . ."

The questioning continued—in English—for an hour or more.

"Right, that's it," he finally announced. "I think I might have to detain you."

A look of real concern flashed across the interpreter's face. I was terrified. I knew that being "detained" was the first stage on the road to being deported.

"But why?" I blurted out. "Why would you detain me? What have I done wrong?"

"You entered the country illegally," he fired back at me. "You came here on a false passport, didn't you?"

"And that means I have to be detained?" I was terrified now. What had I been thinking of, coming here, if this was how they were going to treat me?

"All right, look, maybe there's another way," he announced. "Perhaps we don't have to detain you, after all. But, if we don't, you'll have to report to your local police station, every week, to sign. And that's the best I can do for you." With that he walked out. The Burmese woman seemed shocked by the behavior of the man and tried to make conversation with me, but I was too upset and left immediately.

At least I hadn't been "detained," I told myself as I headed for the exit. Once I was back at Bwa Bwa's place, I told her all that had happened and how horrible it had been. Bwa Bwa gave me a hug and told me not to worry. She had won her claim for refugee status, and so would I. My case was stronger than hers, she said, for by speaking out I had made myself a public enemy of the Burmese junta.

Now that I had claimed asylum, I was banned from working in the United Kingdom. I had no idea why, as newspapers complained about asylum seekers getting government benefits. I wanted to work and pay my own way. Why wouldn't they let me? I still wanted to work with Burma Campaign UK, though, so in autumn 2005 I joined as a volunteer.

It was an exciting time to join the campaign. The demonstration I had been to at the Burmese embassy had been part of a global effort to raise awareness about Burma. It was so successful that the United States raised Burma at the UN Security Council, which had never discussed Burma before.

Russia and China had blocked the talks, saying Burma was not a threat to international peace and security and so the council could not intervene. This prompted South African Archbishop Desmond Tutu and former Czech president Václav Havel to commission a legal study by a U.S. law firm, DLA Piper. The report, published in September 2005, found that Burma did in fact meet the criteria for the Security Council to intervene, as Burma had many of the problems that the council had taken action on in other countries, including the overthrow of a democratically elected government, HIV/AIDS, conflict resulting from its attacks on ethnic minorities, severe human rights violations, refugee outflows, and drug trafficking. The report recommended that the Security Council pass a resolution requiring the restoration of democracy to Burma and an end to the attacks on ethnic civilians. If it were passed, the regime would be forced to stop attacking the Karen or face serious consequences.

Two days after the report was issued, the United States announced that it would support a resolution. I felt so happy; the most powerful country in the world would take up action on my country!

The United Kingdom was sitting on the fence, and our job at the Burma Campaign UK was to get it to support the resolution as well. I learned how to campaign, lobbying members of Parliament, putting pressure on the government through the media, giving public talks. It was challenging, but my confidence was growing. Joining the Burma Campaign UK was the first major decision I had taken for myself, and as I learned how I could make a difference, I was sure my decision had been the right one. It wasn't long before I saw a direct result of our work. After almost three months of campaigning for a resolution, the British government said it would support Burma's being brought before the UN Security Council. Now I saw that campaigning could change things.

In December 2005 we finally got nine countries on the Security Council to support Burma's being discussed, and so, for the very first time in history, the Security Council discussed my country. The discussions mainly were generally about human rights abuses and the need for all sides to sit down and negotiate a transition to democracy, but they were a significant step forward. We kept up the pressure, lobbying members of Parliament and contacting media in countries that were Security Council members. In September 2006 the Security Council held its first formal discussion, another step forward. In January 2007 the United States and United Kingdom put forward a resolution on Burma, simply calling on the regime to enter into negotiations, but

China and Russia vetoed the resolution. Even more shocking was that South Africa voted with them. How could it do that after it had depended so much on international support for its own struggle against apartheid?

During this time I had been doing a lot of public speaking up and down the country. As I got better at it, I could see the impact it was having, with people getting active and supporting the campaign. In December 2005 I finished my MA course with a dissertation on the Karen people. I was so proud that against so many odds I had succeeded in completing the degree. And already I was putting what I had learned into practice.

Throughout it all, I never forgot my journey back into Burma and the people I had met there. In early 2006 the Burmese junta had stepped up its attacks against the Karen. One of the reasons was that it had a plan to build hydropower dams in Karen State and sell the electricity to Thailand, even though most people in Burma had no electricity. All the generals cared about was making money to buy more weapons and build new luxury homes. But some of the planned dams were in KNU-controlled areas, and they wanted to drive the Karen people out of those areas. I was used to hearing horrific reports of abuses against my people, but even for me the reports from local NGOs and my friends on the border were shocking: women and even children were being raped; villagers were being horribly mutilated, with ears, arms, and breasts cut off. There were even beheadings.

Yet the British government and the United Nations ignored this new round of brutality. The new UN envoy to Burma, Ibrahim Gambari, visited Burma, but instead of demanding an end to the killings, which the United Nations later described as breaking the Geneva Conventions, he didn't even mention what was going on. He smiled and posed for pictures with the generals, and just because they had agreed to meet him, he talked about how they had opened a new page in their relations with the world community. I was so angry. How could he be so stupid? How could he believe their lies?

One Friday night I got home and read more e-mails from friends on the border about villagers being tortured and killed and decided that the Burma Campaign UK must let the world know what was going on in this fresh affront to human rights. The junta was making a mockery of international condemnation and had descended to a new low of barbarism. The British government and United Nations must demand they stop the attacks, and we must get the British government to give aid to the thousands of homeless people hiding in the jungle. This was it. Mark had said I could do more to help my people in London than on the border. Now I would see if that was true.

I called Mark to see if the Burma Campaign UK would undertake my plan of action, but I hadn't realized how late it was. I had woken him up. Exhausted from working so hard, he was scheduled to go on vacation the next morning and had to get up at 4 A.M. At first he was grumpy, but after listening to me speak he agreed that the Burma Campaign UK must act. On the plane he drafted a plan, and as soon as he got to his hotel he called me to give me a jobs list. It meant asking lots of people to take action, including Yvette Mahon, the director of the Burma Campaign UK at that time. Mark put me in charge of my first campaign. I was very nervous, knowing that if I wasn't successful more of my people would die. I had to collect facts and pictures to show what was going on and meet members of Parliament and representatives of opposition political parties to ask them to put pressure on the government to act. We mobilized our supporters, asking them to write to the government, and with the Karen community in the United Kingdom we organized a demonstration at the Burmese embassy.

At the demonstration we had a letter we wanted to hand in to the embassy, and I knocked on the door to deliver it. But they refused to answer. "There is no way we will open the door!" they shouted through the speakerphone on the door. I couldn't believe it, what a turnaround. Now the regime was afraid and hiding from me!

Our priority was to get aid to the homeless people in the jungle. The only way to get aid to many of them was across the border, as the regime blocked aid from inside the country. But the Department for International Development, the U.K. aid department, was refusing to fund such aid; it wanted to work only from inside the country. I could not understand why it would not help people who were so desperate and felt even more angry when we found out that another government department was funding a survey of wild bats in the same area. There was no aid for people, but they were counting wild bats.

We talked to our contacts in the media to try to get them to cover the story. The people at BBC *Newsnight* were just as shocked. They interviewed the minister from DFID, who afterward ordered a policy review. But the months dragged on, and still nothing changed.

In October 2006 things were ratcheted up a level. Benedict Rogers, a human rights campaigner working with the campaign group Christian Solidarity Worldwide, contacted me. That year's conference of the Conservative Party, one of the main political parties in the United Kingdom, had wanted to invite Aung San Suu Kyi to speak but hadn't even been able to get the invitation to her because she was being kept under house arrest in Rangoon. Her phone line was cut, her mail intercepted, and no visitors were allowed. So they asked me to speak instead.

I had met Benedict Rogers once before, on the Thailand-Burma border, in 2003, when he had visited my father in the company of other human rights campaigners. We had stayed in touch since then, and he wanted me to speak for six minutes at the conference, which would be a high-profile event. I figured if I prepared well I would be fine, so I agreed.

I chose to wear a white Karen dress for the conference, in order to make a simple statement about my identity. The day before I was scheduled to speak, I traveled by train to Bournemouth, the town where the conference was being held, to collect my conference pass, but it wasn't ready. The police said it would take some time to get clearance to allow me to enter the conference secure zone, especially as I was an asylum seeker. In fact, it wouldn't be possible until the following morning.

As my hotel room was inside the conference center, I now had nowhere to stay. I was tired, stressed, and nervous about my lecture the next day, and all of a sudden I just started crying. The conference organizers apologized profusely, but they had to follow procedures. Luckily, Benedict Rogers was there, and he managed to find me a hotel room.

The next morning my pass was ready, and as soon as I arrived I was taken to the greenroom to get ready. I had hoped to have time to practice my speech again, but in my Karen dress I stood out, and people kept coming up to talk to me.

After almost an hour I was taken into the conference hall itself and instructed to sit on a chair in the front row reserved for speakers. The other guest speaker that morning was John McCain, the soon-to-be U.S. presidential candidate, but I had little time to worry before I was on and was now looking forward to my chance to speak.

I had expected to feel nervous, but I wasn't. I felt calm as I looked at the audience. The conference hall was huge, so big I couldn't even see the faces of people at the back of the room. There were giant backdrops with party slogans and bright lights everywhere. Three floors of sloped seating holding more than a thousand people overlooked the stage. The sound of thousands of people clapping in the enclosed hall translated into a physical feeling, an uplifting energy. I was amazed but undaunted.

After about thirty minutes it was my turn to speak. The chair introduced me, and I walked to the front of the stage. I felt calm as I looked at the audience. A sea of faces stretched before me, and the room was silent as they waited for me to begin.

"Good afternoon, ladies and gentlemen," I said. I gestured behind me at the green wall of the conference hall. "The green background takes me back to my home in the jungle in Burma."

There was a ripple of laughter.

" . . . When I was just fourteen years old, the soldiers came to my village. They opened fire, and then there was no warning. The mortar bombs exploded. We fled for our lives, but many people were killed. My family ran, carrying what we could on our backs. We left everything and our home behind. I still remember the smell of the black smoke as our village was destroyed. . . .

"Ladies and gentlemen, my country, Burma, is ruled by one of the world's most brutal military dictatorships. And it is eleven years since the attack on my village, but nothing has changed. Earlier this year the regime launched a new military offensive against ethnic people of Karen and Karenni . . . shooting children, mutilating and beheading people, forcing twenty thousand people from their homes. And still the British government has done nothing to stop companies investing in Burma. How many more generations will have to suffer while the world looks the other way?

" . . . In many countries trade and investment can have a positive impact, bringing jobs and prosperity and opening up countries to new ideas. But in Burma the opposite happened. The regime used trade and investment to double the size of the army and then reduce spending on health and education. That is why Burmese people are asking for targeted economic sanctions, to cut the economic lifeline keeping this regime afloat.

" . . . What is more important than the basic right for all of us to live in peace, without fear?"

There was applause from the audience, and I felt encouraged.

"How can governments stand by while in Burma innocent children are shot, girls as young as five years old are raped by the soldiers, and while a thousand political prisoners are tortured and facing cruelty every day? And while Aung San Suu Kyi remains under house arrest, and her life in danger?"

I continued speaking and at the end made a simple point, one that came from my heart:

"There are millions and millions of people like me around the world, not just from Burma, who have been forced from their homes by the brutal regimes. We just want to go home. I just want to go home. But I can't without your help. Please help us go home. Thank you."

As I stopped speaking, the audience started to rise to its feet, and all of a sudden thirty-five hundred delegates were giving me—the Karen girl from the jungle—a standing ovation. I had spoken for five minutes freely from the heart. At the end I hadn't even needed my speech notes.

After the session I was asked to do lots of interviews. The next day, *The Times* of London, one of the most respected newspapers in the country, praised my speech, and my quote saying I wanted to go home was the quote of the day in one of the biggest-selling tabloid newspapers, *The Mirror*. In the taxi on the way back to the train station the taxi driver recognized me. He showed me the local newspaper, which had printed my whole speech. With media coverage like that, and even members of the public recognizing me, I hoped I was getting the message across that action needed to be taken to help the people of Burma.

But with this higher profile came greater danger. More than ever now, I was putting myself in the firing line. I still had to sign in at the police station every week, but there seemed to be no further progress in my claim for refugee status. The Home Office wrote to my lawyer, saying they needed proof of my status as a refugee in Thailand. There was no way to prove that, though, as I had been crossed off the UN list in Mae La camp. The Home Office had given no reason why it had to verify my refugee status in Thailand, but that was the reason it was using to justify my claim's taking so long. I had given it my father's phone number, so it could speak to him and verify my story, but I knew from speaking with my father that no one had called him. I lived in daily fear that the Home Office was going to try to deport me to Burma. Sometimes, alone at night, I would cry silent tears.

By February 2007 I was staying at a friend's house in London, returning one evening with Satoko, a Japanese girl I knew from university. Bwa Bwa was also coming for dinner, and I was looking forward to seeing her. Satoko and I walked up the dark, rainy street and approached the door. As I did so, two shadowy shapes detached themselves from a phone box on the street. Suddenly they were upon me.

I felt intense pain as one dragged me by the hair, pulling me back toward the street. I started screaming as loudly as I could. My handbag was on my shoulder, but neither made any attempt to grab it but tried to drag me out toward the road. I screamed for help, Satoko turned to help me, and suddenly my attackers let go of me and ran away.

I was shaking and in shock. My friends helped me inside the house. My hair had been pulled out in great clumps. Because the attackers had worn hooded jackets, their faces had been in shadow and I had not been able to make out their features. All I was certain of is that I hadn't been robbed. My cell phone and my handbag were untouched.

CHAPTER TWENTY-NINE

IN THE FIRING LINE

That August, I moved into a two-bedroom apartment in North London, sharing it with a married couple, both of whom were Karen. The wife, Pasaw Htee—"Mist Water"—was a medical doctor, and her husband, Saw Htoo Tha—"Mr. Golden Fruit"—had already won his refugee status in the United Kingdom and was working full time. They were 100 percent supportive of my work and knew the risks I was taking. They knew my safety was threatened, and we carried out certain measures to make things as secure at the apartment as possible.

As my claim for refugee status ground into its second year, my solicitor applied for judicial review—a process by which the courts can force the Home Office to make a decision. The threat of judicial review finally forced its hand, and later in August 2007 I was finally granted full refugee status in the United Kingdom. I was overjoyed. I felt as if an enormous weight had been taken off my shoulders. At least now I knew that I couldn't be deported to face the vengeance of those who rule my country. It also meant that I could start working full time with the Burma Campaign UK, which would finally be able to pay me a living wage. I was appointed its campaigns officer, with special responsibility for parliamentary work.

My friends at the Burma Campaign UK decided to throw a little party. Mark brought a carrot cake with white icing and little carrot-shaped cookies on top. We had champagne in plastic cups to celebrate. Mark asked everyone to raise a glass for the toast.

"Congratulations, Zoya, on winning your refugee status! It's been a long two years!"

"To Zoya!" everyone echoed. "Congratulations!"

"I'm so happy to finally be a legal person existing in the real world!" I told them. "This day really means so much to me."

Since the age of fourteen I had been a ghost citizen. I had been a refugee of one kind or another, but one with no formal status. Even my UN refugee registration hadn't meant much; I had had no ID card and no passport, and was pretty much bereft of any identity. This was the first time that I had existed, legally and for real, and I was now twenty-six years old. My time as a "nonperson" had been twelve long years. Now I was a "person," like everyone around me. I could open a bank account, work, and rent a home, and soon I could travel abroad—things most people take for granted.

That weekend my sister came to visit, and she, Mist Water, Mr. Golden Fruit, and I had a celebratory meal. I cooked chicken curry spiced with chili, pepper, salt, garlic, coriander, and turmeric. I could afford to buy those things now and to treat my friends and my big sister. And of course we had a big bowl of fish paste. We celebrated the fact that for us four, life seemed to be improving. I had a country to call my home, a house in which to make a home, friends, a job, and an income.

I was sad to be separated from the rest of my family. For now, my brother Slone's home was in Canada. Things for Say Say and my father were pretty much as they had always been. They had no formal ID, no homeland, and no way to travel out of Thailand. Before I left Mae Sot, Say Say had gotten married, and he now had a little son and daughter. His Karen wife had taken up the offer of resettlement under the UN program and moved to Norway with the children. But Say Say had remained on the Thailand-Burma border, working with my father. My new status and my ability to work in the United Kingdom meant that I could now put more of my energy into helping them with their fight for freedom.

The campaign on cross-border aid that I had been given responsibility for was making real progress. We had persuaded the British Parliament's International Development Committee to hold an inquiry into the situation. It issued a report supporting what we had been campaigning for—that aid should go to the internally displaced persons and be delivered cross-border. Once again the Department for International Development reviewed its policy. Finally it agreed to double Britain's aid to Burma and to fund cross-border aid. I was beside myself with joy. This increase in aid might save the lives of thousands of desperate people. But just as I started feeling as if I were really making a difference, tragedy struck again.

In August 2007 the Burmese regime raised the price of fuel by up to 500 percent. For people already living in abject poverty, it was too much. They took to the streets, demanding change. Despite arrests and intimidation by the military, the protests grew until hundreds of thousands were marching the streets. Saffron-robed Buddhist monks led the protests, saying they could no longer ignore the suffering of the people.

The press dubbed the uprisings the "Saffron Revolution." It was headline news, and the Burma Campaign UK was inundated with media inquiries. For days on end I would get up at 4 A.M. to do my first TV interview and then go from studio to studio. We were demanding action from the international community, not just sympathy. As the protests grew, we allowed ourselves to hope that perhaps this was it, the regime would fall. But the junta reacted as it had always done by killing and maiming in the streets. It cut phone lines and Internet links, effectively isolating Burma from the outside world. That made it very hard to get any news out of the country. As it launched its brutal crackdown, my heart wept. No matter how upset I was, though, I had to find the strength to continue speaking out. As the killings and arrests continued on the streets of Rangoon, media interest in Burma reached a massive peak. I rushed from one interview to the next as

Buddhist monasteries were being raided and thousands of monks arrested. It was vital that the world act.

A few days into the terrible conflict, I was in the office and Mark asked if I would take a phone call.

"Who from?" I asked.

"Prime Minister Gordon Brown," he replied. "He's spoken with the Chinese prime minister, the French president, and the U.S. president about the crisis. Now he wants to talk to someone from Burma. He wants to talk to you."

I was honored and asked the prime minister to try to get the UN Security Council to take action and for the European Union to introduce targeted economic sanctions that would stop money from going to the generals. European investment was helping to pay for the bullets we saw being used against the monks on the streets of Rangoon.

On Sunday morning the prime minister issued a statement on Burma. He said he would be pushing for the Security Council to discuss the crisis and for the European Union to impose new sanctions. I felt so encouraged that finally the world might take a strong stand against the generals.

The following weekend there was a big march for Burma in London, followed by a rally in Trafalgar Square, right in the center of London. To show his support, Gordon Brown invited a delegation, including some Buddhist monks living in exile and me, to meet him to discuss the crisis. It was so odd to be sitting in No. 10 Downing Street, when only two years previously I had stood on the pavement outside shouting slogans. Brown promised to do all that he could, and I could see that his concern was genuine.

After that meeting I addressed ten thousand people at the rally in Trafalgar Square, and spoke that night at a concert that the musician Damien Rice was giving in Wembley Arena. It was one of the most amazing days of my life. My journey from the jungle to the world stage had been long and harrowing, but breaking the silence around Burmese oppression finally seemed to be taking effect. After years of being a powerless victim, this was truly the best feeling in the world.

CHAPTER THIRTY

THE ROAD HOME

In November 2007 I was issued a British refugee travel document. At first glance it looks like a normal passport, but it has "TRAVEL DOCUMENT" emblazoned across the front. The Burma Campaign UK was assembling a delegation of politicians and the media to travel to Thailand and the border with Burma. I had been given the job of organizing it and was looking forward to going back to see the situation for myself, and of course to see Say Say and my father.

The plan was to visit Mae La—my old refugee camp—and the clinic that had kept so much of my family alive for so long. Some of us also intended to sneak across the border into Burma, to spend time with those most in need—the internal displaced people. The delegation included a member of Spain's Parliament, Carmen García; a Spanish TV crew and NGOs; an Estonian MP, Silver Meikar; and an Estonian journalist. Radio journalists from the BBC and of course Mark would be going with us also.

When I spoke to my father by telephone about the trip, he told me that the security situation had worsened; his name was now on the top of the regime's hit list, and I would be in danger as well. After

I discussed this with Mark, he decided that we needed more security and arranged for a former Royal Marine soldier named John Rowe to visit the office. John taught us about surveillance and countersurveillance; how to detect a tail and then lose it; how to do basic first aid; plus very basic self-defense. John instructed me what to do if I were grabbed from behind, not knowing that Mark had already shown me one trick—that I should stamp my heel into my assailant's foot. John wasn't expecting that. He cried out in pain. This big marine hadn't expected a small Karen girl to be so strong.

Once more I was heading back into the darkness, but now I was doing so as a known, outspoken opponent of the regime oppressing and enslaving my country. It would have every reason to want to stop us. A few weeks after my self-defense instructions from John, our delegation arrived in the Thai town of Mae Sot. When we arrived at the hotel, I left the others to get settled and rushed downstairs to meet Say Say, who picked me up and took me to my father's house. I was shocked by Say Say's appearance. In the barely three years since I had last seen him, he had aged so much. The constant stress of his work had left him thin, haggard, and exhausted.

My father was waiting for me at the doorway of the house and broke into a smile as soon as he saw me, and I tried to return the warmth and welcome that were in his eyes. But in truth I was shocked at how he, too, had aged. His hair had turned gray, and for the first time he looked like an old man. Clearly, all the pressure he was under was taking its toll: the constant risk of assassination and his responsibilities as general secretary of the KNU. My father represented us Karen to the world and held media interviews every day. He was one of our most respected leaders, and everyone wanted his advice and support.

He hugged me tight. "Oh, wonderful! My Little Daughter has just arrived!"

I hugged him back as hard as I could. And then we went inside and I sat on his lap. I was twenty-seven years old, but I didn't ever intend to stop doing so.

That first night my father invited our entire delegation to his house for a traditional Karen dinner. It was a funny mixture of people around the table. Karen Army commanders and some of my old schoolfriends sat next to MPs from Estonia and Catalonia in Spain, places they had never even heard of. But people soon got to chatting, and the evening went well. Both Estonia and Spain had been under dictators, and my fellow Karen were keen to hear how the dictators had fallen.

Once the delegation had left, my father proceeded to tell me and my friends the story of how he had come to name me "Zoya." I felt I had heard it a hundred times before, but as he spoke, I could see how proud he was of me.

In the morning we set off to visit two IDP camps, both situated on the banks of the Salween River, only just inside Burma, although we had to pass Burmese Army checkpoints to reach them.

On the one hand, it was wonderful to be back there, to see the mountains again, breathe the fresh air, and see and smell familiar plants and flowers. I had missed it so much. But at the same time, I was saddened that the camps were just as they had been on my journey into Burma years before. The suffering was still going on. Things hadn't changed.

In the first camp we met a couple with a newborn baby girl. The father had helped the mother give birth in the jungle, with no doctors or medicines at hand. The mother asked me if I would name the baby. I said I would love to but that we should offer the honor to our foreign guests. The Spanish MP named the girl "Libertat," the word for "freedom" in Catalan.

Another young mother told us that her husband had been shot dead in the attack on their village as she had fled for her life with the children, escaping into the jungle. As a widow, she found it difficult to care for herself and her offspring. We had brought canned fish and cookies with us to give out to the children. Such simple, basic foodstuffs were received with such joy by the half-starved kids in the camp.

More people were on their way to the camp, with Karen soldiers acting as their guides to ensure they reached it safely. But even in the camp they were unsafe. Not far away in the jungle there was a Burmese Army post, from which an attack could happen at any time. In fact, several had occurred during the past year. Before leaving, we visited the school, a tiny bamboo hut with no walls and a bamboo floor, where two teachers taught one hundred students crammed together.

The foreign visitors were horrified at the conditions they saw. Each child had his or her own tragic story to tell, but sadly we had little time to record them in the couple of hours we were there. But we heard enough for our delegates to get a basic understanding of what was going on. For me it was all too familiar. It was as if time had frozen since I had left. I could tell that the foreign visitors were horrified. I didn't need to remind them what this was like when compared with the schools of their childhoods; it was too obvious to require any mention.

The following day we set out for Mae La refugee camp. Officially, we weren't allowed into the camp. Thai authorities rarely let politicians or journalists into refugee camps. But we found a way to get in; it was my first time back there since 2004. It felt so strange entering the camp gates again, knowing that this time I was no longer trapped. There were scores of new arrivals, but most were "ghost refugees."

The dreadful system that my mother, Slone, and so many others had suffered under just seemed to go on and on.

One man, a teacher back in his home village, had been taken by Burmese soldiers, who tortured him and tried to make him confess to being a resistance fighter. First he was beaten with bamboo poles; then he was tied to a tree and left there for days. Every day he would be beaten, and he drifted slowly toward death. He showed me the scars from where he had been whipped. The village headman had saved him by traveling to the army camp to argue for the man's life. He had explained that the man was an innocent teacher, and finally the soldiers had let him go. He was so close to death that he'd had to be carried back to his village by friends. Once he had recovered enough to move, the teacher had fled with his family into the jungle and found his way to

Mae La camp. He told me he could never forgive those who had done this to him.

Some people had been in the camps for twenty years and more. Most of those with any skills—doctors, nurses, and teachers—had left on a UN resettlement program that took long-term refugees to new countries where they could restart their lives. This loss of trained and skilled people further degraded the lives of people in the camps on the Thailand-Burma border, which almost uniquely were run by the refugees themselves, the uneducated farmers and rural villagers who made up the majority of the refugees coming from Burma.

At Dr. Cynthia's clinic we met a mother with a young boy who was very ill. Ordinary villagers from deep inside Burma, without any proper health care, they had walked through the jungle for weeks to get to the clinic, during which the boy's high fever had worsened so much that he was unconscious and close to death by the time they arrived. He had been unconscious for days. This determined mother had heard that Dr. Cynthia's clinic gave free treatment to refugees and IDPs, so she had trekked through the jungle to find it, carrying her unconscious son, who was half her size, in her arms. Her story reminded me of my first almost-dying, except that my mother had only had to make a short dash through the jungle before reaching a clinic. This woman was from the Shan ethnic group, and her journey from the Shan hills to Dr. Cynthia's clinic had taken two weeks.

At the end of the week I held an interview with the media that were with us.

"I first fled Burma when I was fourteen. It is now thirteen years later, and nothing has changed. Nothing. We have seen in the IDP camps that people are still running from bullets and bombs, just as I did years ago. We have seen in the refugee camps that people suffer there, just as I and my family did when we were refugees. Nothing has changed. We need to stop investing in this murderous regime; we need to stop buying their gas and timber and gems; and we need to stop selling them arms with which they go about killing their own people." I believed now, more than ever, that as long as the junta was in power its killings and abuses would continue driving more people into the camps. It was a vicious cycle. We needed measures to break that cycle by getting rid of the ruling regime, and bringing freedom and democracy to Burma.

The delegation departed, and I stayed on for a few days to be with my father and catch up with old friends.

One morning my father, Say Say, and I attended the Karen National Unity Seminar. With Karen inside Burma, in exile on the borders, and being resettled overseas, it was important that we all share information and coordinate our work. We had had to take extra security precautions before leaving home, because a few days before we had learned of a plot to kill my father and me with a roadside bomb as we traveled to this meeting. It was a terrible reminder to me that my father was in real danger.

He and I often spoke of the legacy we would be leaving and how else we could make lasting contributions to the cause. He hadn't told me and hadn't asked for it, but many others had said that he was likely to be nominated as KNU president in elections due toward the end of the year. My father was expected to be elected easily. I had started working on this book and told him that with the proceeds I wanted to set up a charity in memory of my mother, to fulfill our dream of providing proper education for the Karen. My father was so pleased. He said he'd like to write the foreword, if I would allow him to. I laughed at him teasing me.

"But let this book speak about the Karen struggle," he urged me, "and Burma's fight to be free."

On January 31, we attended a ceremony to mark Karen Resistance Day. But that morning, during routine security checks, the people organizing the event discovered a bomb beneath the chair on the stage where my father was going to sit. Nonetheless, my father gave his speech and a press conference, in which he described the continuing military offensive against the Karen people. Later he received a phone call. An unknown voice told my father that he was going to come and kill him.

After that, my father told me to be very careful. He told me that the enemy knew I was there with him and that they also wanted to kill me. He made me promise that I would take care of myself and be careful. He said I'd be much safer when I returned to the United Kingdom.

"They are closing in on me, Little Daughter," he warned me. "And if they cannot get to me, they will try to get to you."

The Pakistani presidential candidate Benazir Bhutto had just recently been assassinated, and I was really worried for my father's safety.

"Look, Pah, you have to recognize that Benazir Bhutto got killed because she didn't take proper precautions," I told him. "I'm worried the same might happen to you."

"I know! I know!" my father replied. "The regime is trying very hard to kill me, so maybe I won't survive for long."

"Pah, don't talk like that!" I said. *"Please."*

"Little Daughter, even if they kill me they won't kill what I stand for, will they?"

"But I still don't like you talking like that. I want you always to be around, Pah, and to live into a grand old age!"

My father seemed to ignore my last comment. "I'm so proud that you are taking such an active role in the struggle now, my Little Daughter. When I meet people, they speak about you so much. They tell me, 'Ah, your little daughter, she is just like you.'"

My father told me that he was tired. He had been fighting for a long, long time and was feeling old. After a few more years of service, he wanted to retire, write a book about his life, and tend his flower gardens. I wanted him to be at my graduation ceremony for my MA, in July, a few months from now. He promised he would try to be there.

I returned to London in early February. Bwa Bwa and I had been invited to the premiere of the movie *Rambo IV*. In the film, Rambo travels into

Karen areas to rescue some missionaries kidnapped by the Burmese soldiers. A lot of blood and mayhem follow, but finally Rambo wins the day, with the help of the Karen resistance. Most people don't believe it when I tell them, but *Rambo IV* accurately portrays the horrors going on in my homeland. When Bwa Bwa and I turned up outside the red-carpeted venue, we were mobbed by the crowd.

"Who do you play?" someone yelled.

"Give us an autograph, will you!"

"Get us in to meet Rambo!"

People thrust autograph books at us. Cameras flashed in our faces. It was all very weird. But I signed away and made sure we took the opportunity to tell them about the plight of the Karen people in Burma.

"We're not in the movie, exactly," I said. "But we are Karen, and the film's all about our people. For decades . . ."

When I came out of the premiere, I gave my father a call, as I had told him we'd be going to the premiere. He'd been so pleased, and I'd promised to call him afterward to tell him all about it. But Pah had crossed into Burma on his own mission, and I couldn't reach him.

I would never get the chance to tell him about the movie.

CHAPTER THIRTY-ONE

THE FINAL CUT

Two days after the movie premiere, I had an early-morning phone call from Bwa Bwa. A reporter had just called her from the BBC World Service. Had she heard news of my father being shot? the reporter had asked. As I listened to Bwa Bwa's words, a text message came in on my cell phone. It was another journalist, asking me if I had heard the same thing.

I got off the phone refusing to believe what I had heard. My father shot? Surely it couldn't be true? I had to hope and pray that the journalists had got it wrong and that my father was all right. I tried calling his cell, but it was turned off. In mounting panic I tried Say Say, but his phone was also unavailable. In desperation I called another friend of the family, Pee La Sein. Pee La Sein confirmed to me that the news was true. He had been shot and had died of his wounds. Our father, Padoh Mahn Sha, had been assassinated by those who for so long had been plotting and striving to kill him. He had been sitting peacefully on the veranda of his house in Mae Sot when three agents of the Burmese regime drove up in a pickup truck. Two ascended the stairs and shot him. Those are the simple facts of his dying.

I let out a cry that brought everyone in the house running. I broke down and sobbed out the news to them. I called Bwa Bwa, who broke down over the phone. Then I called Slone, in Canada, and woke him in the middle of the night. He knew immediately that something was wrong. I cried and cried as I choked out the news to Slone that our father had been killed.

In the greater scheme of things, my father was killed because the Burmese regime feared him. Forever a man of principle and a man of the people, my father had enjoyed enormous support—not just from the Karen but from the Burmese pro-democracy movement as a whole, and from freedom-loving people around the world. As news spread of the killing, more and more Karen turned up at my home. They were all devastated, and I realized some were looking to me for comfort. I thought of my father's iron determination and willed myself to stop crying. I needed to be strong now. They had killed my father because they wanted to kill what he stood for. I was determined not to let that happen.

My father had been my best friend, my inspiration, and my guiding light. Whenever I had felt afraid, his example had kept me strong. But now he was gone, and I was heartbroken.

Bwa Bwa and I returned to Thailand as quickly as we could. It wasn't safe for us to attend the funeral; there were reports that many more assassins had been dispatched to kill Karen leaders and other democracy activists. But we needed to see his body. We were taken to him in They Bay Hta, just inside Karen State. I clasped my hands in front of my face and bowed down three times, the traditional way to pay respect. My father was in a bed surrounded by flowers—the flowers that he had always loved so much when he was alive. He was so pale, but he looked at peace at last.

My sister and I were torn; we wanted to stay for the funeral and knew that our people wanted to see us, but the risks were so great. We were determined to stay alive and carry on his work. We stayed with him all night, and at dawn we had to creep away.

We delayed the funeral as long as we possibly could, but Slone wasn't able to get back to the border in time.

In our animist tradition, after people die, we have a final lunch with them. But because of the security situation poor Say Say was alone when he prepared the final lunch for our father. He set a place for my father and asked him to come eat with him one last time.

Friends described it as the saddest funeral they had ever attended. Thousands turned up to pay their respects. It was a traditional animist funeral, but Christian and Buddhist services were also held. The KNLA held a gunfire salute over my father's body before it was burned on a traditional funeral pyre. His ashes were scattered in the Moei River, under trees, and at the base of a mountain.

Later, we went to clear out our father's papers. In among them I found the letter that I had written when I was sixteen, from Noh Poe refugee camp. Reading it over again, I realized how hurtful it must have been for him to receive it.

Dear Pah, well, I think you must have completely forgotten us—especially your Little Daughter. Well, it's okay, I suppose. . . . But I don't want to be a refugee anymore. Life in the refugee camp is so horrible. Do you know what it's like? What it feels like to be a refugee? The Thai soldiers are so horrible to us.

Some months later I was flicking through his diary and found a poem he had written, dedicated to all women in Burma.

To Beloved Daughter
Against the Current
O my beloved daughter,

In the long journey of life,
In broad daylight, under the sun,
As it's hard to know where north and south are,
There're also those who're standing still.

Though in the middle of the night,
A time hard to see the way,
As north and south are definitely known,
There're those who're journeying toward the destination.

In the stormy wind,
And the waves blasting,
Crying and wailing,
In abandonment,
There're also those who've sunk into depravity.

In the violent storm,
And the stormy sea,
There're also those who are journeying,
Against the current and vicious wind.

O my beloved daughter,
Keep sincerity and conscience,
Alertness and ethics,
Diligence and learning,
Faith and uprightness,
Courage and sacrifice,
As a base and journey on,
With fearlessness,
For the noble cause.

Published in *Thanu Htoo Journal* of January 31, 1999, on the fiftieth
anniversary of the Karen Revolution

My father's life was one of sacrifice and struggle. My mother's, also. When they died they left us no material possessions but something more valuable: they gave us compassion, principles, and strength. While the dictators may have killed my father, they can never kill my father's dream. The Karen, and all the people of Burma, will be free.

STATEMENT BY ZOYA PHAN AND HER SISTERS AND BROTHERS FOR HER FATHER'S FUNERAL

We have lost a great father, and a great leader.

We were lucky to have a father who was caring and full of love. He gave us guidance and support, and taught us tolerance and to stand against injustice. He could not give us wealth or luxury, but ensured that we had an education and the opportunity to fulfill our potential.

He was always humble, yet a strong and brave leader. He dedicated his life to the struggle, and always put the welfare of his people and his country before himself. His example of determination and self-sacrifice to win our freedom won him the love and respect of not just the Karen people, but also the Burmese democracy movement and of freedom-loving people around the world.

He will be remembered by many not only as an inspirational leader, but also on a personal level for the many acts of kindness he performed for those who needed help.

We are proud to be his children, as all Karen people and all people who long for freedom in Burma are proud of him.

Our father lived for the principles of freedom and democracy. He believed in the unity of the Karen people against a common enemy, and in the unity of all the ethnic nationalities and people of Burma, knowing that only together can we bring freedom to our land, protect our culture and traditions, and fight poverty, hunger, and disease.

What the SPDC are trying to do by killing our father is to try to kill what he stood for. We must not let them succeed.

. . . And to the international community: the assassination of our father shows once again that the regime is lying when it says it has a roadmap to democracy. Our father dedicated his life to the struggle for a democratic Burma. That is why they killed him. . . .

We know that many of you are feeling sad and downhearted. That is not what our father would want. He would want you to be strong and unified. If you loved our father, the best way to show it is to fight to fulfill his dream of freedom. Don't let what he stood for die with him.

Our father's death does not leave us weaker. It shows that we are strong. They killed our father because they are afraid of him and what he stood for. . . .

Our father did not live to see freedom for our people, but his dream lives on.

The Karen, and all the people of Burma, will be free.

EPILOGUE

As I write this epilogue I have just received news that the dictatorship has drawn up a new hit list and sent death squads to Thailand to assassinate Karen leaders, as they did with my father and as they did with Saw Ba U Gyi, the founder of the KNU, back in 1950. The suffering and the killing never seem to end. Attacks on civilians are also increasing, as the generals try to crush all opposition ahead of their fake elections scheduled for sometime in 2010.

Zipporah Sein, my former teacher, has been elected to replace my father as general secretary of the Karen National Union. She is a strong and experienced leader, and I am pleased it is she who has taken over from my father. She is the first female leader of the KNU in its history. With Aung San Suu Kyi and many other strong women leaders in our struggle, ours is a movement increasingly led by women. Zipporah has described the new constitution that will come into force after the 2010 "elections" as "a death sentence for ethnic diversity in Burma."

Yet even as ethnic people are slaughtered by the dictatorship, women and children gang-raped and killed, and tens of thousands forced to run for their lives, some governments even suggest that the "elections" could bring change and that sanctions and pressure should be lifted. How can they be so foolish and naive as to believe the lies of the generals over and over again? How can they ignore what happens to the ethnic people of Burma? Would a regime interested in reform send its soldiers to gang-rape and kill an eight-months-pregnant teenage woman? I am so angry.

I am the international coordinator at the Burma Campaign UK now. My task is to help link up campaigners around the world, building the international campaign to help my country. Former antiapartheid activists, who campaigned for the freedom of the people in South Africa and to free Nelson Mandela, tell me the situation in Burma is much worse than it was in South Africa. But there isn't the same-scale international campaign for Burma as there was for South Africa.

I have visited many countries to tell governments, MPs, and the public what is going on in my country. I have met politicians, present and former presidents, and prime ministers. Sometimes I have to pinch myself to make sure that it is all real; it's hard to believe that the girl from the jungle is really meeting these people and having these opportunities to speak out. I feel such responsibility to make the most of the opportunities I have been given, because I know that lives depend on it. Sometimes I find it depressing that there is still so little awareness among governments and that so few are willing to take action. But as my father said, freedom won't be given to us; we will have to work for it.

Many of my Karen friends who appear in this book are now scattered all over the world. Tens of thousands of people, mostly Karen, have been resettled: some to Australia, others to the United States, and some even to the frozen landscapes of northern Finland. One ethnic Karenni woman in her forties whom I met on a lobbying trip to Finland told me she felt she hadn't been born until she arrived there. She had lived her entire life in fear, she said. But she also said what everyone else says if you talk to them long enough: I want to go home. While the UN resettlement program is giving people a chance to escape from the misery of the refugee camps and start a new life in safety, I can't help thinking that the Burmese generals must be delighted with the United Nations for doing this. Instead of taking action to stop the attacks, the United Nations whisks the refugees thousands of miles away. In a way, the UN resettlement program is cooperating with the ethnic cleansing policy of the regime. And no matter how many people it resettles, more come to the camps to fill their place, because the attacks haven't stopped and the United Nations isn't trying to stop them.

Our struggle isn't just against dictatorship and oppression. It is also a fight for a better Burma, a better place for all to live. Regardless of our ethnicity, we are one people, and we are engaged in one struggle for our country to be free. My dream is of a Burma where never again will a mother put her children to bed crying because they have not had enough to eat. I dream of a Burma where no more children die of preventable diseases because the government has spent money on guns instead of medicine. I dream of a Burma where no farmer lives in fear of being shot because of his ethnicity or used as slave labor. I dream of a Burma with no political prisoners, where we can choose our leaders. I dream of a Burma where we celebrate our cultures, different but equal. If every one of us takes action, no matter how small or big we are, together we will be an unstoppable force, and we will win our freedom. United, our will and determination will be stronger than guns and bullets.

I hope that this book has been interesting for you to read. Maybe you will feel sorry for me after what I have been through in my life. Don't. I am one of the lucky ones. I am lucky I am still alive. I am lucky I haven't been raped. I am lucky that I am not still in a refugee camp with no work, no freedom, and the same food for breakfast, lunch, and dinner for year after year after year. And I am lucky to be able to work to help my people. I don't want you to feel sorry for me, I want you to feel angry, and I want you to do something about it.

A British actress once introduced me at an event as a woman who would wrap my hands around your heart. But I told the audience, I don't want your heart, I want you to take action. I say the same to you now. So few people know what is going on in my country, but you do now. Will you do something about it or just pick up another book? On the following pages are details of organizations working to help my people. I ask you to support them. We need your help.

I want to go home. Please help me.

THE PHAN FOUNDATION

The Phan Foundation was founded by Zoya Phan, her sister, Bwa Bwa, and her brothers, Say Say and Slone. It is dedicated to the memory of their parents, Padoh Mahn Sha Lah Phan and Nant Kyin Shwe.

The foundation has four main objectives:

To alleviate poverty
To provide education
To promote human rights
To protect Karen culture

For the Karen people of Burma.

It helps people in Burma and refugees forced to flee their homes. It also aims to protect and promote the culture of the Karen, a culture that is being systematically destroyed as part of the Burmese regime's policy of ethnic cleansing. In meeting its objectives, the foundation has a particular focus on young people, encouraging and supporting a new generation of grassroots activists who will work to help their people.

Zoya's experiences described in this book are not unique. Each year tens of thousands more people are driven from their homes. The poverty is as bad as in the worst conflict-hit African countries, but the Burmese regime will not allow the United Nations or aid agencies to deliver aid to millions of people in desperate poverty. Parents are forced to watch their children die of measles, malaria, or dysentery, when cheap medicines would save their lives. Children grow up without access to education. But there are ways to get aid in, through underground networks. A small amount of money can make a big difference.

Please support the Phan Foundation. You can donate online at www.phanfoundation.org. For more information, send an e-mail to info@phanfoundation.org.

Other Organizations Working to Help Free Burma

Zoya is the international coordinator of the Burma Campaign UK, which campaigns for human rights, democracy, and development in Burma. Find out more at www.burmacampaign.org.uk.

In the United States you can visit www.uscampaignforburma.org.

You can find out if there is a Burma Campaign in your country at www.burmacampaign.org.uk/links.html.

The Mae Tao Clinic on the Thailand-Burma border saved Zoya's life several times: www.maetaoclinic.org.

The Thailand-Burma Border Consortium provides assistance to refugees who have been forced to flee to Thailand: www.tbbc.org.

The Karen Women's Organisation provides assistance to refugees and internally displaced people, and promotes democracy and human rights: www.karenwomen.org.

The Karen National Union is the organization that Zoya's parents dedicated their lives to. It leads the Karen struggle for human rights and democracy: www.karennationalunion.net.

You can also follow Zoya's activities on her own Web site, www.zoya phan.com, and on her Facebook page: www.facebook.com/zoya phanpage.

Acknowledgments

Special thanks to Mark Farmaner and Anna Roberts, for helping make this book possible. Special thanks to my literary agent, Felicity Bryan, and international agents, George Lucas and Andrew Nurnberg, for your enthusiasm and belief in my story. Very special thanks to Mike Jones and Katherine Stanton at my British publisher, Simon & Schuster; Carolin Graehl, at my German publisher, Droemer; my American editors, Leslie Meredith and Leah Miller, Free Press (Simon & Schuster); and my Canadian publisher, Penguin. Special thanks to my sister, Nant Bwa Bwa Phan, my older brother, Saw Say Say Phan, and my younger brother, Slone Phan, for their support and encouragement. Special thanks to David Lewis and Leslie Lewis for their preparation of the French retreat in which I worked on the manuscript. Thanks to Mrs. Christine and David Major for the Dorset writing retreat and the wonderful cooking, and to Sue Wreford for the comfort and calm of her Wynford Eagle country house in which to work.

One of the ways in which the regime ruling Burma keeps hold of power is through denying education to its people. Without education

I would not be able to do the work I do now to try to help my people. I was very lucky to be able to attend college, and for that I must thank the Open Society Institute Scholarship Program, Prospect Burma, Burma Education Scholarship Trust, and other individuals, including Lisa Houston, Martin Panter, Michael Woods, Paul Sztumpf, and Steve Bates.

INDEX

Note: Burmese personal names appear in this index under the first word of the name (except that names preceded by the term of respect "U" are alphabetized according to what follows "U").

ABOUT THE AUTHORS

Zoya Phan is a refugee living in London and one of the leading Burmese democracy activists in Europe. She is regularly interviewed by major national and international media, including BBC, CNN, Sky, and Al Jazeera.

Damien Lewis is an award-winning, best-selling British author and filmmaker.